An Introduction to
Computational Learning Theory

An Introduction to
Computational Learning Theory

Michael J. Kearns
Umesh V. Vazirani

The MIT Press

Cambridge, Massachusetts

London, England

©1994 Massachusetts Institute of Technology

This book was typeset by the authors and was printed and bound in the United States of America.

Library of Congress Cataloging-in-Publication Data

Kearns, Michael J.
    An introduction to computational learning theory / Michael J. Kearns, Umesh V. Vazirani.
        p.   cm.
    Includes bibliographical references and index.
    ISBN 0-262-11193-4
    1. Machine learning.   2. Artificial intelligence.   3. Algorithms.
4. Neural networks.   I. Vazirani, Umesh Virkumar.   II. Title.
Q325.5.K44   1994
006.3—dc20   94-16588
                                                            CIP

Contents

Preface

In the Fall term of 1990, we jointly taught a graduate seminar in computational learning theory in the computer science department of the University of California at Berkeley. The material that is presented here has its origins in that course, both in content and exposition. Rather than attempt to give an exhaustive overview of this rapidly expanding and changing area of research, we have tried to carefully select fundamental topics that demonstrate important principles that may be applicable in a wider setting than the one examined here. In the technical sections, we have tried to emphasize intuition whenever possible, while still providing precise arguments.

The book is intended for researchers and students in artificial intelligence, neural networks, theoretical computer science and statistics, and anyone else interested in mathematical models of learning. It is appropriate for use as the central text in a specialized seminar course, or as a supplemental text in a broader course that perhaps also studies the viewpoints taken by artificial intelligence and neural networks. While Chapter 1 lays a common foundation for all the subsequent material, the later chapters are essentially self-contained and may be read selectively and in any order. Exercises are provided at the end of each chapter.

Some brief comments on the expected background of the reader are appropriate here. Familiarity with some basic tools of the formal analysis of algorithms is necessary, as is familiarity with only the most elementary notions of complexity theory, such as NP-completeness. For the reader unfamiliar with these topics, the books of Cormen, Leiserson and Rivest [27], Garey and Johnson [38] and Aho, Hopcroft and Ullman [2] provide classic background reading. Some background in probability theory and statistics is desirable but not necessary. In an Appendix in Chapter 9 we have gathered in one place the simple tools of probability theory that we will invoke repeatedly throughout our study.

We are deeply indebted to many colleagues for the advice, feedback and support they gave to us during the writing of this book. We are especially grateful to Ron Rivest of M.I.T. for using preliminary versions of the book for two years as a text in his machine learning course. The comments that resulted from this course were invaluable, and we thank Jay Alsam of M.I.T. for improving several derivations.

We give warm thanks to Dana Angluin of Yale for a detailed critique of a preliminary version. We incorporated practically all of her suggestions, and they greatly improved the presentation. We are very grateful to Les Valiant of Harvard for his many comments and continuing support of the project.

For many suggested improvements and discussions of the material, we thank Scott Decatur of Harvard, John Denker of Bell Labs, Sally Goldman of Washington University, David Haussler of U.C. Santa Cruz, Esther Levin of Bell Labs, Marina Meila of M.I.T., Fernando Pereira of Bell Labs, Stuart Russell of U.C. Berkeley, Rob Schapire of Bell Labs, Donna Slonim of M.I.T., and Manfred Warmuth of U.C. Santa Cruz. Thanks to Danuta Sowinska-Khan and the Art Department of Bell Labs for their preparation of the figures.

We give warm thanks to Terry Ehling of The MIT Press for bringing this project to fruition, and for her enthusiastic support from beginning to end.

An Introduction to
Computational Learning Theory

1

The Probably Approximately Correct Learning Model

1.1   A Rectangle Learning Game

Consider a simple one-player learning game. The object of the game is to learn an unknown axis-aligned rectangle R — that is, a rectangle in the Euclidean plane $\Re^2$ whose sides are parallel with the coordinate axes. We shall call R the **target** rectangle. The player receives information about R only through the following process: every so often, a random point p is chosen in the plane according to some fixed probability distribution $\mathcal{D}$. The player is given the point p together with a label indicating whether p is contained in R (a positive example) or not contained in R (a negative example). Figure 1.1 shows the unknown rectangular region R along with a sample of positive and negative examples.

The goal of the player is to use as few examples as possible, and as little computation as possible, to pick a **hypothesis** rectangle R' which is a close approximation to R. Informally, the player's knowledge of R is tested by picking a new point at random from the same probability distribution $\mathcal{D}$, and checking whether the player can correctly decide whether the point falls inside or outside of R. Formally, we measure the

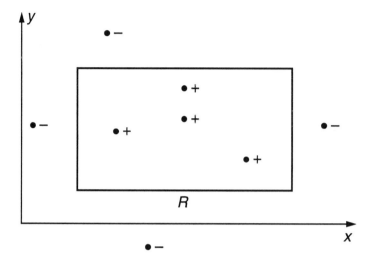

Figure 1.1: *The target rectangle R in the plane along with a sample of positive and negative examples.*

error of R' as the probability that a randomly chosen point from $\mathcal{D}$ falls in the region $R\Delta R'$, where $R\Delta R' = (R - R') \cup (R' - R)$.

To motivate the rectangle learning game, consider a slightly more concrete scenario that can be expressed as an instance of the game. Suppose that we wanted to learn the concept of "men of medium build". Assume that a man is of medium build if his height and weight both lie in some prescribed ranges — for instance, if his height is between five feet six inches and six feet, and his weight is between 150 pounds and 200 pounds. Then each man's build can be represented by a point in the Euclidean plane, and the concept of medium build is represented by an axis-aligned rectangular region of the plane. Thus, during an initial training phase, the learner is told for each new man he meets whether that man is of medium build or not. Over this period, the learner must form some model or hypothesis of the concept of medium build.

Now assume that the learner encounters every man in his city with equal probability. Even under this assumption, the corresponding points in the plane may not be uniformly distributed (since not all heights and weights are equally likely, and height and weight may be highly dependent quantities), but will instead obey some fixed distribution $\mathcal{D}$ which may be quite difficult to characterize. For this reason, in our learning game, we allow the distribution $\mathcal{D}$ to be arbitrary, but we assume that it is fixed, and that each example is drawn independently from this distribution. (Note that once we allow $\mathcal{D}$ to be arbitrary, we no longer need to assume that the learner encounters every man in his city with equal probability.) To evaluate the hypothesis of the learner, we are simply evaluating its success in classifying the build of men in future encounters, still assuming that men are encountered according to the same probability distribution as during the training phase.

There is a simple and efficient strategy for the player of the rectangle learning game. The strategy is to request a "sufficiently large" number m of random examples, then choose as the hypothesis the axis-aligned rectangle R' which gives the tightest fit to the positive examples (that is, that rectangle with the smallest area that includes all of the positive examples and none of the negative examples). If no positive examples are drawn, then $R' = \emptyset$. Figure 1.2 shows the tightest-fit rectangle defined by the sample shown in Figure 1.1.

We will now show that for any target rectangle R and any distribution $\mathcal{D}$, and for any small values ϵ and δ ($0 < \epsilon, \delta \leq 1/2$), for a suitably chosen value of the sample size m we can assert that with probability at least $1 - \delta$, the tightest-fit rectangle has error at most ϵ with respect to R and $\mathcal{D}$.

First observe that the tightest-fit rectangle R' is always contained in the target rectangle R (that is, $R' \subseteq R$ and so $R \triangle R' = R - R'$). We can express the difference $R - R'$ as the union of four rectangular strips. For instance, the topmost of these strips, which is shaded and denoted T' in Figure 1.3, is the region above the upper boundary of R' extended to the left and right, but below the upper boundary of R. Note that there is some overlap between these four rectangular strips at the corners. Now

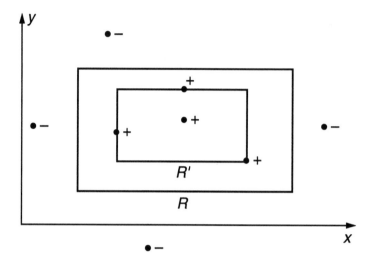

Figure 1.2: *The tightest-fit rectangle R' defined by the sample.*

if we can guarantee that the weight under $\mathcal{D}$ of each strip (that is, the probability with respect to $\mathcal{D}$ of falling in the strip) is at most $\epsilon/4$, then we can conclude that the error of R' is at most $4(\epsilon/4) = \epsilon$. (Here we have erred on the side of pessimism by counting each overlap region twice.)

Let us analyze the weight of the top strip T'. Define T to be the rectangular strip along the inside top of R which encloses *exactly* weight $\epsilon/4$ under $\mathcal{D}$ (thus, we sweep the top edge of R downwards until we have swept out weight $\epsilon/4$; see Figure 1.3). Clearly, T' has weight exceeding $\epsilon/4$ under $\mathcal{D}$ if and only if T' includes T (which it does not in Figure 1.3). Furthermore, T' includes T if and only if no point in T appears in the sample S — since if S does contain a point $p \in T$, this point has a positive label since it is contained in R, and then by definition of the tightest fit, the hypothesis rectangle R' must extend upwards into T to cover p.

By the definition of T, the probability that a single draw from the distribution $\mathcal{D}$ misses the region T is exactly $1 - \epsilon/4$. Therefore the

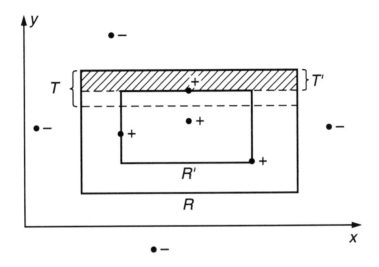

Figure 1.3: *Analysis of the error contributed by the top shaded strip T'. The strip T has weight exactly $\epsilon/4$ under $\mathcal{D}$.*

probability that m independent draws from $\mathcal{D}$ all miss the region T is exactly $(1 - \epsilon/4)^m$. Here we are using the fact that the probability of a conjunction of independent events is simply the product of the probabilities of the individual events. The same analysis holds for the other three rectangular regions of $R - R'$, so by the **union bound**, the probability that any of the four strips of $R - R'$ has weight greater than $\epsilon/4$ is at most $4(1 - \epsilon/4)^m$. By the union bound, we mean the fact that if A and B are any two events (that is, subsets of a probability space), then

$$\mathbf{Pr}[A \cup B] \leq \mathbf{Pr}[A] + \mathbf{Pr}[B].$$

Thus, the probability that one of the four error strips has weight exceeding $\epsilon/4$ is at most four times the probability that a fixed error strip has weight exceeding $\epsilon/4$.

Provided that we choose m to satisfy $4(1 - \epsilon/4)^m \leq \delta$, then with probability $1 - \delta$ over the m random examples, the weight of the error region $R - R'$ will be bounded by ϵ, as claimed. Using the inequality

$$(1 - x) \leq e^{-x}$$

(which we shall appeal to frequently in our studies) we see that any value
of m satisfying $4e^{-\epsilon m/4} \leq \delta$ also satisfies the previous condition. Dividing
by 4 and taking natural logarithms of both sides gives $-\epsilon m/4 \leq \ln(\delta/4)$,
or equivalently $m \geq (4/\epsilon) \ln(4/\delta)$.

In summary, provided our tightest-fit algorithm takes a sample of at
least $(4/\epsilon) \ln(4/\delta)$ examples to form its hypothesis rectangle R', we can
assert that with probability at least $1 - \delta$, R' will misclassify a new point
(drawn according to the same distribution from which the sample was
chosen) with probability at most ϵ.

A few brief comments are appropriate. First, note that the analysis
really does hold for any fixed probability distribution. We only needed
the independence of successive points to obtain our bound. Second, the
sample size bound behaves as we might expect, in that as we increase
our demands on the hypothesis rectangle — that is, as we ask for greater
accuracy by decreasing ϵ or greater **confidence** by decreasing δ — our
algorithm requires more examples to meet those demands. Finally, the
algorithm we have analyzed is efficient: the required sample size is a
slowly growing function of $1/\epsilon$ and $1/\delta$ (linear and logarithmic, respectively), and once the sample is given, the computation of the tightest-fit
hypothesis can be carried out rapidly.

1.2   A General Model

In this section, we introduce the model of learning that will be the central
object for most of our study: the **Probably Approximately Correct**
or **PAC** model of learning. There are a number of features of the rectangle learning game and its solution that are essential to the PAC model,
and bear highlighting before we dive into the general definitions.

- The goal of the learning game is to learn an unknown target set, but the target set is not arbitrary. Instead, there is a known and rather strong constraint on the target set — it is a rectangle in the plane whose sides are parallel to the axes.

- Learning occurs in a probabilistic setting. Examples of the target rectangle are drawn randomly in the plane according to a fixed probability distribution which is unknown and unconstrained.

- The hypothesis of the learner is evaluated relative to the *same* probabilistic setting in which the training takes place, and we allow hypotheses that are only approximations to the target. The tightest-fit strategy might not find the target rectangle exactly, but will find one with only a small probability of disagreement with the target.

- We are interested in a solution that is efficient: not many examples are required to obtain small error with high confidence, and we can process those examples rapidly.

We wish to state a general model of learning from examples that shares and formalizes the properties we have listed. We begin by developing and motivating the necessary definitions.

1.2.1 Definition of the PAC Model

Let X be a set called the **instance space**. We think of X as being a set of encodings of instances or objects in the learner's world. In our rectangle game, the instance space X was simply the set of all points in the Euclidean plane $\Re^2$. As another example, in a character recognition application, the instance space might consist of all 2-dimensional arrays of binary pixels of a given width and height.

A **concept** over X is just a subset $c \subseteq X$ of the instance space. In the rectangle game, the concepts were axis-aligned rectangular regions.

Continuing our character recognition example, a natural concept might
be the set of all pixel arrays that are representations of the letter "A"
(assuming that every pixel array either represents an "A", or fails to
represent an "A").

A concept can thus be thought of as the set of all instances that
positively exemplify some simple or interesting rule. We can equivalently
define a concept to be a boolean mapping $c : X \rightarrow \{0, 1\}$, with $c(x) = 1$
indicating that x is a positive example of c and $c(x) = 0$ indicating that
x is a negative example. For this reason, we also sometimes call X the
input space.

A **concept class** $\mathcal{C}$ over X is a collection of concepts over X. In the
rectangle game, the target rectangle was chosen from the class $\mathcal{C}$ of all
axis-aligned rectangles. Ideally, we are interested in concept classes that
are sufficiently expressive for fairly general knowledge representation. As
an example in a logic-based setting, suppose we have a set $x_1, \ldots, x_n$
of n boolean variables, and let X be the set of all assignments to these
variables (that is, $X = \{0, 1\}^n$). Suppose we consider concepts c over
$\{0, 1\}^n$ whose positive examples are exactly the satisfying assignments
of some boolean formulae f_c over $x_1, \ldots, x_n$. Then we might define an
interesting concept class $\mathcal{C}$ by considering only those boolean formulae f_c
that meet some natural syntactic constraints, such as being in disjunctive
normal form (DNF) and having a small number of terms.

In our model, a learning algorithm will have access to positive and
negative examples of an unknown **target concept** c, chosen from a
known concept class $\mathcal{C}$. The learning algorithm will be judged by its
ability to identify a hypothesis concept that can accurately classify instances as positive or negative examples of c. Before specifying the learning protocol further, it is important to note that in our model, learning
algorithms "know" the target class $\mathcal{C}$, in the sense that the designer of the
learning algorithm is guaranteed that the target concept will be chosen
from $\mathcal{C}$ (but must design the algorithm to work for any $c \in \mathcal{C}$).

Let $\mathcal{D}$ be any fixed probability distribution over the instance space X.

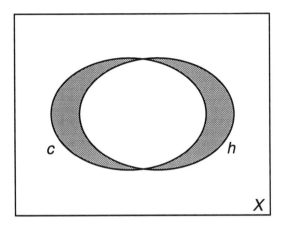

Figure 1.4: *Venn diagram of two concepts, with symmetric difference shaded.*

We will refer to $\mathcal{D}$ as the **target distribution**. If h is any concept over X, then the distribution $\mathcal{D}$ provides a natural measure of **error** between h and the target concept c: namely, we define

$$error(h) = \mathbf{Pr}_{x \in \mathcal{D}}[c(x) \neq h(x)].$$

Here we regard the concepts c and h as boolean functions, and we have introduced a notational convention that we shall use frequently: the subscript $x \in \mathcal{D}$ to $\mathbf{Pr}[\cdot]$ indicates that the probability is taken with respect to the random draw of x according to $\mathcal{D}$. Note that $error(h)$ has an implicit dependence on c and $\mathcal{D}$ that we will usually omit for brevity when no confusion will result.

A useful alternative way to view $error(h)$ is represented in Figure 1.4. Here we view the concepts c and h as sets rather than as functions, and we have drawn an abstract Venn diagram showing the positive examples of c and h, which of course lie within the entire instance space X. Then $error(h)$ is simply the probability with respect to $\mathcal{D}$ that an instance is drawn falling in the shaded region.

Let $EX(c, \mathcal{D})$ be a procedure (we will sometimes call it an *oracle*) that runs in unit time, and on each call returns a labeled example $\langle x, c(x) \rangle$, where x is drawn randomly and independently according to $\mathcal{D}$. A learning algorithm will have access to this oracle when learning the target concept $c \in \mathcal{C}$. Ideally, the learning algorithm will satisfy three properties:

- The number of calls to $EX(c, \mathcal{D})$ is small, in the sense that it is bounded by a fixed polynomial in some parameters to be specified shortly.

- The amount of computation performed is small.

- The algorithm outputs a **hypothesis concept** h such that $error(h)$ is small.

Note that the number of calls made by a learning algorithm to $EX(c, \mathcal{D})$ is bounded by the running time of the learning algorithm.

We are now ready to give the definition of Probably Approximately Correct learning. We designate it as our preliminary definition, since we shall soon make some important additions to it.

Definition 1 *(The PAC Model, Preliminary Definition) Let $\mathcal{C}$ be a concept class over X. We say that $\mathcal{C}$ is **PAC learnable** if there exists an algorithm L with the following property: for every concept $c \in \mathcal{C}$, for every distribution $\mathcal{D}$ on X, and for all $0 < \epsilon < 1/2$ and $0 < \delta < 1/2$, if L is given access to $EX(c, \mathcal{D})$ and inputs ϵ and δ, then with probability at least $1 - \delta$, L outputs a hypothesis concept $h \in \mathcal{C}$ satisfying $error(h) \leq \epsilon$. This probability is taken over the random examples drawn by calls to $EX(c, \mathcal{D})$, and any internal randomization of L.*

*If L runs in time polynomial in $1/\epsilon$ and $1/\delta$, we say that $\mathcal{C}$ is **efficiently** PAC learnable. We will sometimes refer to the input ϵ as the **error parameter**, and the input δ as the **confidence parameter**.*

The hypothesis $h \in \mathcal{C}$ of the PAC learning algorithm is thus "approximately correct" with high probability, hence the name Probably Approximately Correct learning.

Two important comments regarding the PAC learning model are now in order. First, the error and confidence parameters ϵ and δ control the two types of failure to which a learning algorithm in the PAC model is inevitably susceptible. The error parameter ϵ is necessary since, for example, there may be only a negligible probability that a small random sample will distinguish between two competing hypotheses that differ on only one improbable point in the instance space. The confidence parameter δ is necessary since the learning algorithm may occasionally be extremely unlucky, and draw a terribly "unrepresentative" sample of the target concept — for instance, a sample consisting only of repeated draws of the same instance despite the fact that the distribution is spread evenly over all instances. The best we can hope for is that the probability of both types of failure can be made arbitrarily small at a modest cost.

Second, notice that we demand that a PAC learning algorithm perform well with respect to any distribution $\mathcal{D}$. This strong requirement is moderated by the fact that we only evaluate the hypothesis of the learning algorithm with respect to the same distribution $\mathcal{D}$. For example, in the rectangle learning game discussed earlier, this means that if the distribution gives negligible weight to some parts of the Euclidean plane, then the learner does not have to be very careful in learning the boundary of the target rectangle in that region.

Definition 1, then, is our tentative definition of PAC learning, which will be the model forming the bulk of our studies. As previously mentioned, we shall make a couple of important refinements to this definition before we begin the serious investigation. Before doing so, however, we pause to note that we have already proven our first result in this model. Recall that our algorithm for the rectangle learning game required the ability to store real numbers and perform basic operations on them, such as comparisons. In the following theorem, and throughout our study, whenever necessary we will assume a model of computation that allows storage of a single real number in a single memory location, and that charges one unit of computation time for a basic arithmetic operation (addition, multiplication or division) on two real numbers.

Theorem 1.1 *The concept class of axis-aligned rectangles over the Euclidean plane $\Re^2$ is efficiently PAC learnable.*

1.2.2 Representation Size and Instance Dimension

An important issue was swept under the rug in our definition of PAC learning. This is the fundamental distinction between a concept (which is just a set or a boolean function) and its representation (which is a symbolic encoding of that set or function). Consider a class of concepts defined by the satisfying assignments of boolean formulae. A concept from this class — that is, the set of satisfying assignments for some boolean formula f — can be represented by the formula f, by a truth table, or by another boolean formula f' that is logically equivalent to f. Although all of these are representations of the same underlying concept, they may differ radically in representational size.

For instance, it is not hard to prove that for all n, the boolean parity function $f(x_1, \ldots, x_n) = x_1 \oplus \cdots \oplus x_n$ (where $\oplus$ denotes the exclusive-or operation) can be computed by a circuit of $\wedge$, $\vee$ and $\neg$ gates whose size is bounded by a fixed polynomial in n, but to represent this same function as a disjunctive normal form (abbreviated DNF) formula requires size exponential in n. As another example, in high-dimensional Euclidean space $\Re^n$, we may choose to represent a convex polytope either by specifying its vertices, or by specifying linear equations for its faces, and these two representation schemes can differ exponentially in size.

In each of these examples, we are fixing some representation scheme — that is, a precise method for encoding concepts — and then examining the size of the encoding for various concepts. Other natural representation schemes that the reader may be familiar with include decision trees and neural networks. As with boolean formulae, in these representation schemes there is an obvious mapping from the representation (a decision tree or a neural network) to the set or boolean function that is being represented. There is also a natural measure of the size of a given representation in the scheme (for instance, the number of nodes in the decision tree or the number of weights in a neural network).

Since a PAC learning algorithm only sees examples of the functional (that is, input-output) behavior of the target concept, it has absolutely no information about which, if any, of the many possible representations is actually being used to represent the target concept in reality. However, it matters greatly which representation the algorithm chooses for its hypothesis, since the time to write this representation down is obviously a lower bound on the running time of the algorithm.

Formally speaking, a **representation scheme** for a concept class $\mathcal{C}$ is a function $\mathcal{R} : \Sigma^* \rightarrow \mathcal{C}$, where Σ is a finite alphabet of symbols. (In cases where we need to use real numbers to represent concepts, such as axis-aligned rectangles, we allow $\mathcal{R} : (\Sigma \cup \Re)^* \rightarrow \mathcal{C}$.) We call any string $\sigma \in \Sigma^*$ such that $\mathcal{R}(\sigma) = c$ a **representation** of c (under $\mathcal{R}$). Note that there may be many representations of a concept c under the representation scheme $\mathcal{R}$.

To capture the notion of representation size, we assume that associated with $\mathcal{R}$ there is a mapping $size : \Sigma^* \rightarrow N$ that assigns a natural number $size(h)$ to each representation $h \in \Sigma^*$. Note that we allow $size(\cdot)$ to be any such mapping; results obtained under a particular definition for $size(\cdot)$ will be meaningful only if this definition is natural. Perhaps the most realistic setting, however, is that in which $\Sigma = \{0, 1\}$ (thus, we have a binary encoding of concepts) and we define $size(h)$ to be the length of h in bits. (For representations using real numbers, it is often natural to charge one unit of size for each real number.) Although we will use other definitions of size when binary representations are inconvenient, our definition of $size(\cdot)$ will always be within a polynomial factor of the binary string length definition. For example, we can define the size of a decision tree to be the number of nodes in the tree, which is always within a polynomial factor of the length of the binary string needed to encode the tree in any reasonable encoding method.

So far our notion of size is applicable only to representations (that is, to strings $h \in \Sigma^*$). We would like to extend this definition to measure the size of a target concept $c \in C$. Since the learning algorithm has access only to the input-output behavior of c, in the worst case it must assume that the simplest possible mechanism is generating this behavior. Thus, we define $size(c)$ to be $size(c) = \min_{\mathcal{R}(\sigma)=c}\{size(\sigma)\}$. In other words, $size(c)$ is the size of the smallest representation of the concept c in the underlying representation scheme $\mathcal{R}$. Intuitively, the larger $size(c)$ is, the more "complex" the concept c is with respect to the chosen representation scheme. Thus it is natural to modify our notion of learning to allow more computation time for learning more complex concepts, and we shall do this shortly.

For a concept class C, we shall refer to the **representation class C** to indicate that we have in mind some fixed representation scheme $\mathcal{R}$ for C. In fact, we will usually *define* the concept classes we study by their representation scheme. For instance, we will shortly examine the concept class in which each concept is the set of satisfying assignments of some conjunction of boolean variables. Thus, each concept can be represented by a list of the variables in the associated conjunction.

It is often convenient to also introduce some notion of size or dimension for the elements of the instance space. For example, if the instance space X_n is the n-dimensional Euclidean space $\Re^n$, then each example is specified by n real numbers, and so it is natural to say that the size of the examples is n. The same comments apply to the instance space $X_n = \{0, 1\}^n$. It turns out that these are the only two instance spaces that we will ever need to consider in our studies, and in the spirit of asymptotic analysis we will want to regard the instance space dimension n as a parameter of the learning problem (for example, to allow us to study the problem of learning axis-aligned rectangles in $\Re^n$ in time polynomial in n). Now if we let $\mathcal{C}_n$ be the class of concepts over X_n, and write $X = \cup_{n\geq 1} X_n$ and $\mathcal{C} = \cup_{n\geq 1} \mathcal{C}_n$, then X and $\mathcal{C}$ define an infinite family of learning problems of increasing dimension.

To incorporate the notions of target concept size and instance space dimension into our model, we make the following refined definition of PAC learning:

Definition 2 *(The PAC Model, Modified Definition) Let $\mathcal{C}_n$ be a representation class over X_n (where X_n is either $\{0,1\}^n$ or n-dimensional Euclidean space $\Re^n$), and let $X = \cup_{n\geq 1} X_n$ and $\mathcal{C} = \cup_{n\geq 1} \mathcal{C}_n$. The modified definition of PAC learning is the same as the preliminary definition (Definition 1), except that now we allow the learning algorithm time polynomial in n and $size(c)$ (as well as $1/\epsilon$ and $1/\delta$ as before) when learning a target concept $c \in \mathcal{C}_n$.*

Since in our studies X_n will always be either $\{0,1\}^n$ or n-dimensional Euclidean space, the value n is implicit in the instances returned by $EX(c, \mathcal{D})$. We assume that the learner is provided with the value $size(c)$ as an input. (However, see Exercise 1.5.)

We emphasize that while the target concept may have many possible representations in the chosen scheme, we only allow the learning algorithm time polynomial in the size of the smallest such representation. This provides a worst-case guarantee over the possible representations of c, and is consistent with the fact that the learning algorithm has no idea which representation is being used for c, having only functional information about c.

Finally, we note that for several concept classes the natural definition of $size(c)$ is already bounded by a polynomial in n, and thus we really seek an algorithm running in time polynomial in just n. For instance, if we look at the representation class of all DNF formulae with at most 3 terms, any such formula has length at most $3n$, so polynomial dependence on the size of the target formula is the same as polynomial dependence on n.

1.3   Learning Boolean Conjunctions

We now give our second result in the PAC model, showing that **conjunctions of boolean literals** are efficiently PAC learnable. Here the instance space is $X_n = \{0,1\}^n$. Each $a \in X_n$ is interpreted as an assignment to the n boolean variables $x_1, \ldots, x_n$, and we use the notation a_i to indicate the ith bit of a. Let the representation class $\mathcal{C}_n$ be the class of all conjunctions of literals over $x_1, \ldots, x_n$ (a **literal** is either a variable x_i or its negation $\overline{x}_i$). Thus the conjunction $x_1 \wedge \overline{x}_3 \wedge x_4$ represents the set $\{a \in \{0,1\}^n : a_1 = 1, a_3 = 0, a_4 = 1\}$. It is natural to define the size of a conjunction to be the number of literals in that conjunction. Then clearly $size(c) \leq 2n$ for any conjunction $c \in \mathcal{C}_n$. (We also note that a standard binary encoding of any conjunction $c \in \mathcal{C}_n$ has length $O(n \log n)$.) Thus for this problem, we seek an algorithm that runs in time polynomial in n, $1/\epsilon$ and $1/\delta$.

Theorem 1.2 *The representation class of conjunctions of boolean literals is efficiently PAC learnable.*

Proof: The algorithm we propose begins with the hypothesis conjunction

$$h = x_1 \wedge \overline{x}_1 \wedge \cdots \wedge x_n \wedge \overline{x}_n.$$

Note that initially h has no satisfying assignments. The algorithm simply ignores any negative examples returned by $EX(c, \mathcal{D})$. Let $\langle a, 1 \rangle$ be a positive example returned by $EX(c, \mathcal{D})$. In response to such a positive example, our algorithm updates h as follows: for each i, if $a_i = 0$, we delete x_i from h, and if $a_i = 1$, we delete $\overline{x}_i$ from h. Thus, our algorithm deletes any literal that "contradicts" the positive data.

For the analysis, note that the set of literals appearing in h at any time always contains the set of literals appearing in the target concept c. This is because we begin with h containing all literals, and a literal is only deleted from h when it is set to 0 in a positive example; such a literal clearly cannot appear in c. The fact that the literals of h always include those of c implies that h will never err on a negative example of c (that is, h is more specific than c).

Thus, consider a literal z that occurs in h but not in c. Then z causes h to err only on those positive examples of c in which $z = 0$; also note that it is exactly such positive examples that would have caused our algorithm to delete z from h. Let $p(z)$ denote the total probability of such instances under the distribution $\mathcal{D}$, that is,

$$p(z) = \mathbf{Pr}_{a \in \mathcal{D}}[c(a) = 1 \wedge z \text{ is } 0 \text{ in } a].$$

Since every error of h can be "blamed" on at least one literal z of h, by the union bound we have $error(h) \leq \sum_{z \in h} p(z)$. We say that a literal is *bad* if $p(z) \geq \epsilon/2n$. If h contains no bad literals, then $error(h) \leq \sum_{z \in h} p(z) \leq 2n(\epsilon/2n) = \epsilon$. We now upper bound the probability that a bad literal will appear in h.

For any *fixed* bad literal z, the probability that this literal is not deleted from h after m calls of our algorithm to $EX(c, \mathcal{D})$ is at most $(1 - \epsilon/2n)^m$, because the probability the literal z is deleted by a single call to $EX(c, \mathcal{D})$ is $p(z)$ (which is at least $\epsilon/2n$ for a bad literal). From this we may conclude that the probability that there is *some* bad literal that is not deleted from h after m calls is at most $2n(1 - \epsilon/2n)^m$, where we have used the union bound over the $2n$ possible literals.

Thus to complete our analysis we simply need to solve for the value of m satisfying $2n(1 - \epsilon/2n)^m \leq \delta$, where $1 - \delta$ is the desired confidence. Using the inequality $1 - x \leq e^{-x}$, it suffices to pick m such that $2ne^{-m\epsilon/2n} \leq \delta$, which yields $m \geq (2n/\epsilon)(\ln(2n) + \ln(1/\delta))$.

Thus, if our algorithm takes at least this number of examples, then with probability at least $1 - \delta$ the resulting conjunction h will have error at most ϵ with respect to c and $\mathcal{D}$. Since the algorithm takes linear time to process each example, the running time is bounded by mn, and hence is bounded by a polynomial in n, $1/\epsilon$ and $1/\delta$, as required. $\square$(Theorem 1.2)

1.4   Intractability of Learning 3-Term DNF Formulae

We next show that a slight generalization of the representation class of boolean conjunctions results in an intractable PAC learning problem. More precisely, we show that the class of disjunctions of three boolean conjunctions (known as **3-term disjunctive normal form (DNF) formulae**) is not efficiently PAC learnable unless every problem in *NP* can be efficiently solved in a worst-case sense by a randomized algorithm — that is, unless for every language A in *NP* there is a randomized algorithm taking as input any string α and a parameter $\delta \in [0,1]$, and that with probability at least $1 - \delta$ correctly determines whether $\alpha \in A$ in time polynomial in the length of α and $1/\delta$. The probability here is taken only with respect to the coin flips of the randomized algorithm. In technical language, our hardness result for 3-term DNF is based on the widely believed assumption that $RP \neq NP$.

The representation class $\mathcal{C}_n$ of 3-term DNF formulae is the set of all disjunctions $T_1 \vee T_2 \vee T_3$, where each T_i is a conjunction of literals over the boolean variables $x_1, \ldots, x_n$. We define the size of such a representation to be sum of the number of literals appearing in each term (which is always bounded by a fixed polynomial in the length of the bit string needed to represent the 3-term DNF in a standard encoding). Then $size(c) \leq 6n$ for any concept $c \in \mathcal{C}_n$ because there are at most $2n$ literals in each of the three terms. Thus, an efficient learning algorithm for this problem is required to run in time polynomial in n, $1/\epsilon$ and $1/\delta$.

Theorem 1.3 *If $RP \neq NP$, the representation class of 3-term DNF* *formulae is not efficiently PAC learnable.*

Proof: The high-level idea of the proof is to reduce an *NP*-complete language A (to be specified shortly) to the problem of PAC learning 3-term DNF formulae. More precisely, the reduction will efficiently map any string α, for which we wish to determine membership in A, to a set S_α of labeled examples. The cardinality $|S_\alpha|$ will be bounded by a polynomial in the string length $|\alpha|$. We will show that given a PAC learning algorithm L for 3-term DNF formulae, we can run L on S_α, in a manner to be described, to determine (with high probability) if α belongs to A or not.

The key property we desire of the mapping of α to S_α is that $\alpha \in A$ if and only if S_α is **consistent** with some concept $c \in \mathcal{C}$. The notion of a concept being consistent with a sample will recur frequently in our studies.

Definition 3 *Let* $S = \{\langle x_1, b_1 \rangle, \ldots, \langle x_m, b_m \rangle\}$ *be any labeled set of instances, where each* $x_i \in X$ *and each* $b_i \in \{0, 1\}$. *Let* c *be a concept over* X. *Then we say that* c *is* **consistent** *with* S *(or equivalently,* S *is consistent with* c*) if for all* $1 \leq i \leq m$, $c(x_i) = b_i$.

Before detailing our choice for the *NP*-complete language A and the mapping of α to S_α, just suppose for now that we have managed to arrange things so that $\alpha \in A$ if and only if S_α is consistent with some concept in $\mathcal{C}$. We now show how a PAC learning algorithm L for $\mathcal{C}$ can be used to *determine* if there exists a concept in $\mathcal{C}$ that is consistent with S_α (and thus whether $\alpha \in A$) with high probability. This is achieved by the following general method: we set the error parameter $\epsilon = 1/(2|S_\alpha|)$ (where $|S_\alpha|$ denotes the number of labeled pairs in S_α), and answer each request of L for a random labeled example by choosing a pair $\langle x_i, b_i \rangle$ uniformly at random from S_α. Note that if there is a concept $c \in \mathcal{C}$ consistent with S_α, then this simulation emulates the oracle $EX(c, \mathcal{D})$, where $\mathcal{D}$ is uniform over the (multiset of) instances appearing in S_α. In this case, by our choice of ϵ, we have guaranteed that any hypothesis h with error less that ϵ must in fact be consistent with S_α, for if h errs on even a single example in S_α, its error with respect to c and $\mathcal{D}$ is at least $1/|S_\alpha| = 2\epsilon > \epsilon$. On the other hand, if there is no concept in $\mathcal{C}$ consistent with S_α, L cannot possibly find one. Thus we can simply check the output of L for consistency with S_α to determine with confidence $1 - \delta$ if there exists a consistent concept in $\mathcal{C}$.

Combined with the assumed mapping of a string α to a set S_α, we thus can determine (with probability at least $1 - \delta$) the membership of α in A by simulating the PAC learning algorithm on S_α. This general method of using a PAC learning algorithm to determine the existence of a concept that is consistent with a labeled sample is quite common in the computational learning theory literature, and the main effort comes in choosing the right NP-complete language A, and finding the desired mapping from instances α of A to sets of labeled examples S_α, which we now undertake.

To demonstrate the intractability of learning 3-term DNF formulae, the NP-complete language A that we shall use is Graph 3-Coloring:

The Graph 3-Coloring Problem. Given as input an undirected graph $G = (V, E)$ with vertex set $V = \{1, \ldots, n\}$ and edge set $E \subseteq V \times V$, determine if there is an assignment of a color to each element of V such that at most 3 different colors are used, and for every edge $(i, j) \in E$, vertex i and vertex j are assigned different colors.

We now describe the desired mapping from an instance $G = (V, E)$ of Graph 3-Coloring to a set S_G of labeled examples. S_G will consist of a set S_G^+ of positively labeled examples and a set S_G^- of negatively labeled examples, so $S_G = S_G^+ \cup S_G^-$. For each $1 \leq i \leq n$, S_G^+ will contain the labeled example $\langle v(i), 1 \rangle$, where $v(i) \in \{0, 1\}^n$ is the vector with a 0 in the ith position and 1's everywhere else. These examples intuitively encode the vertices of G. For each edge $(i, j) \in E$, the set S_G^- will contain the labeled example $\langle e(i, j), 0 \rangle$, where $e(i, j) \in \{0, 1\}^n$ is the vector with 0's in the ith and jth positions, and 1's everywhere else. Figure 1.5 shows

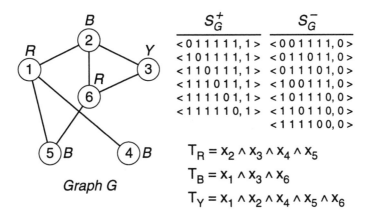

Figure 1.5: *A graph G with a legal 3-coloring, the associated sample, and the terms defined by the coloring.*

an example of a graph G along with the resulting sets S_G^+ and S_G^-. The figure also shows a legal 3-coloring of G, with R, B and Y denoting red, blue and yellow.

We now argue that G is 3-colorable if and only if S_G is consistent with some 3-term DNF formula. First, suppose G is 3-colorable and fix a 3-coloring of G. Let R be the set of all vertices colored red, and let T_R be the conjunction of all variables in $x_1, \ldots, x_n$ whose index does *not* appear in R (see Figure 1.5). Then for each $i \in R$, $v(i)$ must satisfy T_R because the variable x_i does not appear in T_R. Furthermore, no $e(i,j) \in S_G^-$ can satisfy T_R because since both i and j cannot be colored red, one of x_i and x_j must appear in T_R. We can define terms that are satisfied by the non-blue and non-yellow $v(i)$ in a similar fashion, with no negative examples being accepted by any term.

For the other direction, suppose that the formula $T_R \vee T_B \vee T_Y$ is consistent with S_G. Define a coloring of G as follows: the color of vertex i is red if $v(i)$ satisfies T_R, blue if $v(i)$ satisfies T_B, and yellow if $v(i)$ satisfies T_Y (we break ties arbitrarily if $v(i)$ satisfies more than one term). Since the formula is consistent with S_G, every $v(i)$ must satisfy some term, and so every vertex must be assigned a color by this process. We now argue that it is a legal 3-coloring. To see this, note that if i and j ($i \neq j$) are assigned the same color (say red), then both $v(i)$ and $v(j)$ satisfy T_R. Since the ith bit of $v(i)$ is 0 and the ith bit of $v(j)$ is 1, it follows that neither x_i nor $\overline{x}_i$ can appear in T_R. Since $v(j)$ and $e(i,j)$ differ only in their ith bits, if $v(j)$ satisfies T_R then so does $e(i,j)$, implying $e(i,j) \notin S_G^-$ and hence $(i,j) \notin E$. $\square$(Theorem 1.3)

Thus, we see that 3-term DNF formulae are not efficiently PAC learnable under the assumption that *NP*-complete problems cannot be solved with high probability by a probabilistic polynomial-time algorithm (technically, under the assumption $RP \neq NP$). With some more elaborate technical gymnastics, the same statement can in fact be made for 2-term DNF formulae, and for k-term DNF formulae for any constant $k \geq 2$.

However, note that our reduction relied critically on our demand in the definition of PAC learning that the learning algorithm output a hypothesis from the same representation class from which the target formula is drawn — we used each term of the hypothesis 3-term formula to define a color class in the graph. In the next section we shall see that this demand is in fact necessary for this intractability result, since its removal permits an efficient learning algorithm for this same class. This will motivate our final modification of the definition of PAC learning.

1.5   Using 3-CNF Formulae to Avoid Intractability

We conclude this chapter by showing that if we allow the learning algorithm to output a more expressive hypothesis representation, then the class of 3-term DNF formulae *is* efficiently PAC learnable. In combination with Theorem 1.3, this motivates our final modification to the definition of PAC learning.

We can use the fact that for boolean algebra, $\vee$ distributes over $\wedge$ (that is, $(u \wedge v) \vee (w \wedge x) = (u \vee w) \wedge (u \vee x) \wedge (v \vee w) \wedge (v \vee x)$ for boolean variables u, v, w, x) to represent any 3-term DNF formula over $x_1, \ldots, x_n$ by an equivalent conjunctive normal form (CNF) formulae over $x_1, \ldots, x_n$ in which each clause contains at most 3 literals (we will call such formulae **3-CNF formulae**):

$$T_1 \vee T_2 \vee T_3 \equiv \bigwedge_{u \in T_1, v \in T_2, w \in T_3} (u \vee v \vee w).$$

Here the conjunction is over all clauses choosing one literal from each term.

We can *reduce* the problem of PAC learning 3-CNF formulae to the problem of PAC learning conjunctions, for which we already have an efficient algorithm. The high-level idea is as follows: given an oracle for random examples of an unknown 3-CNF formula, there is a simple and efficient method by which we can transform each positive or negative example into a corresponding positive or negative example of an unknown conjunction (over a larger set of variables). We then give the transformed examples to the learning algorithm for conjunctions that we have already described in Section 1.3. The hypothesis output by the learning algorithm for conjunctions can then be transformed into a good hypothesis for the unknown 3-CNF formula.

To describe the desired transformation of examples, we regard a 3-CNF formula as a conjunction over a new and larger variable set. For every triple of literals u, v, w over the original variable set $x_1, \ldots, x_n$, the new variable set contains a variable $y_{u,v,w}$ whose value is defined by $y_{u,v,w} = u \vee v \vee w$. Note that when $u = v = w$, then $y_{u,v,w} = u$, so all of the original variables are present in the new set. Also, note that the number of new variables $y_{u,v,w}$ is $(2n)^3 = O(n^3)$.

Thus for any assignment $a \in \{0, 1\}^n$ to the original variables $x_1, \ldots, x_n$, we can in time $O(n^3)$ compute the corresponding assignment a' to the new variables $\{y_{u,v,w}\}$. Furthermore, it should be clear that any 3-CNF formula c over $x_1, \ldots, x_n$ is equivalent to a simple conjunction c' over the new variables (just replace any clause $(u \lor v \lor w)$ by an occurrence of the new variable $y_{u,v,w}$). Thus, we can run our algorithm for conjunctions from Section 1.3, expanding each assignment to $x_1, \ldots, x_n$ that is a positive example of the unknown 3-CNF formula into an assignment for the $y_{u,v,w}$, and giving this expanded assignment to the algorithm as a positive example of an unknown conjunction over the $y_{u,v,w}$. We can then convert the resulting hypothesis conjunction h' over the $y_{u,v,w}$ back to a 3-CNF h in the obvious way, by expanding an occurrence of the variable $y_{u,v,w}$ to the clause $(u \lor v \lor w)$.

Formally, we must argue that if c and $\mathcal{D}$ are the target 3-CNF formula and distribution over $\{0, 1\}^n$, and c' and $\mathcal{D}'$ are the corresponding conjunction over the $y_{u,v,w}$ and induced distribution over assignments a' to the $y_{u,v,w}$, then if h' has error less than ϵ with respect to c' and $\mathcal{D}'$, h has error less than ϵ with respect to c and $\mathcal{D}$. This is most easily seen by noting that our transformation of instances is one-to-one: if a_1 is mapped to a'_1 and a_2 is mapped to a'_2, then $a_1 \neq a_2$ implies $a'_1 \neq a'_2$. Thus each vector a' on which h' differs from c' has a unique preimage a on which h differs from c, and the weight of a under $\mathcal{D}$ is exactly that of a' under $\mathcal{D}'$. It is worth noting, however, that our reduction is exploiting the fact that our conjunctions learning algorithm works for any distribution $\mathcal{D}$, as the distribution is "distorted" by the transformation. For example, even if $\mathcal{D}$ was the uniform distribution over $\{0, 1\}^n$, $\mathcal{D}'$ would not be uniform over the transformed assignments a'.

We have just given an example of a **reduction** between two learning problems. A general notion of reducibility in PAC learning will be formalized and studied in Chapter 7.

We have proven:

Theorem 1.4 *The representation class of 3-CNF formulae is efficiently PAC learnable.*

Thus, because we have already shown that any 3-term DNF formula can be written as a 3-CNF formula, we can PAC learn 3-term DNF formulae if we allow the hypothesis to be represented as a 3-CNF formula, but not if we insist that it be represented as a 3-term DNF formula! The same statement holds for any constant $k \geq 2$ for k-term DNF formulae and k-CNF formulae. This demonstrates an important principle that often appears in learning theory: even for a fixed concept class from which target concepts are chosen, the choice of hypothesis representation can sometimes mean the difference between efficient algorithms and intractability. The specific cause of intractability here is worth noting: the problem of just predicting the classification of new examples of a 3-term DNF formula is tractable (we can use a 3-CNF formula for this purpose), but expressing the prediction rule in a particular form (namely, 3-term DNF formulae) is hard.

This state of affairs motivates us to generalize our basic definition one more time, to allow the learning algorithm to use a more expressive hypothesis representation than is strictly required to represent the target concept. After all, we would not have wanted to close the book on the learnability of 3-term DNF formulae after our initial intractability result just because we were constrained by an artificial definition that insisted that learning algorithms use some particular hypothesis representation. Thus our final modification to the definition of PAC learning lets the hypothesis representation used be a parameter of the PAC learning problem.

Definition 4 *(The PAC Model, Final Definition) If C is a concept class over X and $\mathcal{H}$ is a representation class over X, we will say that C is* **(efficiently) PAC learnable using $\mathcal{H}$** *if our basic definition of PAC learning (Definition 2) is met by an algorithm that is now allowed to output a hypothesis from $\mathcal{H}$. Here we are implicitly assuming that $\mathcal{H}$ is at least as expressive as C, and so there is a representation in $\mathcal{H}$ of every function in C. We will refer to $\mathcal{H}$ as the* **hypothesis class** *of the PAC learning algorithm.*

While for the reasons already discussed we do not want to place un-

necessary restrictions on $\mathcal{H}$, neither do we want to leave $\mathcal{H}$ entirely unconstrained. In particular, it would be senseless to study a model of learning
in which the learning algorithm is constrained to run in polynomial time,
but the hypotheses output by this learning algorithm could not even be
evaluated in polynomial time. This motivates the following definition.

Definition 5 *We say that the representation class $\mathcal{H}$ is **polynomially
evaluatable** if there is an algorithm that on input any instance $x \in X_n$
and any representation $h \in \mathcal{H}_n$, outputs the value $h(x)$ in time polynomial
in n and $size(h)$.*

Throughout our study, we will always be implicitly assuming that
PAC learning algorithms use polynomially evaluatable hypothesis classes.
Using our new language, our original definition was for PAC learning $\mathcal{C}$ using $\mathcal{C}$, and now we shall simply say that $\mathcal{C}$ is **efficiently PAC learnable**
to mean that $\mathcal{C}$ is efficiently PAC learnable using $\mathcal{H}$ for some polynomially
evaluatable hypothesis class $\mathcal{H}$.

The main results of this chapter are summarized in our new language
by the following theorem.

Theorem 1.5 *The representation class of 1-term DNF formulae (conjunctions) is efficiently PAC learnable using 1-term DNF formulae. For
any constant $k \geq 2$, the representation class of k-term DNF formulae is not efficiently PAC learnable using k-term DNF formulae (unless
$RP = NP$), but is efficiently PAC learnable using k-CNF formulae.*

1.6 Exercises

1.1. Generalize the algorithm for the rectangle learning game to prove
that if $\mathcal{C}_n$ is the class of all axis-aligned hyperrectangles in n-dimensional
Euclidean space $\Re^n$, then $\mathcal{C}$ is efficiently PAC learnable.

1.2. Let $f(\cdot)$ be an integer-valued function, and assume that there does not exist a randomized algorithm taking as input a graph G and a parameter $0 < \delta \leq 1$ that runs in time polynomial in $1/\delta$ and the size of G, and that with probability at least $1 - \delta$ outputs "no" if G is not k-colorable and outputs an $f(k)$-coloring of G otherwise. Then show that for some $k \geq 3$, k-term DNF formulae are not efficiently PAC learnable using $f(k)$-term DNF formulae.

1.3. Consider the following **two-oracle** variant of the PAC model: when $c \in C$ is the target concept, there are separate and arbitrary distributions $\mathcal{D}_c^+$ over only the positive examples of c and $\mathcal{D}_c^-$ over only the negative examples of c. The learning algorithm now has access to two oracles $EX(c, \mathcal{D}_c^+)$ and $EX(c, \mathcal{D}_c^-)$ that return a random positive example or a random negative example in unit time. For error parameter ϵ, the learning algorithm must find a hypothesis satisfying $\mathbf{Pr}_{x \in \mathcal{D}_c^+}[h(x) = 0] \leq \epsilon$ and $\mathbf{Pr}_{x \in \mathcal{D}_c^-}[h(x) = 1] \leq \epsilon$. Thus, the learning algorithm may now explicitly request either a positive or negative example, but must find a hypothesis with small error on both distributions.

Let C be any concept class and $\mathcal{H}$ be any hypothesis class. Let h_0 and h_1 be representations of the identically 0 and identically 1 functions, respectively. Prove that C is efficiently PAC learnable using $\mathcal{H}$ in the original one-oracle model if and only if C is efficiently PAC learnable using $\mathcal{H} \cup \{h_0, h_1\}$ in the two-oracle model.

1.4. Let C be any concept class and $\mathcal{H}$ be any hypothesis class. Let h_0 and h_1 be representations of the identically 0 and identically 1 functions, respectively. Show that if there is a randomized algorithm for efficiently PAC learning C using $\mathcal{H}$, then there is a deterministic algorithm for efficiently PAC learning C using $\mathcal{H} \cup \{h_0, h_1\}$.

1.5. In Definition 2, we modified the PAC model to allow the learning algorithm time polynomial in n and $size(c)$, and also provided the value $size(c)$ as input. Prove that this input is actually unnecessary: if there is an efficient PAC learning algorithm for C that is given $size(c)$ as input, then there is an efficient PAC learning algorithm for C that is not given this input.

1.7   Bibliographic Notes

The PAC model was defined in the seminal paper of L.G. Valiant [92], and was elaborated upon in his two subsequent papers [91, 93]. Much of this book is devoted to results in this probabilistic model. Papers by Haussler [45, 46, 47, 44] and Kearns, Li, Pitt and Valiant [59] describe some results in the PAC model from an artificial intelligence perspective.

In addition to defining the model, Valiant's original paper [92] proposed and analyzed the algorithm for PAC learning boolean conjunctions that we presented in Section 1.3. The informal rectangle game which began our study was formally analyzed in the PAC model in another important paper due to Blumer, Ehrenfeucht, Haussler and Warmuth [22], whose main results are the topic of Chapter 3.

The importance of hypothesis representation was first explored by Pitt and Valiant [71]. They showed that k-term DNF is not efficiently PAC learnable using a hypothesis class of k-term DNF, but is efficiently PAC learnable using k-CNF. The general techniques we outlined in Section 1.4 have been used to obtain representation-dependent hardness theorems for many classes, including various neural network architectures (Blum and Rivest [16, 20], Judd [53]). Intractability results for PAC learning neural networks that do not rely on hypothesis class restrictions will be given in Chapter 6. The earliest intractability results for learning that can be translated into the PAC model are those for deterministic finite automata due to Gold [40], who showed that the problem of finding the smallest finite state machine consistent with a labeled sample is *NP*-hard. This result was dramatically improved to obtain a hardness result for even approximating the smallest machine by Pitt and Warmuth [72]. In Chapter 6 we shall give even stronger hardness results for PAC learning finite automata.

Since Valiant introduced the PAC model, there have been a dizzying number of extensions and variants proposed in the computational learning theory. Some of these variants leave what is efficiently learnable essentially unchanged, and were introduced primarily for technical convenience. Others are explicitly designed to change the PAC model in a significant way, for example by providing the learner with more power or a weaker learning criterion. Later we shall study some of these variants. The paper of Haussler, Kearns, Littlestone and Warmuth [49] contains many theorems giving equivalences and relationships between some of the different models in the literature. For instance, the solutions to Exercises 1.3, 1.4 and 1.5 are contained in this paper. Exercise 1.1 is from the Blumer et al. paper [22], and Exercise 1.2 is from Pitt and Valiant [71].

2

Occam's Razor

The PAC model introduced in Chapter 1 defined learning directly in terms of the predictive power of the hypothesis output by the learning algorithm. It was possible to apply this measure of success to a learning algorithm because we made the assumption that the instances are drawn independently from a *fixed* probability distribution $\mathcal{D}$, and then measured predictive power with respect to this same distribution.

In this chapter, we consider a rather different definition of learning that makes no assumptions about how the instances in a labeled sample are chosen. (We still assume that the labels are generated by a target concept chosen from a known class.) Instead of measuring the *predictive* power of a hypothesis, the new definition judges the hypothesis by how succinctly it explains the *observed* data (a labeled sample). The crucial difference between PAC learning and the new definition is that in PAC learning, the random sample drawn by the learning algorithm is intended only as an aid for reaching an accurate model of some external process (the target concept and distribution), while in the new definition we are concerned only with the fixed sample before us, and not any external process.

This new definition will be called *Occam learning*, because it formalizes a principle that was first expounded by the theologian William

of Occam, and which has since become a central doctrine of scientific
methodology. The principle is often referred to as *Occam's Razor* to indicate that overly complex scientific theories should be subjected to a
simplifying knife.

If we equate "simplicity" with representational succinctness, then another way to interpret Occam's principle is that learning is the act of
finding a pattern in the observed data that facilitates a compact representation or compression of this data. In our simple concept learning
setting, succinctness is measured by the size of the representation of the
hypothesis concept. Equivalently, we can measure succinctness by the
cardinality of the hypothesis class used by the algorithm, for if this class
is small then a typical hypothesis from the class can be represented by
a short binary string, and if this class is large then a typical hypothesis
must be represented by a long string. Thus an algorithm is an *Occam
algorithm* if it finds a short hypothesis consistent with the observed data.

Despite its long and illustrious history in the philosophy of science
and its extreme generality, there is something unsatisfying about the
notion of an Occam algorithm. After all, the primary goal of science
(or more generally, of the learning process) is to formulate theories that
accurately predict future observations, not just to succinctly represent
past observations. In this chapter, we will prove that when restricted to
the probabilistic setting of the PAC model, Occam algorithms do indeed
have predictive power. This provides a formal justification of the Occam
principle, albeit in a restricted setting.

Thus, under appropriate conditions, any algorithm that always finds
a succinct hypothesis that is consistent with a given input sample is
automatically a PAC learning algorithm. In addition to the philosophical
interpretation we have just discussed, this reduction of PAC learning
to Occam learning provides a new method of designing PAC learning
algorithms.

2.1 Occam Learning and Succinctness

As in Chapter 1, let $X = \cup_{n \geq 1} X_n$ be the instance space, let $\mathcal{C} = \cup_{n \geq 1} \mathcal{C}_n$ be the target concept class, and let $\mathcal{H} = \cup_{n \geq 1} \mathcal{H}_n$ be the hypothesis representation class. In this chapter we will assume, unless explicitly stated otherwise, that the hypothesis representation scheme of $\mathcal{H}$ uses a binary alphabet, and we define $size(h)$ to be the length of the bit string h. Also, recall that for a concept $c \in \mathcal{C}$, $size(c)$ denotes the size of the smallest representation of c in $\mathcal{H}$.

Let $c \in \mathcal{C}_n$ denote the target concept. A labeled sample S of cardinality m is a set of pairs:

$$S = \{\langle x_1, c(x_1) \rangle, \ldots, \langle x_m, c(x_m) \rangle\}.$$

An Occam algorithm L takes as input a labeled sample S, and outputs a "short" hypothesis h that is consistent with S. By consistent we mean that $h(x_i) = c(x_i)$ for each i, and by "short" we mean that $size(h)$ is a sufficiently slowly growing function of n, $size(c)$ and m. This is formalized in the following definition.

Definition 6 *Let $\alpha \geq 0$ and $0 \leq \beta < 1$ be constants. L is an (α, β)-* **Occam algorithm for $\mathcal{C}$ using $\mathcal{H}$** *if on input a sample S of cardinality m labeled according to $c \in \mathcal{C}_n$, L outputs a hypothesis $h \in \mathcal{H}$ such that:*

- *h is consistent with S.*

- *$size(h) \leq (n \cdot size(c))^{\alpha} m^{\beta}$.*

We say that L is an **efficient** *(α, β)-Occam algorithm if its running time is bounded by a polynomial in n, m and $size(c)$.*

In what sense is the output h of an Occam algorithm succinct? First let us assume that $m \gg n$, so that the above bound can be effectively simplified to $size(h) < m^\beta$ for some $\beta < 1$. Since the hypothesis h is consistent with the sample S, h allows us to reconstruct the m labels $c(x_1) = h(x_1), \ldots, c(x_m) = h(x_m)$ given only the unlabeled sequence of instances $x_1, \ldots, x_m$. Thus the m bits $c(x_1), \ldots, c(x_m)$ have been effectively *compressed* into a much shorter string h of length at most m^β. Note that the requirement $\beta < 1$ is quite weak, since a consistent hypothesis of length $O(mn)$ can always be achieved by simply storing the sample S in a table (at a cost of $n + 1$ bits per labeled example) and giving an arbitrary (say negative) answer for instances that are not in the table. We would certainly not expect such a hypothesis to have any predictive power.

Let us also observe that even in the case $m << n$, the shortest consistent hypothesis in $\mathcal{H}$ may in fact be the target concept, and so we must allow $size(h)$ to depend at least linearly on $size(c)$. The definition of succinctness above is considerably more liberal than this in terms of the allowed dependence on n, and also allows a generous dependence on the number of examples m. We will see cases where this makes it easier to efficiently find a consistent hypothesis — by contrast, computing the shortest hypothesis consistent with the data is often a computationally hard problem.

The next theorem, which is the main result of this chapter, states that any efficient Occam algorithm is also an efficient PAC learning algorithm.

Theorem 2.1 *(Occam's Razor) Let L be an efficient (α, β)-Occam algorithm for C using $\mathcal{H}$. Let $\mathcal{D}$ be the target distribution over the instance space X, let $c \in C_n$ be the target concept, and $0 < \epsilon, \delta \leq 1$. Then there is a constant $a > 0$ such that if L is given as input a random sample S of m examples drawn from $EX(c, \mathcal{D})$, where m satisfies*

$$m \geq a \left(\frac{1}{\epsilon} \log \frac{1}{\delta} + \left(\frac{(n \cdot size(c))^\alpha)}{\epsilon} \right)^{\frac{1}{1-\beta}} \right)$$

then with probability at least $1 - \delta$ the output h of L satisfies $error(h) \leq \epsilon$. Moreover, L runs in time polynomial in n, $size(c)$, $1/\epsilon$ and $1/\delta$.

Notice that as β tends to 1, the exponent in the bound for m tends to infinity. This corresponds with our intuition that as the length of the hypothesis approaches that of the data itself, the predictive power of the hypothesis is diminishing.

For the applications we give later, it turns out to be most convenient to state and prove Theorem 2.1 in a slightly more general form, in which we measure representational succinctness by the cardinality of the hypothesis class rather than by the bit length $size(h)$. We then prove Theorem 2.1 as a special case. To make this precise, let $\mathcal{H}_n = \cup_{m \geq 1} \mathcal{H}_{n,m}$. Consider a learning algorithm for $\mathcal{C}$ using $\mathcal{H}$ that on input a labeled sample S of cardinality m outputs a hypothesis from $\mathcal{H}_{n,m}$. The following theorem shows that if $|\mathcal{H}_{n,m}|$ is small enough, then the hypothesis output by L has small error with high confidence.

Theorem 2.2 *(Occam's Razor, Cardinality Version) Let $\mathcal{C}$ be a concept class and $\mathcal{H}$ a representation class. Let L be an algorithm such that for any n and any $c \in \mathcal{C}_n$, if L is given as input a sample S of m labeled examples of c, then L runs in time polynomial in n, m and $size(c)$, and outputs an $h \in \mathcal{H}_{n,m}$ that is consistent with S. Then there is a constant $b > 0$ such that for any n, any distribution $\mathcal{D}$ over X_n, and any target concept $c \in \mathcal{C}_n$, if L is given as input a random sample from $EX(c, \mathcal{D})$ of m examples, where $|\mathcal{H}_{n,m}|$ satisfies*

$$\log |\mathcal{H}_{n,m}| \leq b\epsilon m - \log \frac{1}{\delta}$$

(or equivalently, where m satisfies $m \geq (1/b\epsilon)(\log |\mathcal{H}_{n,m}| + \log(1/\delta))$) then L is guaranteed to find a hypothesis $h \in \mathcal{H}_n$ that with probability at least $1 - \delta$ obeys $error(h) \leq \epsilon$.

Note that here we do not necessarily claim that L is an *efficient* PAC learning algorithm. In order for the theorem to apply, we must (if possible) pick m large enough so that $b\epsilon m$ dominates $\log |\mathcal{H}_{n,m}|$. Moreover, since the running time of L has a polynomial dependence on m, in order to assert that L is an efficient PAC algorithm, we also have to bound m by some polynomial in n, $size(c)$, $1/\epsilon$ and $1/\delta$. The proof of Theorem 2.1 relies on the fact that in the case of an (α, β)-Occam algorithm, $\log |\mathcal{H}_{n,m}|$ grows only as m^β, and therefore given any ϵ, this is smaller than $b\epsilon m$ for a small value of m.

We first give a proof of Theorem 2.2.

Proof: We say that a hypothesis $h \in \mathcal{H}_{n,m}$ is *bad* if $error(h) > \epsilon$, where the error is of course measured with respect to the target concept c and and the target distribution $\mathcal{D}$. Then by the independence of the random examples, the probability that a fixed bad hypothesis h is consistent with a randomly drawn sample of m examples from $EX(c, \mathcal{D})$ is at most $(1 - \epsilon)^m$. Using the union bound, this implies that if $\mathcal{H}' \subseteq \mathcal{H}_{n,m}$ is the set of *all* bad hypotheses in $\mathcal{H}_{n,m}$, then the probability that some hypothesis in $\mathcal{H}'$ is consistent with a random sample of size m is at most $|\mathcal{H}'|(1 - \epsilon)^m$. We want this to be at most δ; since $|\mathcal{H}'| \leq |\mathcal{H}_{n,m}|$ we get a stronger condition if we solve for $|\mathcal{H}_{n,m}|(1 - \epsilon)^m \leq \delta$. Taking logarithms, we obtain $\log |\mathcal{H}_{n,m}| \leq m \log(1/(1 - \epsilon)) - \log(1/\delta)$. Using the fact that $\log(1/(1 - \epsilon)) = \Theta(\epsilon)$, we get the statement of the theorem.

$\square$(Theorem 2.2)

We now prove Theorem 2.1:

Proof: Let $\mathcal{H}_{n,m}$ denote the set of all possible hypothesis representations that the (α, β)-Occam algorithm L might output when given as input a labeled sample S of cardinality m. Since L is an (α, β)-Occam algorithm, every such hypothesis has bit length at most $(n \cdot size(c))^\alpha m^\beta$, thus implying that $|\mathcal{H}_{n,m}| \leq 2^{(n \cdot size(c))^\alpha m^\beta}$. By Theorem 2.2, the output of L has error at most ϵ with confidence at least $1 - \delta$ provided

$$\log |\mathcal{H}_{n,m}| \leq b\epsilon m - \log \frac{1}{\delta}.$$

Transposing, we want m such that

$$m \geq \frac{1}{b\epsilon} \log |\mathcal{H}_{n,m}| + \frac{1}{b\epsilon} \log \frac{1}{\delta}$$

The above condition can be satisfied by picking m such that both $m \geq (2/b\epsilon) \log |\mathcal{H}_{n,m}|$ and $m \geq (2/b\epsilon) \log(1/\delta)$ hold. Choosing $a = 2/b$ yields the statement of the theorem. $\qquad \square$(Theorem 2.1)

2.2 Improving the Sample Size for Learning Conjunctions

As an easy warm-up to some more interesting applications of Occam's Razor, we first return to the problem of PAC learning conjunctions of boolean literals, and apply Theorem 2.2 to slightly improve the sample size bound (and therefore the running time bound) of the learning algorithm we presented for this problem in Section 1.3.

Thus as in Section 1.3, we let $X_n = \{0,1\}^n$. Each $a \in \{0,1\}^n$ is interpreted as an assignment to the n boolean variables $x_1, \ldots, x_n$. Let $\mathcal{C}_n$ be the class of conjunctions of literals over $x_1, \ldots, x_n$. Recall that our learning algorithm started with a hypothesis that is the conjunction of all the $2n$ literals. Given as input a set of m labeled examples, the algorithm ignored negative examples, and on each positive example $\langle a, 1 \rangle$, the algorithm deleted any literal z such that $z = 0$ in a. Note that this ensures that upon receiving the positive example a, the hypothesis is updated to be consistent with this example. Furthermore, any future deletions will not alter this consistency, since deletions can only increase the set of positive examples of the hypothesis. Finally, recall that we already argued in Section 1.3 that this algorithm never misclassifies any negative example of the target conjunction c. Thus, if we run the algorithm on an arbitrary sample S of labeled examples of some target conjunction, it always outputs a hypothesis conjunction that is consistent with S, and thus it is an Occam algorithm. Note that in this simple example, $size(h)$ (or equivalently, $\log |\mathcal{H}_{n,m}|$) depends only on n and not on m or $size(c)$.

Now the number of conjunctions over $x_1, \ldots, x_n$ is bounded by 3^n (each variable occurs positively or negatively or is absent entirely), so applying Theorem 2.2, we see that $O((1/\epsilon)\log(1/\delta) + n/\epsilon)$ examples are sufficient to guarantee that the hypothesis output by the learning algorithm has error less than ϵ with confidence at least $1 - \delta$. This is an improvement by a logarithmic factor over the bound given in Chapter 1.

2.3   Learning Conjunctions with Few Relevant Variables

Despite the efficiency of our algorithm for PAC learning boolean conjunctions, we can still imagine improvements. Let us define $size(c)$ be the number of literals appearing in the target conjunction c. Notice that $size(c) \leq n$, but the size of the sample drawn by our learning algorithm for conjunctions is proportional to n independent of how small $size(c)$ might be. In this section, we give a new algorithm that reduces the number of examples to nearly $size(c)$. It can be argued that it is often realistic to assume that $size(c) << n$, since we typically describe an object by describing only a few attributes out of a large list of potential attributes.

Even though we greatly improve the sample size for the case of small $size(c)$, we should point out that the running time of the new learning algorithm still grows with n, since the instances are of length n, and the algorithm must take enough time to read each instance. An interesting feature of the new algorithm is that it makes use of the negative examples, unlike our previous algorithm for learning conjunctions.

In order to describe the new algorithm, we need to introduce a combinatorial problem and a well-known algorithm for its approximate solution. This approximation algorithm has many applications in computational learning theory.

The Set Cover Problem. Given as input a collection $\mathcal{S}$ of subsets of $U = \{1, \ldots, m\}$, find a subcollection $\mathcal{T} \subseteq \mathcal{S}$ such that $|\mathcal{T}|$ is minimized, and the sets in $\mathcal{T}$ form a **cover** of U:

$$\bigcup_{t \in \mathcal{T}} t = U.$$

We assume, of course, that the entire collection $\mathcal{S}$ is itself a cover. For any instance $\mathcal{S}$ of the Set Cover Problem, we let $opt(\mathcal{S})$ denote the number of sets in a minimum cardinality cover.

Finding an optimal cover is a well-known *NP*-hard problem. However, there is an efficient greedy heuristic that is guaranteed to find a cover $\mathcal{R}$ of cardinality at most $O(opt(\mathcal{S}) \log m)$.

The greedy heuristic initializes $\mathcal{R}$ to be the empty collection. It first adds to $\mathcal{R}$ the set s^* from $\mathcal{S}$ with the largest cardinality, and then updates $\mathcal{S}$ by replacing each set s in $\mathcal{S}$ by $s - s^*$. It then repeats the process of choosing the remaining set of largest cardinality and updating $\mathcal{S}$ until all the elements of $\{1, \ldots, m\}$ are covered by $\mathcal{R}$.

The greedy heuristic is based on the following fact: let $U^* \subseteq U$. Then there is always a set t in $\mathcal{S}$ such that $|t \cap U^*| \geq |U^*|/opt(\mathcal{S})$. To see why this is true, just observe that U^* has a cover of size at most $opt(\mathcal{S})$ (since U does), and at least one of the sets in the optimal cover must cover a $1/opt(\mathcal{S})$ fraction of U^*.

Let $U_i \subseteq U$ denote the set of elements still not covered after i steps of the greedy heuristic. Then

$$|U_{i+1}| \leq |U_i| - \frac{|U_i|}{opt(\mathcal{S})} = |U_i| \left(1 - \frac{1}{opt(\mathcal{S})} \right).$$

So by induction on i:

$$|U_i| \leq \left(1 - \frac{1}{opt(\mathcal{S})} \right)^i m.$$

Choosing $i \geq opt(\mathcal{S}) \log m$ suffices to drive this upper bound below 1. Thus all the elements of U are covered after the algorithm has chosen $opt(\mathcal{S}) \log m$ sets.

We now return to the problem of PAC learning conjunctions with few relevant variables. We shall describe our new algorithm as an Occam algorithm and apply Theorem 2.2 to obtain the required sample size for PAC learning. Thus, given a sample S of m examples of a target conjunction, the new Occam algorithm starts by applying our original conjunctions algorithm — which uses only the positive examples — to S in order to produce a hypothesis conjunction h. This conjunction will have the property that it is consistent with S, since the old algorithm was indeed an Occam algorithm. The new algorithm will then use the negative examples in S to exclude several additional literals from h in a manner described below, to compute a new hypothesis conjunction h' containing at most $size(c) \log m$ of the literals appearing in h. This new smaller hypothesis will still be consistent with S, and so the sample size bound for PAC learning can be derived from Theorem 2.2.

Recall that excluding literals from h does not affect consistency with the positive examples in S, since the set of positive examples of h only grows as we delete literals. However, the new algorithm has to carefully choose which literals of h it excludes in order to ensure that the hypothesis is still consistent with all the negative examples in S. To do this, we cast the problem as an instance of the Set Cover Problem and apply the greedy algorithm.

For each literal z appearing in h, we can identify a subset $N_z \subseteq S$ of the negative examples in S with the property that inclusion of z in the hypothesis conjunction is sufficient to guarantee consistency with N_z. The set N_z is just those negative examples in $\langle a, 0 \rangle \in S$ for which the value of z is 0 in a. Thus, we can think of the inclusion of z in our hypothesis conjunction as "covering" the set N_z of negative examples. If we have a collection of N_z that covers all the negative examples of S, and each z appears in h, then the conjunction h' of this collection will still form a hypothesis consistent with S.

Our goal is thus reduced to covering the set of all negative examples in S with the minimum number of the sets N_z. Applying the greedy heuristic to this problem, and noting that among the literals of h, a cover of $size(c)$ sets exists (since the literals that occur in the target conjunction must form a cover), we get a cover of size $size(c) \log m$; in other words, our hypothesis class $\mathcal{H}_{n,m}$ is the set of all conjunctions of at most $size(c) \log m$ literals. Using the fact that a conjunction of ℓ literals over n variables can be encoded using $\ell \log n$ bits, and setting $\ell = size(c) \log m$, we get a bound of $size(c) \log m \log n$ on the number of bits needed to represent our hypothesis, and thus $|\mathcal{H}_{n,m}| \leq 2^{size(c) \log m \log n}$. Applying the condition $m = \Omega((1/\epsilon) \log |\mathcal{H}_{n,m}|)$ required by Theorem 2.2, we obtain the constraint $m \geq c_1((1/\epsilon) size(c) \log m \log n)$ for some constant $c_1 > 0$. It is easily verified that this is satisfied provided $m \geq c_1((1/\epsilon) size(c) \log n \log(size(c) \log n))$. Thus, the overall sample size required by the new algorithm is

$$m \geq c_1 \left(\frac{1}{\epsilon} \log \frac{1}{\delta} + \frac{size(c) \log n(\log size(c) + \log \log n)}{\epsilon} \right).$$

Note that this bound has a slightly superlinear dependence on $size(c)$, but only an approximately logarithmic dependence on the total number of variables n.

In fact, a slight modification of this algorithm that we shall now sketch quite briefly gives a better bound. The basic idea behind the modification is that rather than running the greedy cover heuristic until the hypothesis covers all of the negative examples, we shall run it only until the hypothesis misclassifies fewer than $\epsilon m/2$ negative examples. Thus, our resulting hypothesis will be almost but not quite consistent with its input sample, where the degree of consistency is controlled by the desired error bound ϵ.

For the analysis, observe that now the halting condition for the greedy heuristic is $(1 - 1/size(c))^i m < (\epsilon/2)m$ instead of $(1 - 1/size(c))^i m < 1$ as before; here we are using the correspondence between $opt(\mathcal{S})$ in the covering problem and $size(c)$ in the PAC learning problem. Thus, we halt with a hypothesis of $i = size(c) \log(2/\epsilon)$ literals instead of $i = size(c) \log m$ literals. This gives a smaller hypothesis class cardinality of $2^{size(c) \log(2/\epsilon) \log n}$.

Now we just need a lemma stating that the probability that a fixed conjunction h such that $error(h) \geq \epsilon$ is consistent with at least a fraction $1 - \epsilon/2$ of m random examples is bounded by some exponentially decreasing function of m (that is, we need the analogue of the bound $(1 - \epsilon)^m$ on the probability that a hypothesis of error greater than ϵ is completely consistent with the sample). It turns out that we can state a bound of $e^{-\epsilon m/16}$ on this probability, and this is discussed in the section on Chernoff Bounds in the Appendix of Chapter 9. For our immediate problem, given this bound we can now apply the same arguments as those in the proof of Theorem 2.2, and by solving $2^{size(c) \log(2/\epsilon) \log n} e^{-\epsilon m/16} \leq \delta$ we obtain a sample size bound of

$$ m \geq c_1 \left(\frac{1}{\epsilon} \log \frac{1}{\delta} + \frac{size(c) \log(2/\epsilon) \log n}{\epsilon} \right). $$

2.4   Learning Decision Lists

Our final application of Occam learning is to an algorithm for PAC learning **decision lists** over the boolean variables $x_1, \ldots, x_n$. A decision list may be thought of as an ordered sequence of if-then-else statements. The sequence of conditions in the decision list are tested in order, and the answer associated with the first satisfied condition is output.

Formally, a k-**decision list** over the boolean variables $x_1, \ldots, x_n$ is an ordered sequence $L = (c_1, b_1), \ldots, (c_l, b_l)$ and a bit b, in which each c_i is a conjunction of at most k literals over $x_1, \ldots, x_n$, and each $b_i \in \{0, 1\}$. For any input $a \in \{0, 1\}^n$, the value $L(a)$ is defined to be b_j, where j is the smallest index satisfying $c_j(a) = 1$; if no such index exists, then $L(a) = b$. Thus, b is the "default" value in case a falls off the end of the list. We call b_i the bit *associated* with the condition c_i. Figure 2.1 shows an example of a 2-decision list along with its evaluation on a particular input.

First let us consider the expressive power of k-decision lists. We

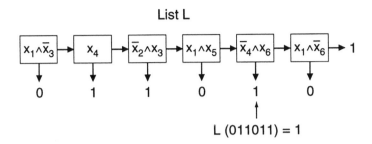

Figure 2.1: *A 2-decision list and the path followed by an input. Evaluation starts at the leftmost item and continues to the right until the first condition is satisfied, at which point the binary value below becomes the final result of the evaluation.*

observe that if a concept c can be represented as a k-decision list, then so can $\neg c$ (simply complement the values of the b_i). Clearly, any k-DNF formula can be represented as a k-decision list of the same length (choose an arbitrary order in which to evaluate the terms of the k-DNF, setting all the b_i to 1 and the default b to 0). Since k-decision lists are closed under complementation, they can also represent k-CNF formulae. Furthermore, in Exercise 2.1 we demonstrate that for each k there exist functions that can be represented by a k-decision list, but not by either a k-DNF or a k-CNF formula. Thus, k-decision lists strictly generalize these classes.

Theorem 2.3 *For any fixed $k \geq 1$, the representation class of k-decision lists is efficiently PAC learnable.*

Proof: We give an Occam algorithm and apply Theorem 2.2. We present the algorithm for 1-decision lists; the problem for general k can easily be reduced to this problem, exactly as the k-CNF PAC learning problem was reduced to the problem of PAC learning conjunctions in Chapter 1.

Given an input sample S of m examples of some 1-decision list, our Occam algorithm starts with the empty decision list as its hypothesis. In each step, it finds some literal z such that the set $S_z \subseteq S$, which we define to be the set of examples (positive or negative) in which z in set to 1, is both non-empty and has the property that it contains either only positive examples of the target concept, or only negative examples. We call such a z a *useful* literal. The algorithm then adds this literal (with the associated bit 1 if S_z contained only positive examples, and the associated bit 0 if S_z contained only negative examples) as the last condition in the current hypothesis decision list, updates S to be $S - S_z$, and iterates the process until $S = \emptyset$ and therefore all examples are correctly classified by the hypothesis decision list.

To prove that the algorithm always succeeds in finding a consistent hypothesis, it suffices to show that it always succeeds in finding a useful literal z at each step as long as $S \neq \emptyset$. But this is true because the target decision correctly classifies every element of S, and so the first condition z in the target decision list such that S_z is non-empty is a useful literal.

Since any decision list on n variables can be encoded in $O(n \log n)$ bits, we can apply Theorem 2.2 to obtain a sample size bound of $m \geq c_1((1/\epsilon)(\log(1/\delta) + n \log n))$ for PAC learning. Since the Occam algorithm clearly runs in time polynomial in m, we have efficient PAC learning.

$\square$(Theorem 2.3)

2.5   Exercises

2.1. Show that for each k, there exists a function that can be represented as a k-decision list, but not by a k-CNF or k-DNF formula.

2.2. A **decision tree** is similar to a 1-decision list, except now we allow the (single-literal) decision conditions to be placed in a binary tree, with the decision bits placed only at the leaves. To evaluate such a tree T on input $a \in \{0, 1\}^n$, we simply follow the path through T defined by starting at the root of T and evaluating the literal at each node on input a, going left if the evaluation yields 0 and right if it yields 1. The value $T(a)$ is the bit value stored at the leaf reached by this path. Figure 2.2 shows an example of a decision tree along with its evaluation on an input.

We define the **rank** of a decision tree T recursively as follows: the rank of a tree consisting of a single node is 0. If the ranks of T's left subtrees and right subtrees are r_L and r_R respectively, then if $r_L = r_R$ the rank of T is $r_L + 1$; otherwise, it is $\max(r_L, r_R)$. The rank is a measure of how "unbalanced" the tree is.

Compute the rank of the decision tree given in Figure 2.2, and show that the class of functions computed by rank r decision trees is included in the class of functions computed by r-decision lists. Thus, for any fixed r we can efficiently PAC learn rank r decision trees.

2.3. Let $\mathcal{C}$ be any concept class. Show that if $\mathcal{C}$ is efficiently PAC learnable, then for some constants $\alpha \geq 1$ and $\beta < 1$ there is an (α, β)-Occam algorithm for $\mathcal{C}$. Hint: construct an appropriate simulation of the PAC learning algorithm L in which the accuracy parameter depends on the degree of the polynomial running time of L.

2.4. Recall that following our final definition of PAC learning (Definition 4), we emphasized the importance of restricting our attention to PAC learning algorithms that use polynomially evaluatable hypothesis classes $\mathcal{H}$ (see Definition 5). Suppose that we consider relaxing this restriction, and let $\mathcal{H}$ be the class of all Turing machines (not necessarily polynomial time) — thus, the output of the learning algorithm can be any program. Show that if $\mathcal{C}_n$ is the class of all boolean circuits of size at most $p(n)$ for some fixed polynomial $p(\cdot)$, then $\mathcal{C}$ is efficiently PAC learnable using $\mathcal{H}$. Argue that your solution shows that this relaxation trivializes the model of learning.

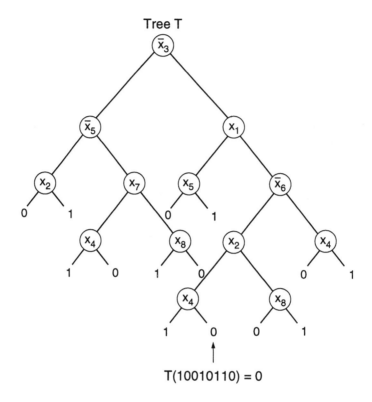

Figure 2.2: *A decision tree and the path followed by an input.*

2.6   Bibliographic Notes

The notion of Occam learning as we have formalized it and our main theorems stating that Occam learning implies PAC learning are due to Blumer, Ehrenfeucht, Haussler and Warmuth [21]. There is a converse to Theorem 2.1 which establishes that $\mathcal{C}$ is PAC learnable if and only if there is an Occam algorithm for $\mathcal{C}$. This was the topic of Exercise 2.3, whose intended solution is due to Board and Pitt [23]. A considerably stronger converse is a consequence of the equivalence between weak and strong PAC learning due to Schapire [84, 85] (see also the work of Freund [35, 36] and Helmbold and Warmuth [52]). We shall study this equivalence in Chapter 4.

The predictive power of Occam algorithms continues to hold for several variants of the PAC model and for more general notions of hypothesis complexity. These include models for PAC learning in the presence of various types of errors (Angluin and Laird [10], Kearns and Li [57, 55]), learning probabilistic concepts (Kearns and Schapire [61, 85]), and function learning (Natarajan [70]). In Chapter 3 we will consider a very general notion of hypothesis complexity, the Vapnik-Chervonenkis dimension (Vapnik [94]; Blumer, Ehrenfeucht, Haussler and Warmuth [22]), and we again prove the predictive power of algorithms finding a consistent hypothesis with limited complexity. The predictive power of Occam algorithms in a setting where the examples are not independent but obey a Markovian constraint is examined by Aldous and Vazirani [3].

The algorithm for learning conjunctions with few relevant literals is due to Haussler [45], who also provides a lucid discussion of Occam learning and inductive bias from the artificial intelligence perspective. The analysis of the greedy set cover approximation algorithm is due to Chvatal [26]. The modification of the covering algorithm to only nearly cover the sample is due to M. Warmuth. The problem of learning when there are many irrelevant variables present has also been carefully examined by Littlestone [65, 66] and Blum [17] in on-line models of learning. The decision list learning algorithm is due to Rivest [78], and Exercise 2.2 is due to A. Blum (see also the paper Ehrenfeucht and Haussler [32]).

Relationships between various measures of hypothesis complexity and generalization ability have been proposed and examined in a a large and fascinating literature that predates the PAC model results given here. Two dominant theories along these lines are the structural risk minimization of Vapnik [94] and the minimum description length principle of Rissanen [77]. The papers of Quinlan and Rivest [75] and DeSantis, Markowsky and Wegman [29] examine variants of the minimum description length principle from a computational learning theory viewpoint. It has frequently been observed that the minimum description length criterion has a Bayesian interpretation in which representational length determines the prior distribution. This viewpoint is further explored in the paper of Evans, Rajagopalan and Vazirani [34], where the notion of an Occam algorithm is generalized to arbitrary stochastic processes.

3

The Vapnik-Chervonenkis Dimension

3.1 When Can Infinite Classes Be Learned with a Finite Sample?

In this chapter, we consider the following question: How many random examples does a learning algorithm need to draw before it has sufficient information to learn an unknown target concept chosen from the concept class C? We should emphasize that we will temporarily ignore issues of computational efficiency while studying this question (or equivalently, we assume that the learning algorithm has infinite computing power to process the finite random sample it has drawn). We first note that the results of the previous chapter can be used to give such a bound in the case that C is a concept class of finite cardinality. If the learning algorithm simply draws a random sample of $O((1/\epsilon) \log(|C|/\delta))$ examples, and finds any $h \in C$ consistent with these examples (say, by exhaustive search), then Theorem 2.2 guarantees that h will meet the PAC model criteria. Notice that this bound is not meaningful if C has infinite cardinality. Are there any non-trivial infinite concept classes that are learnable from a finite sample?

Actually, our PAC learning algorithm for axis-aligned rectangles in the Euclidean plane given in Section 1.1 is an example of such a class. In the analysis of that PAC learning algorithm, we made critical use of the fact that axis-aligned rectangles have simple boundaries: the target rectangle is always completely specified by four real numbers that indicate the locations of the four bounding edges, and this allowed us to partition the error of the tightest-fit hypothesis into four simple rectilinear regions. It is tempting to say that the "complexity" of this concept class is four, because the boundary of any concept in the class can be described by four real numbers.

In this chapter, we are interested in a general measure of complexity for concept classes of infinite cardinality. We would like this measure to play the same role in the sample complexity of PAC learning infinite classes that the quantity $\log |\mathcal{C}|$ (which we saw in Chapter 2 was closely related to the size of representations) plays in the sample complexity of PAC learning finite classes. We will define a purely combinatorial measure of concept class complexity known as the *Vapnik-Chervonenkis dimension*, a measure that assigns to each concept class $\mathcal{C}$ a single number that characterizes the sample size needed to PAC learn $\mathcal{C}$.

3.2   The Vapnik-Chervonenkis Dimension

For the remainder of this chapter, $\mathcal{C}$ will be a concept class over instance space X, and both $\mathcal{C}$ and X may be infinite. The first thing we will need is a way to discuss the behavior of $\mathcal{C}$ when attention is restricted to a finite set of points $S \subseteq X$.

Definition 7 *For any concept class $\mathcal{C}$ over X, and any $S \subseteq X$,*

$$\Pi_{\mathcal{C}}(S) = \{c \cap S : c \in \mathcal{C}\}.$$

Equivalently, if $S = \{x_1, \ldots, x_m\}$ then we can think of $\Pi_\mathcal{C}(S)$ as the set of vectors $\Pi_\mathcal{C}(S) \subseteq \{0,1\}^m$ defined by

$$\Pi_\mathcal{C}(S) = \{(c(x_1), \ldots, c(x_m)) : c \in \mathcal{C}\}.$$

Thus, $\Pi_\mathcal{C}(S)$ is the set of all the **behaviors** or **dichotomies** on S that are induced or **realized** by $\mathcal{C}$. We will use the descriptions of $\Pi_\mathcal{C}(S)$ as a collection of subsets of S and as a set of vectors interchangeably.

Definition 8 *If $\Pi_\mathcal{C}(S) = \{0,1\}^m$ (where $m = |S|$), then we say that S is **shattered** by $\mathcal{C}$. Thus, S is shattered by $\mathcal{C}$ if $\mathcal{C}$ realizes all possible dichotomies of S.*

Now we are ready for our key definition.

Definition 9 *The **Vapnik-Chervonenkis (VC) dimension** of $\mathcal{C}$, denoted as $VCD(\mathcal{C})$, is the cardinality d of the largest set S shattered by $\mathcal{C}$. If arbitrarily large finite sets can be shattered by $\mathcal{C}$, then $VCD(\mathcal{C}) = \infty$.*

3.3   Examples of the VC Dimension

Let us consider a few natural geometric concept classes, and informally calculate their VC dimension. It is important to emphasize the nature of the existential and universal quantifiers in the definition of VC dimension: in order to show that the VC dimension of a class is at least d, we must simply find some shattered set of size d. In order to show that the VC dimension is at most d, we must show that no set of size $d+1$ is shattered. For this reason, proving upper bounds on the VC dimension is usually considerably more difficult than proving lower bounds. The following examples are not meant to be precise proofs of the stated bounds on

Figure 3.1: *A dichotomy unrealizable by intervals.*

the VC dimension, but are simply illustrative exercises to provide some practice thinking about the VC dimension.

Intervals of the real line. For this concept class, any set of two points can be shattered, so the VC Dimension is at least two, but no set of three points can be shattered: label the three points as shown in Figure 3.1, a labeling which cannot be induced by any interval. Thus the VC dimension for this class is two.

Linear halfspaces in the plane. For this concept class, any three points that are not collinear can be shattered. Figure 3.2(a) shows how one dichotomy out of the possible 8 dichotomies can be realized by a halfspace; the reader can easily verify that the remaining 7 dichotomies can be realized by halfspaces. To see that no set of four points can be shattered, we consider two cases. In the first case (shown in Figure 3.2(b)), all four points lie on the convex hull defined by the four points. In this case, if we label one "diagonal" pair positive and the other "diagonal" pair negative as shown in Figure 3.2(b), no halfspace can induce this labeling. In the second case (shown in Figure 3.2(c)), three of the four points define the convex hull of the four points, and if we label the interior point negative and the hull points positive, again no halfspace can induce the dichotomy. Thus the VC dimension here is three. In general, for halfspaces in $\Re^d$, the VC dimension is $d + 1$.

Axis-aligned rectangles in the plane. For this concept class, we can shatter the four points shown in Figure 3.3(a), where we have again indicated how a single dichotomy can be realized and left the remainder to the reader. However, not *all* sets of four points can be shattered, as indicated by the unrealizable dichotomy shown in Figure 3.3(b). Still, the existence of a single shattered set of size four is sufficient to lower bound

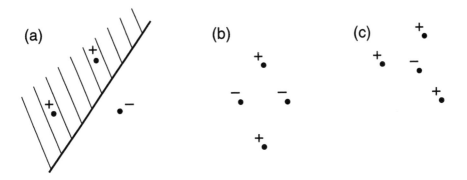

Figure 3.2: (a) *A dichotomy and its realization by a halfspace, with the shaded region indicating the positive side.* (b) and (c) *Dichotomies unrealizable by halfspaces.*

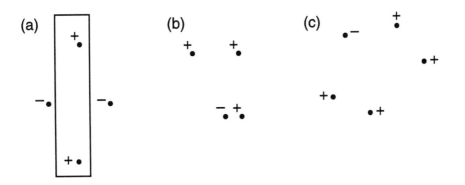

Figure 3.3: (a) *A dichotomy and its realization by an axis-aligned rectangle.* (b) and (c) *Dichotomies unrealizable by axis-aligned rectangles.*

the VC dimension. Now for any set of five points in the plane, there must be some point that is neither the extreme left, right, top or bottom point of the five (see Figure 3.3(c)). If we label this non-extremal point negative and the remaining four extremal point positive, no rectangle can realize the dichotomy. Thus the VC dimension is four.

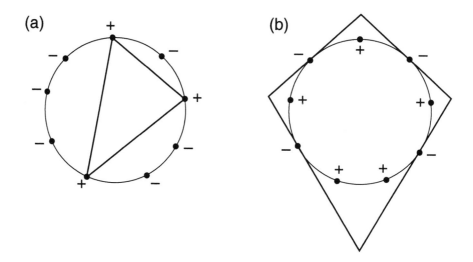

Figure 3.4: (a) *Realizing a dichotomy with a polygon when there are fewer positive labels.* (b) *When there are fewer negative labels.*

Convex polygons in the plane. For convex d-gons in the plane, the VC dimension is $2d + 1$. For the lower bound, we can induce any labeling of any $2d + 1$ points on a circle using a d-gon as follows: if there are more negative labels than positive labels, use the positive points as the vertices as shown in Figure 3.4(a). Otherwise, use tangents to the negative points as edges as shown in Figure 3.4(b). For the upper bound, it can be shown that choosing the points to lie on a circle does in fact maximize the number of points that can be shattered, and we can force $d + 1$ sides using $2d + 2$ points on a circle by alternating positive and negative labels.

3.4 A Polynomial Bound on $|\Pi_{\mathcal{C}}(S)|$

Definition 10 *For any natural number m we define*

$$\Pi_{\mathcal{C}}(m) = \max\{|\Pi_{\mathcal{C}}(S)| : |S| = m\}.$$

The function $\Pi_{\mathcal{C}}(m)$ can be thought of as a measure of the complexity of $\mathcal{C}$: the faster this function grows, the more behaviors on sets of m points that can be realized by $\mathcal{C}$ as m increases. Now clearly, if $\mathcal{C}$ does not have finite VC dimension, then $\Pi_{\mathcal{C}}(m) = 2^m$ for all m since we can shatter arbitrarily large finite sets. In this section, we prove a surprising and beautiful result, namely that despite the fact that we might naively expect $\Pi_{\mathcal{C}}(m)$ to grow as rapidly as an exponential function of m, it is actually bounded by a polynomial in m of degree d, where d is the VC dimension of $\mathcal{C}$. In other words, depending on whether the VC dimension is finite or infinite, the function $\Pi_{\mathcal{C}}(m)$ is either eventually polynomial or forever exponential. For the more interesting and typical case of finite VC dimension, we shall eventually translate the polynomial upper bound on $\Pi_{\mathcal{C}}(m)$ into an upper bound on the sample complexity of PAC learning that is linear in d.

We begin by proving that $\Pi_{\mathcal{C}}(m)$ is bounded by the function $\Phi_d(m)$ defined below. We then show a polynomial bound on $\Phi_d(m)$.

Definition 11 *For any natural numbers m and d, the function $\Phi_d(m)$ is defined inductively by*

$$\Phi_d(m) = \Phi_d(m-1) + \Phi_{d-1}(m-1)$$

with initial conditions $\Phi_d(0) = \Phi_0(m) = 1$.

Lemma 3.1 *If $VCD(\mathcal{C}) = d$, then for any m, $\Pi_{\mathcal{C}}(m) \leq \Phi_d(m)$.*

Proof: By induction on both d and m. For the base cases, the lemma is easily established when $d = 0$ and m is arbitrary, and when $m = 0$ and d is arbitrary. We assume for induction that for all m', d' such that $m' \leq m$ and $d' \leq d$ and at least one of the two inequalities is strict, we have $\Pi_{\mathcal{C}}(m') \leq \Phi_{d'}(m')$. We now show that this inductive assumption establishes the desired statement for d and m.

Given any set S of size m, let $x \in S$ be a distinguished point. Let us first compute $|\Pi_{\mathcal{C}}(S - \{x\})|$. This is easy since by induction (note that $S - \{x\}$ is a set of size $m - 1$) we have $|\Pi_{\mathcal{C}}(S - \{x\})| \leq \Phi_d(m-1)$.

The difference between $\Pi_{\mathcal{C}}(S)$ and $\Pi_{\mathcal{C}}(S-\{x\})$ is that pairs of distinct sets in $\Pi_{\mathcal{C}}(S)$ that differ only on their labeling of x are identified (that is, merged) in $\Pi_{\mathcal{C}}(S - \{x\})$. Thus let us define

$$\mathcal{C}' = \{c \in \Pi_{\mathcal{C}}(S) : x \notin c, c \cup \{x\} \in \Pi_{\mathcal{C}}(S)\}.$$

Then $|\mathcal{C}'|$ counts the number of pairs of sets in $\Pi_{\mathcal{C}}(S)$ that are collapsed to a single representative in $\Pi_{\mathcal{C}}(S - \{x\})$. Note that $\mathcal{C}' = \Pi_{\mathcal{C}'}(S - \{x\})$ because $\mathcal{C}'$ consists only of subsets of $S - \{x\}$. This yields the simple equality

$$|\Pi_{\mathcal{C}}(S)| = |\Pi_{\mathcal{C}}(S - \{x\})| + |\Pi_{\mathcal{C}'}(S - \{x\})|.$$

We now show that $VCD(\mathcal{C}') \leq d - 1$. To see this, let $S' \subseteq S - \{x\}$ be shattered by $\mathcal{C}'$. Then $S' \cup \{x\}$ is shattered by $\mathcal{C}$. Thus we must have $|S'| \leq d - 1$. Now by induction we have $|\mathcal{C}'| = |\Pi_{\mathcal{C}'}(S - \{x\})| \leq \Phi_{d-1}(m-1)$.

Our total count is thus bounded by $\Phi_d(m-1) + \Phi_{d-1}(m-1) = \Phi_d(m)$, as desired. $\square$(Lemma 3.1)

Lemma 3.2 $\Phi_d(m) = \sum_{i=0}^{d} \binom{m}{i}$.

Proof: By induction; the base cases are easy to check. For the induction step, we have:

$$
\begin{aligned}
\Phi_d(m) &= \Phi_d(m-1) + \Phi_{d-1}(m-1) \\
&= \sum_{i=0}^{d} \binom{m-1}{i} + \sum_{i=0}^{d-1} \binom{m-1}{i} \\
&= \sum_{i=0}^{d} \left[\binom{m-1}{i} + \binom{m-1}{i-1} \right] \\
&= \sum_{i=0}^{d} \binom{m}{i}
\end{aligned}
$$

where the second equality is by induction and we define $\binom{m-1}{-1} = 0$ for the third equality. $\square$(Lemma 3.2)

Now for $m \leq d$, $\Phi_d(m) = 2^m$. For $m > d$, since $0 \leq d/m \leq 1$, we may write:

$$\left(\tfrac{d}{m}\right)^d \sum_{i=0}^{d} \binom{m}{i} \leq \sum_{i=0}^{d} \left(\tfrac{d}{m}\right)^i \binom{m}{i} \leq \sum_{i=0}^{m} \left(\tfrac{d}{m}\right)^i \binom{m}{i} = \left(1 + \tfrac{d}{m}\right)^m \leq e^d.$$

Dividing both sides by $\left(\tfrac{d}{m}\right)^d$ yields

$$\Phi_d(m) = \sum_{i=0}^{d} \binom{m}{i} \leq \left(\frac{em}{d}\right)^d = O(m^d)$$

which is polynomial in m for fixed d, giving us the promised polynomial bound for the case $m > d$.

3.5 A Polynomial Bound on the Sample Size for PAC Learning

3.5.1 The Importance of ϵ-Nets

Let us now fix the target concept $c \in \mathcal{C}$, and define the class of **error regions** with respect to c and $\mathcal{C}$ by $\Delta(c) = \{c \Delta c' : c' \in \mathcal{C}\}$. It is easy to show that $VCD(\mathcal{C}) = VCD(\Delta(c))$. To see this, for any set S we can map each element $c' \in \Pi_{\mathcal{C}}(S)$ to $c' \Delta(c \cap S) \in \Pi_{\Delta(c)}(S)$. Since this is a bijective mapping of $\Pi_{\mathcal{C}}(S)$ to $\Pi_{\Delta(c)}(S)$, $|\Pi_{\Delta(c)}(S)| = |\Pi_{\mathcal{C}}(S)|$. Since this holds for any set S, $VCD(\mathcal{C}) = VCD(\Delta(c))$ follows.

We may further refine the definition of $\Delta(c)$ to consider only those error regions with weight at least ϵ under the fixed target distribution $\mathcal{D}$. Thus, let $\Delta_\epsilon(c) = \{r \in \Delta(c) : \mathbf{Pr}_{x \in \mathcal{D}}[x \in r] \geq \epsilon\}$. We can now make the following important definition:

Definition 12 *For any $\epsilon > 0$, we say that a set S is an ϵ-net for $\Delta(c)$ if every region in $\Delta_\epsilon(c)$ is "hit" by a point in S, that is, if for every $r \in \Delta_\epsilon(c)$ we have $S \cap r \neq \emptyset$.*

An ϵ-net for $\Delta(c)$ is thus a set that hits all of the ϵ-heavy regions of $\Delta(c)$. As an example, suppose X is the closed interval $[0, 1]$ and let $\mathcal{D}$ be the uniform density on X. Suppose that $\mathcal{C}$ consists of all closed intervals on $[0, 1]$ as well as the empty set $\emptyset$, and that the target concept $c = \emptyset$. Then $\Delta(c)$ is again the set of all closed intervals on $[0, 1]$. For any interval I under the uniform density, $\mathbf{Pr}_{x \in \mathcal{D}}[x \in I]$ is just the length of I. Any interval whose probability is greater than ϵ will have length greater than ϵ, so the set of all points $k\epsilon$, for natural numbers $1 \leq k \leq \lceil 1/\epsilon \rceil$, is an ϵ-net for $\Delta(c)$.

The notion of ϵ-nets has actually been implicit in some of our earlier analyses, in particular those of Occam's Razor in Chapter 2. The important property of ϵ-nets is that if the sample S drawn by a learning algorithm forms an ϵ-net for $\Delta(c)$, and the learning algorithm outputs a hypothesis $h \in \mathcal{C}$ that is consistent with S, then this hypothesis must have error less than ϵ: since $c\Delta h \in \Delta(c)$ was not hit by S (otherwise h would not be consistent with S), and S is an ϵ-net for $\Delta(c)$, we must have $c\Delta h \notin \Delta_\epsilon(c)$ and therefore $error(h) \leq \epsilon$.

Thus if we can bound the probability that the random sample S fails to form an ϵ-net for $\Delta(c)$, then we have bounded the probability that a hypothesis consistent with S has error greater than ϵ. For the case of finite $\mathcal{C}$, the analysis of Occam's Razor obtained such a bound by a simple counting argument that we sketch again here in our new notation: for any fixed error region $c\Delta h \in \Delta_\epsilon(c)$, the probability that we fail to hit $c\Delta h$ in m random examples is at most $(1 - \epsilon)^m$. Thus the probability that we fail to hit some $c\Delta h \in \Delta_\epsilon(c)$ is bounded above by $|\Delta(c)|(1-\epsilon)^m$, which in turn is bounded by $|\mathcal{C}|(1 - \epsilon)^m$.

Alternatively, we can carry out the above analysis replacing $|\mathcal{C}|$ by $\Phi_d(|X|)$. This follows immediately from the fact that $\mathcal{C} = \Pi_{\mathcal{C}}(X)$ and

Lemma 3.1. This gives us a bound of $\Phi_d(|X|)(1-\epsilon)^m$ on the probability of failing to draw an ϵ-net for $\Delta(c)$. However, this does not represent any progress over the state of affairs in which we began this chapter, since if X is infinite then $\Phi_d(|X|)$ is infinite as well. Ideally, we would like to carry out a similar analysis that instead of considering the entire domain X considers only the small random subset S observed by the learning algorithm.

3.5.2   A Small ϵ-Net from Random Sampling

We now show that if we draw a small set of examples from the oracle $EX(c, \mathcal{D})$, then they form an ϵ-net with high probability. The important property is that the size of the required sample depends on the VC dimension d and ϵ and δ, but is independent of $|\mathcal{C}|$ and $|X|$. From the preceding discussion, this will immediately lead to an upper bound on the number of examples required for PAC learning that depends only on these same quantities.

Suppose that we draw a multiset S_1 of m random examples from $\mathcal{D}$, and let A denote the event that the elements of S_1 fail to form an ϵ-net for $\Delta(c)$. Clearly, our goal is to upper bound the probability of event A. If event A occurs, then by the definition of ϵ-nets, S_1 misses some region $r \in \Delta_\epsilon(c)$. Let us fix this missed region r, and suppose we now draw an additional multiset S_2 of m random examples from $\mathcal{D}$. Since each element of S_2 has probability at least ϵ of hitting r, if $m = O(1/\epsilon)$ the probability S_2 hits r at least $\epsilon m/2$ times is at least $1/2$ by Markov's inequality (see the Appendix in Chapter 9).

If we let B be the combined event over the random draws of S_1 and S_2 that A occurs on the draw of S_1 (so S_1 is not an ϵ-net) *and* S_2 has at least $\epsilon m/2$ hits in a region of $\Delta_\epsilon(c)$ that is missed by S_1, then we have argued that $\mathbf{Pr}[B|A] \geq 1/2$. Since the definition of event B already requires that event A occurs on S_1, we also have $\mathbf{Pr}[B] = \mathbf{Pr}[B|A]\mathbf{Pr}[A]$, so $2\mathbf{Pr}[B] \geq \mathbf{Pr}[A]$.

Thus, we can upper bound the probability of event A by upper bounding the probability of event B. The principal advantage of event B over event A for the purposes of our analysis can be described as follows. To directly analyze the probability of event A, we must consider all regions of the uncountably infinite class $\Delta_\epsilon(c)$ that S_1 might miss. To analyze the probability of event B, we need only consider the regions of $\Pi_{\Delta_\epsilon(c)}(S_1 \cup S_2)$. This is because the occurrence of event B is equivalent to saying that there is some $r \in \Pi_{\Delta_\epsilon(c)}(S_1 \cup S_2)$ such that $|r| \geq \epsilon m/2$ and $r \cap S_1 = \emptyset$.

To bound the probability that such an r exists, rather than drawing S_1 at random and then drawing S_2 at random, we can instead first draw a multiset S of $2m$ instances at random, and then randomly divide S into S_1 and S_2. The resulting distribution of S_1 and S_2 is the same in both experiments, since each draw from $\mathcal{D}$ is independent and identically distributed. Now once S is drawn and fixed (but before it is divided randomly into S_1 and S_2), we may also fix a region $r \in \Pi_{\Delta_\epsilon(c)}(S)$ satisfying $|r| \geq \epsilon m/2$. For this fixed S and fixed r, we now analyze the probability (with respect only to the random partitioning of S into S_1 and S_2) that $r \cap S_1 = \emptyset$. We will then obtain a bound on the probability of event B by summing over all possible fixed $r \in \Pi_{\Delta_\epsilon(c)}(S)$ and applying the union bound.

Our problem is now reduced to the following simple combinatorial experiment: we have $2m$ balls (the multiset S), each colored red or blue, with exactly $\ell \geq \epsilon m/2$ red balls (these are the instances of S that fall in r). We divide these balls randomly into two groups of equal size S_1 and S_2, and we are interested in bounding the probability that all ℓ of the red balls fall in S_2 (that is, the probability that $r \cap S_1 = \emptyset$).

Equivalently, we can first divide $2m$ uncolored balls into S_1 and S_2, and then randomly choose ℓ of the balls to be marked red, the rest being marked blue. Then the probability that all ℓ of the red marks fall on balls S_2 is exactly $\binom{m}{\ell} / \binom{2m}{\ell}$ — this is simply the number of ways we can choose the ℓ red marks in S_2 divided by the number of ways the ℓ red marks can be chosen without constraints. But $\binom{m}{\ell}/\binom{2m}{\ell} \leq 1/2^\ell$. This is because

$$\frac{\binom{m}{\ell}}{\binom{2m}{\ell}} = \Pi_{i=0}^{\ell-1} \frac{(m-i)}{(2m-i)} \leq \Pi_{i=0}^{\ell-1} \left(\frac{1}{2}\right) = \frac{1}{2^\ell}.$$

Thus, for any fixed S and $r \in \Pi_{\Delta_\epsilon(c)}(S)$ satisfying $|r| \geq \epsilon m/2$, the probability that the random partitioning of S results in $r \cap S_1 = \emptyset$ is at most $2^{-\epsilon m/2}$. The probability that this occurs for *some* $r \in \Pi_{\Delta_\epsilon(c)}(S)$ satisfying $|r| \geq \epsilon m/2$ (and thus $\mathbf{Pr}[B]$) is at most

$$|\Pi_{\Delta_\epsilon(c)}(S)|2^{-\frac{\epsilon m}{2}} \leq |\Pi_{\Delta(c)}(S)|2^{-\frac{\epsilon m}{2}} \leq |\Pi_C(S)|2^{-\frac{\epsilon m}{2}}$$

$$\leq \Phi_d(2m)2^{-\frac{\epsilon m}{2}} \leq \left(\frac{2em}{d}\right)^d 2^{-\frac{\epsilon m}{2}}.$$

Finally, $\mathbf{Pr}[A] \leq 2\mathbf{Pr}[B] \leq 2(2em/d)^d 2^{-\epsilon m/2}$, which is less than δ for

$$m = O\left(\frac{1}{\epsilon}\log\frac{1}{\delta} + \frac{d}{\epsilon}\log\frac{1}{\epsilon}\right).$$

We have proved the main result of this chapter:

Theorem 3.3 *Let C be any concept class of VC dimension d. Let L be any algorithm that takes as input a set S of m labeled examples of a concept in C, and produces as output a concept $h \in C$ that is consistent with S. Then L is a PAC learning algorithm for C provided it is given a random sample of m examples from $EX(c, \mathcal{D})$, where m obeys*

$$m \geq c_0\left(\frac{1}{\epsilon}\log\frac{1}{\delta} + \frac{d}{\epsilon}\log\frac{1}{\epsilon}\right)$$

for some constant $c_0 > 0$.

Recall that in Chapter 1, we saw that for computational reasons there may sometimes be a great advantage in using a hypothesis class $\mathcal{H}$ that is more powerful than the class C from which the target is chosen. The reader can verify that the same proof used to establish Theorem 3.3 can be used to prove the following analogue:

Theorem 3.4 *Let C be any concept class. Let $\mathcal{H}$ be any representation class of VC dimension d. Let L be any algorithm that takes as input a set S of m labeled examples of a concept in C, and produces as output a concept $h \in \mathcal{H}$ that is consistent with S. Then L is a PAC learning algorithm for C using $\mathcal{H}$ provided it is given a random sample of m examples from $EX(c, \mathcal{D})$, where m obeys*

$$m \geq c_0 \left(\frac{1}{\epsilon} \log \frac{1}{\delta} + \frac{d}{\epsilon} \log \frac{1}{\epsilon} \right)$$

for some constant $c_0 > 0$.

Thus, to obtain an algorithm for PAC learning C using $\mathcal{H}$, we take a number of examples on the order of the VC dimension of $\mathcal{H}$ (which is at least as large as the VC dimension of C if $\mathcal{H} \supset C$). This shows that while we may reduce our computation time by choosing a more powerful hypothesis representation, we may also increase the number of examples required.

3.6 Sample Size Lower Bounds

We now show that the upper bound on the sample complexity of PAC learning given by Theorem 3.3 is tight within a factor of $O(\log 1/\epsilon)$ (ignoring the dependence on δ). First we show a lower bound of $\Omega(d)$ on the number of examples required for PAC learning using a fairly simple argument, then we present a refined argument that improves the bound to $\Omega(d/\epsilon)$.

Theorem 3.5 *Any algorithm for PAC learning a concept class of Vapnik-Chervonenkis dimension d must use $\Omega(d/\epsilon)$ examples in the worst case.*

Proof: Consider a concept class C such that $VCD(C) = d$. Let $S = \{x_1, \ldots, x_d\}$ be shattered by C. To show a lower bound, we construct a particular distribution that forces any PAC learning algorithm to take many examples. Thus, let $\mathcal{D}$ give probability $1/d$ to each point in S, and probability 0 to points not in S. For this distribution, we can assume without loss of generality that $\mathcal{C} = \Pi_\mathcal{C}(S)$ (that is, $X = S$), so $\mathcal{C}$ is a finite class and $|\mathcal{C}| = 2^d$.

Note that we have arranged things so that for all of the 2^d possible binary labelings of the points in S, there is exactly one concept in $\mathcal{C}$ that induces this labeling. Thus, choosing the target concept c randomly from $\mathcal{C}$ is equivalent to flipping a fair coin d times to determine the labeling induced by c on S.

Now let L be any PAC learning algorithm for $\mathcal{C}$. Set the error parameter $\epsilon \leq 1/8$, and consider running L when the target concept $c \in \mathcal{C}$ is chosen randomly and the input distribution is $\mathcal{D}$. Suppose that after drawing $m < d$ examples from $EX(c, \mathcal{D})$, L has drawn $m' \leq m$ different instances; without loss of generality, let these be $x_1, \ldots, x_{m'}$. Then from the above observations, it is clear that the problem of predicting the correct label of any unseen instance x_j for $j > m'$ is equivalent to predicting the outcome of a fair coin, since each label of c on S is determined by an independent coin flip. Thus the expected error (over the random choice of c and the sample of points) of L's hypothesis is $(d - m')/2d$, and by Markov's inequality (see the Appendix in Chapter 9) is at least $(d - m')/4d$ with probability at least $1/2$. For $m = d/2$ we obtain that the error of L's hypothesis is at least $1/8$ with probability at least $1/2$ (over the random choice of c and the sample). Since this shows that L must fail when c is chosen randomly, there must certainly be some fixed target concept on which L fails, thus giving the $\Omega(d)$ sample complexity lower bound.

To refine this argument to get a lower bound that incorporates ϵ, we simply scale the above coin flipping construction to a region of the distribution that is small but still too large to be "ignored" by the algorithm. Thus, we modify $\mathcal{D}$ to let the distinguished instance x_1 have probability $1 - 8\epsilon$ under $\mathcal{D}$ (we are essentially "giving" this instance along with its correct label to L), and let $x_2, \ldots, x_d$ each have probability $8\epsilon/(d - 1)$

under $\mathcal{D}$ (this is the coin flipping region). Now by simply scaling our previous calculation to the coin flipping region, the expected error of L after seeing at most $d/2$ different instances is at least $(1/8)8\epsilon = \epsilon$ with probability at least $1/2$. But it is not difficult to show that now drawing $d/2$ different points requires $\Omega(d/\epsilon)$ examples, because our problem is reduced to obtaining $d/2$ "successes" in independent trials, each with probability of success only 4ϵ. $\qquad\qquad\square$(Theorem 3.5)

3.7   An Application to Neural Networks

We conclude this chapter by giving a useful general lemma that bounds $VCD(\mathcal{C})$ when each concept in the class $\mathcal{C}$ is actually a **composition** of simpler concepts. Such classes arise frequently — for instance, a DNF formulae is simply a (very constrained) composition of boolean conjunctions (the constraint being that we can only compute disjunctions of conjunctions). After giving this lemma, we then apply it to obtain upper bounds on the sample size required for PAC learning neural networks.

To formalize a general notion of concept composition, let G be a **layered** directed acyclic graph. By this we mean that the nodes of G can be partitioned into layers, and the directed edges of G go only from a node at layer ℓ to a node at layer $\ell+1$. We let n be the number of nodes at layer 0, and we assume that all of these have indegree 0. We think of these n layer 0 nodes as being the inputs to the graph. We also assume that there is only a single node of outdegree 0 at the highest level of the graph, and we think of this node as being the output node of the graph. All internal (that is, non-input) nodes have the same indegree r, and we let s denote the number of internal nodes. Figure 3.5 shows an example of such a layered graph with $n = 8$, $s = 8$ and $r = 3$.

Now let $\mathcal{C}$ be a concept class over r-dimensional Euclidean space $\Re^r$. Suppose we take such a layered graph G, and we label each internal (that is, non-input) node N_i with a concept $c_i \in \mathcal{C}$. Then such a labeled

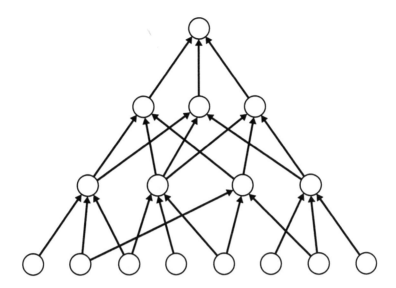

Figure 3.5: *A layered directed acyclic graph.*

graph represents a concept over n-dimensional Euclidean space $\Re^n$ in the obvious way: if we label each of the n input nodes at layer 0 with a real number, then starting with layer 1 we can compute the value at each node N_i by applying the concept c_i labeling node N_i to the values computed at the nodes feeding N_i. (Note that although concepts in $\mathcal{C}$ are defined over $\Re^r$, the input values feeding nodes at level 2 and higher will actually only be from $\{0,1\}^r$.) The output of the entire labeled graph is the binary value computed at the output node. We will call the class of all concepts over $\Re^n$ that can be obtained by labeling G with concepts from $\mathcal{C}$ the G-**composition of** $\mathcal{C}$, which we denote $\mathcal{C}_G$.

Theorem 3.6 *Let G be a layered directed acyclic graph with n input nodes and $s \geq 2$ internal nodes, each of indegree r. Let $\mathcal{C}$ be a concept class over $\Re^r$ of VC dimension d, and let $\mathcal{C}_G$ be the G-composition of $\mathcal{C}$. Then $VCD(\mathcal{C}_G) \leq 2ds \log(es)$.*

Proof: The idea is to first bound the function $\Pi_{\mathcal{C}_G}(m)$. Let us fix any set S of m input vectors $\vec{x}_1, \ldots, \vec{x}_m \in \Re^n$ to the graph G (thus, each $\vec{x}_i$ determines a complete setting of the n input nodes of G). For this fixed input set S, if we now also label each node in G with a concept from $\mathcal{C}$, then for each $\vec{x}_i$ we have completely determined the binary values that will be computed at every node of G when the input is $\vec{x}_i$. Let us call the collection of all the values computed at each node, for each $\vec{x}_i \in S$, a *computation* of G on S. Thus, a computation can be represented by labeling each internal node with the vector in $\{0,1\}^m$ of the values computed at that node on the m vectors in S. Then the set of all possible computations of G on S is obtained by ranging over all possible choices of labels from $\mathcal{C}$ for the nodes of G. Note that two computations of G on S differ if and only if the value computed at some node on some input from S differs in the two computations. Clearly, $|\Pi_{\mathcal{C}_G}(S)|$ is bounded by the total number of possible computations of G on S, which we shall denote $T_{\mathcal{C}_G}(S)$.

To bound $T_{\mathcal{C}_G}(S)$, let G' be the subgraph obtained by removing the output node N_o from G. Let $T_{\mathcal{C}_{G'}}(S)$ denote the total number of computations of G' on S. Each fixed computation of G' can be extended to at most $\Pi_{\mathcal{C}}(m)$ computations of G, because fixing the computation of G' determines for each $1 \leq i \leq m$ the input $\vec{y}_i \in \{0,1\}^r$ that is fed to N_o when $\vec{x}_i$ is fed to G, and at most $\Pi_{\mathcal{C}}(m)$ labelings of $\vec{y}_1, \ldots, \vec{y}_m$ can be obtained at N_o by varying the choice of concept from $\mathcal{C}$ placed at N_o. Thus we obtain that for any S, $T_{\mathcal{C}_G}(S) \leq T_{\mathcal{C}_{G'}}(S) \times \Pi_{\mathcal{C}}(m)$, and a simple inductive argument establishes

$$|\Pi_{\mathcal{C}_G}(S)| \leq T_{\mathcal{C}_G}(S) \leq (\Pi_{\mathcal{C}}(m))^s \leq \left(\frac{em}{d}\right)^{ds}$$

where the second inequality comes from the polynomial bound on the $\Pi_{\mathcal{C}}(m)$ given in Section 3.4. Since S was arbitrary, this bound in fact holds for $\Pi_{\mathcal{C}_G}(m)$.

Thus in order for $\mathcal{C}_G$ to shatter m points, the inequality $(em/d)^{ds} \geq 2^m$ must hold. Conversely, if $(em/d)^{ds} < 2^m$ for some m, then m is an upper bound on $VCD(\mathcal{C}_G)$. It is easy to verify that this latter inequality holds for $m = 2ds \log(es)$ provided $s \geq 2$. $\qquad \square$(Theorem 3.6)

To apply Theorem 3.6 to the problem of PAC learning neural networks, we simply let the function at each node in the graph G be a **linear threshold function**. If the indegree is r, such a function is defined by real **weights** $w_1, \ldots, w_r \in \Re$ and a **threshold** $\Theta \in \Re$. On inputs $x_1, \ldots, x_r \in \Re$ the function outputs 1 if $\sum_{i=1}^{r} w_i x_i \geq \Theta$, and outputs 0 otherwise. We call G the underlying **architecture** of the neural network.

Now as we mentioned in Section 3.3, it is known that the VC dimension of the class of linear threshold on r inputs is $r + 1$. By Theorem 3.6 we find that the Vapnik-Chervonenkis of the class of neural networks with architecture G is at most $2(rs + s)\log(es)$, and combined with Theorem 3.3, we obtain:

Theorem 3.7 *Let G be any directed acyclic graph, and let $\mathcal{C}_G$ be the class of neural networks on an architecture G with indegree r and s internal nodes. Then the number of examples required to learn $\mathcal{C}_G$ is*

$$O\left(\frac{1}{\epsilon}\log\frac{1}{\delta} + \frac{(rs + s)\log s}{\epsilon}\log\frac{1}{\epsilon}\right).$$

3.8 Exercises

3.1. Compute the VC dimension of the class of boolean conjunctions of literals over $\{0, 1\}^n$.

3.2. Consider the concept class over the Euclidean plane $\Re^2$ consisting of the interior regions of circles; thus, the positive examples of each concept form a disk in the plane. Compute the VC dimension of this class. Compute the VC dimension of the class of interiors of triangles in the plane.

3.3. Show that there is no 1-decision list over $\{0, 1\}^n$ computing the exclusive-or function $x_1 \oplus x_2$. Then show that the VC dimension of

1-decision lists over $\{0,1\}^n$ is $\Theta(n)$, and that the VC dimension of k-decision lists is $\Theta(n^k)$. Hint: show that 1-decision lists over $\{0,1\}^n$ compute linearly separable functions (halfspaces). You may use the fact that the VC dimension of halfspaces over $\Re^n$ is linear in n.

3.4. Let $P_{d,k}$ be the class of concepts over $\Re^d$ defined by convex polytopes with k sides; thus, each the positive examples of each concept in $P_{d,k}$ are defined by the convex intersection of k halfspaces in $\Re^d$. Give the best upper and lower bounds that you can on $VCD(P_{d,k})$. You may use the fact that the VC dimension of halfspaces over $\Re^d$ is linear in d.

3.5. Let C be any concept class of VC dimension d over X, and let $\mathcal{D}$ be any distribution over X. Suppose we are given access to a source of random (unlabeled) instances drawn according to $\mathcal{D}$, and also access to an oracle that for any labeled sample of points will return "Yes" if there is a concept in C that is consistent with the labeled sample, and will return "No" otherwise. Describe an algorithm that on input any finite set of instances $S \subseteq X$ and any $\epsilon, \delta > 0$ will output either the answer "Yes, S in an ϵ-net for C with respect to $\mathcal{D}$", or the answer "No, S is not an $\epsilon/4$-net for C with respect to $\mathcal{D}$". Moreover, the algorithm must give a correct answer with probability at least $1 - \delta$. The algorithm need not be efficient. (The quantity $\epsilon/4$ in the "No" condition can in fact be replaced by $\alpha\epsilon$ for any fixed constant $\alpha < 1$, giving an arbitrarily refined test.)

3.6. Prove that the bound of $\Phi_d(m)$ on $\Pi_C(m)$ is tight: that is, for any concept class C of VC dimension d and any m, there exists a set S of m points such that $|\Pi_C(S)| = \Phi_d(m)$.

3.7. In this exercise we consider the two-oracle model of PAC learning defined in Exercise 1.3 of Chapter 1. We say that a concept class C is **PAC learnable from positive examples alone** if it is PAC learnable by an algorithm that only draws from the oracle $EX(c, \mathcal{D}_c^+)$ when learning target concept $c \in C$ (the hypothesis must still meet the two-sided error criterion). We have already seen in Chapter 1 that boolean conjunctions are efficiently PAC learnable from positive examples alone. This exercise ignores computational considerations, and concentrates on the number of examples required for learning from positive examples alone.

We say that a subclass $C' \subseteq C$ has **unique negative examples** if for every $c \in C'$, there is an instance $x_c \in X$ such that $x_c \notin c$ but $x_c \in c'$ for every other $c' \in C'$. We define the **unique negative dimension** of the class C, $UND(C)$, to be the cardinality of the largest subclass C' that has unique negative examples.

Prove that any algorithm learning C from positive examples alone (regardless of computation time or the hypothesis class used) requires $\Omega(UND(C)/\epsilon)$ positive examples.

Then prove that $O(UND(C)/\epsilon)$ positive examples are sufficient for learning from positive examples alone by the following steps. Consider the algorithm that takes a sample S of positive examples of the target concept and returns the hypothesis

$$ h = \min_C(S) = \bigcap_{c \in C : S \subseteq c} c. $$

Note that h may not be contained in C, and also that this algorithm will never err on a negative example of the target concept.

First show that if on random samples S of size d/ϵ (where $d = UND(C)$) from $EX(c, \mathcal{D}_c^+)$, the expected error of $\min_C(S)$ with respect to $\mathcal{D}_c^+$ exceeds ϵ, then there must exist a set $S^* \subseteq c$ of size $d/\epsilon + 1$ with the property that for a fraction at least ϵ of the $x \in S^*$, $x \notin \min_C(S^* - \{x\})$. Then show that this implies that $UND(C) > d$, a contradiction.

Thus, $\Theta(UND(C)/\epsilon)$ positive examples are necessary and sufficient for learning from positive examples alone, and the unique negative dimension plays a role analogous to the Vapnik-Chervonenkis dimension for this model of learning.

3.9   Bibliographic Notes

The classic paper on the VC dimension, and the one in which the main elements of the proof of Theorem 3.3 are first introduced, is by Vapnik and Chervonenkis [95]. These ideas were introduced into the computational learning theory literature and elaborated upon in the influential work of Blumer, Ehrenfeucht, Haussler and Warmuth [22]. Vapnik has also written an excellent book [94] that greatly extends the original ideas into a theory known as structural risk minimization.

The VC dimension and its attendant theorems have been influential in the neural network and artificial intelligence machine learning communities. The calculation of the VC dimension of neural networks is due to Baum and Haussler [13], and Abu-Mostafa [1] and Tesauro and Cohn [89] examine VC dimension issues from a neural network perspective. Haussler [45] examines the VC dimension as a form of inductive bias from an artificial intelligence viewpoint.

The value of the VC dimension as a measure of the sample complexity of learning transcends the PAC model; many authors have shown that the VC dimension provides upper or lower bounds on the resources required for learning in many models. These include on-line models of learning (Haussler, Littlestone and Warmuth [51]; Maass and Turán [69]; Littlestone [66]), models of query learning (Maass and Turán [69]); and many others.

The VC dimension has also been generalized to give combinatorial complexity measures that characterize the sample complexity of learning in various extensions of the PAC model. Perhaps the most general work along these lines in the computational learning theory literature has been undertaken by Haussler [48], who draws on work in statistics, notably the work of Pollard [74] and of Dudley [31]. Haussler's general framework is examined carefully in the context of learning probabilistic concept by Kearns and Schapire [61], who prove that a certain generalization of the VC dimension provides a lower bound on sample size for learning in this model, and by Alon et al. [4], who give an upper bound.

The VC dimension and its generalizations are only one of the many ways that computational learning theory and statistics attempt to quantify the behavior of *learning curves*, that is, the error of the hypothesis as a function of the number of examples seen. For instance, among the many alternative methods of analysis are theories based on tools from information theory and statistical physics [50, 86].

The $\Omega(d/\epsilon)$ sample size lower bound is due to Ehrenfeucht et al. [33], who also give the solution to Exercise 3.3. Exercise 3.7 is due to Gereb-Graus [39].

4

Weak and Strong Learning

4.1 A Relaxed Definition of Learning?

There are two parameters that quantify and control the performance of a PAC learning algorithm — the error parameter ϵ and the confidence parameter δ. The smaller the values of these parameters, the stronger the guarantee on the quality of the hypothesis output by the learning algorithm. In our definition of PAC learning, we demanded that a learning algorithm be able to achieve arbitrarily small values for ϵ and δ, and that the running time be polynomially bounded in $1/\epsilon$ and $1/\delta$ (as well as n and $size(c)$).

Suppose that instead of a PAC learning algorithm, we had in our possession a weaker but perhaps still useful algorithm L that could achieve the PAC criteria not for any ϵ and δ but only for some fixed, constant values ϵ_0 and δ_0. Thus, for any target concept $c \in \mathcal{C}$ and any distribution $\mathcal{D}$, L manages to find a hypothesis h that with probability at least $1 - \delta_0$ satisfied $error(h) \leq \epsilon_0$, and now L runs in time polynomial in just n and $size(c)$. Is there any way we could use L as a subroutine to obtain an improved algorithm L' that achieved the PAC criteria any values for ϵ and δ?

In this chapter, we show that the answer to this question is positive in the strongest possible sense: even an efficient algorithm whose hypotheses are only slightly better than "random guessing" can be used to obtain an efficient algorithm meeting the definition of PAC learning. By slightly better than random guessing, we mean hypotheses that correctly classify an instance with probability just exceeding $1/2$. Note that if all we desired was the ability to correctly classify instances with probability *exactly* $1/2$, we could always accomplish this by skipping the learning process altogether, and simply flipping a fair coin to classify each new instance! Thus, a hypothesis of error strictly less than $1/2$ is the least nontrivial criterion we could ask a learning algorithm to meet.

More precisely, let C be a concept class, and let L be an algorithm that is given access to $EX(c, \mathcal{D})$ for target concept $c \in \mathcal{C}_n$ and distribution $\mathcal{D}$. We say that L is a **weak PAC learning algorithm for C using** $\mathcal{H}$ if there are fixed polynomials $p(\cdot, \cdot)$ and $q(\cdot, \cdot)$ such that L outputs a hypothesis $h \in \mathcal{H}$ that with probability at least $1/q(n, size(c))$ satisfies $error(h) \leq 1/2 - 1/p(n, size(c))$. Thus, with only inverse polynomial confidence, L outputs a hypothesis whose predictive ability has only an inverse polynomial advantage over $1/2$.

With this definition, we can now more formally verify that weak PAC learning really is the weakest demand we could place on an algorithm in the PAC setting without trivializing the learning problem. For instance, over the boolean domain $\{0, 1\}^n$ we can always obtain error bounded by $1/2 - 1/e(n)$ for some *exponentially* growing function $e(n)$ just by taking a small random sample S of the target concept, and letting our hypothesis be the randomized mapping that classifies an instance according to S if the instance appears in S, and otherwise flips a fair coin to classify the instance. Note that in polynomial time, we could not even detect that this hypothesis gave a slight predictive advantage over random guessing.

Thus, our definition demands that the hypothesis of a weak PAC learning algorithm achieve the least nontrivial generalization from the sample — that is, the least ability to predict the label of instances outside the observed sample. Furthermore, in keeping with our notion that n

and $size(c)$ are natural measures of the complexity of the target concept, we even allow the confidence and the advantage of the hypothesis over random guessing to diminish to 0 as the complexity of the target concept increases.

We will sometimes refer to our original definition of PAC learning as **strong PAC learning** to distinguish it from this new notion. The somewhat surprising main result of this chapter is that if $\mathcal{C}$ is efficiently weakly PAC learnable, then $\mathcal{C}$ is efficiently strongly PAC learnable.

We prove the equivalence of weak and strong learning by providing an explicit and efficient transformation of a weak PAC learning algorithm into a strong PAC learning algorithm. If ϵ and δ are the desired error and confidence parameters for the strong learning algorithm, the overhead in running time of this transformation is a surprisingly slowly growing function of $1/\epsilon$ and $1/\delta$. The transformation for achieving greater confidence (that is, reducing δ) is entirely straightforward, as we shall see momentarily. The transformation for reducing the error is much more involved, and forms the bulk of this chapter.

An important consequence of the construction used to prove the equivalence is that it shows that any class that is efficiently PAC learnable is in fact efficiently PAC learnable with specific upper bounds on the required resources. For example, using the construction we can prove that if a concept class is efficiently PAC learnable, then it is efficiently PAC learnable by an algorithm whose required memory is (of course) bounded by a polynomial in n and $size(c)$, but by an only *polylogarthmic* function of $1/\epsilon$. (By this we mean polynomial in $\log(1/\epsilon)$.) When contrasted with the lower bound of $\Omega(1/\epsilon)$ on the number of examples required for PAC learning given by Theorem 3.5 (ignoring for now the dependence on all quantities other than ϵ), this shows that there are no concept classes for which efficient PAC learnability requires that the entire sample be contained in memory at one time — there is always another algorithm that "forgets" most of the sample.

Another consequence of the construction is that if $\mathcal{C}$ is efficiently PAC learnable, then there is an efficient algorithm taking a sample of m labeled examples of any $c \in \mathcal{C}$, and finding a consistent hypothesis whose size is polynomial in $size(c)$ but only polylogarithmic in m. This gives a strong converse to the results on Occam's Razor presented in Chapter 2.

These and several other interesting consequences of the construction are explored in the exercises at the end of the chapter.

4.2 Boosting the Confidence

We begin our proof of the equivalence of weak and strong learning with the easy part: namely, showing that we can efficiently boost the confidence of a learning algorithm from an inverse polynomial to a value arbitrarily close to 1. Without loss of generality, and for simplicity in the following argument, let us fix a value ϵ for the error parameter, and suppose we have an algorithm L such that for any target concept $c \in \mathcal{C}$ and any distribution $\mathcal{D}$, L outputs h such that $error(h) \leq \epsilon$ with probability only at least $\delta_0 = 1/q(n, size(c))$ for some fixed polynomial $q(\cdot, \cdot)$.

We now show that if we are willing to tolerate the slightly higher hypothesis error $\epsilon + \gamma$ (for $\gamma > 0$ arbitrarily small), then we can achieve arbitrarily high confidence $1 - \delta$ (that is, arbitrarily small confidence parameter δ).

Our new algorithm L' will simulate algorithm L a total of k times (where k will be determined shortly), using an independent sample from $EX(c, \mathcal{D})$ for each simulation. Let $h_1, \ldots, h_k$ denote the hypotheses output by L on these k runs. Then because the simulations are independent, the probability that all of $h_1, \ldots, h_k$ have error larger than ϵ is at most $(1 - \delta_0)^k$. Solving $(1 - \delta_0)^k \leq \delta/2$ yields $k \geq (1/\delta_0) \ln(2/\delta)$ for our choice of k.

The remaining task of L' can now be expressed as follows: given the hypotheses $h_1, \ldots, h_k$, and assuming that at least one has error bounded by ϵ, output one which has error at most $\epsilon + \gamma$ with probability at least $1 - \delta/2$. This is easily accomplished by drawing a sufficiently large sample of labeled examples S from $EX(c, \mathcal{D})$, and choosing the h_i that makes the fewest mistakes on S. We will choose S large enough so that with confidence at least $1 - \delta/2$, the empirical error of each h_j on S is within $\gamma/2$ of its true value $error(h_j)$ with respect to c and $\mathcal{D}$. This will ensure that with confidence $1 - \delta/2$ the hypothesis that is output has error at most $\epsilon + \gamma$.

For any fixed hypothesis h_j, whether h_j makes a mistake on a randomly drawn example from $EX(c, \mathcal{D})$ can be regarded as a biased coin flip with probability of heads equal to $error(h_i)$. By the Chernoff bounds discussed in the Appendix in Chapter 9 the empirical error of h_j on S is an estimate for $error(h_j)$ that is accurate to within an additive factor of $\gamma/2$ with confidence at least $1 - \delta/2k$ provided that the number of examples m in S satisfies $m \geq (c_0/\gamma^2) \log(2k/\delta)$ for some appropriate constant $c_0 > 0$.

Now by the union bound, the probability that any of the k hypotheses has empirical error on S deviating from its true error by more than $\gamma/2$ is at most $k(\delta/2k) = \delta/2$. Note that we have arranged things so that the total failure probability — the probability that we fail to get at least one hypothesis of error less than ϵ out of the k runs of L, plus the probability that we fail to choose a hypothesis of error less than $\epsilon + \gamma$ — is at most $\delta/2 + \delta/2 = \delta$.

In summary, the algorithm to boost the confidence from $1/q(n, size(c))$ to $1 - \delta$ (at the expense of an additive factor of γ in the error) is:

- Run L a total of $k = \lceil (1/q(n, size(c))) \ln(2/\delta) \rceil$ times to obtain hypotheses $h_1, \ldots, h_k$.

- Choose a sample S of size $(c_0/\gamma^2) \log(2k/\delta)$ from $EX(c, \mathcal{D})$, and output the h_i that makes fewest mistakes on S.

It is easily verified that the running time is polynomial in n, $size(c)$,

$\log(1/\delta)$, $1/\epsilon$ and $1/\gamma$. To eliminate the parameter γ from this argument, if ϵ is our desired error bound, we can make each run of L using the smaller value $\epsilon' = \epsilon/2$ as the error parameter given to L, and then set $\gamma = \epsilon/2$.

4.3   Boosting the Accuracy

We now turn to the harder problem of decreasing the error. Let us assume for now that we are given an algorithm L for $\mathcal{C}$ that with high probability outputs a hypothesis with error at most $\beta < 1/2$, where β is fixed for the moment. We would like to transform L into an algorithm that with high probability outputs a hypothesis with error at most ϵ, where $0 \leq \epsilon < \beta$ is any given error parameter. We will eventually substitute the value $1/2 - 1/p(n, size(c))$ for β in accordance with the definition of weak learning.

It should be readily apparent that the problem of boosting the accuracy is much harder than the problem of confidence boosting. In the confidence boosting problem, the available learning algorithm did manage to output an acceptable hypothesis (that is, one with the desired error bound ϵ) with probability $1/q(n, size(c))$, so a small pool of independent hypotheses contained an acceptable hypothesis with high probability, and thus confidence boosting involved simply identifying a good hypothesis from the small pool. In contrast, we are now faced with the situation where the available learning algorithm might *always* output a hypothesis with an unacceptably high error (that is, error larger than ϵ).

At first glance, this might make our stated goal seem impossible to achieve. The key to obtaining the result lies in the fact that even though the available learning algorithm L may output hypotheses with unacceptably large error β, it is guaranteed to do so for any distribution on the input space. The idea will be to run L many times, not only on the target distribution $\mathcal{D}$, but also on other related probability distributions which somehow "focus the attention" of L on regions in which the hypotheses of previous runs perform poorly. For example, after running L once to obtain a hypothesis h of error at most β with respect to $\mathcal{D}$, we could then run L again, but only giving L those inputs from $\mathcal{D}$ on which h errs — the intuition being that the second run of L is forced to learn something "new". While this idea does not quite work, a variation of it will, and the many hypotheses output by L on multiple runs will be judiciously combined to yield a new hypothesis with error at most ϵ on the original distribution $\mathcal{D}$.

We will present the accuracy boosting construction in two parts. First, we define and analyze a simple and modest accuracy boosting procedure. Given a learning algorithm L that outputs hypotheses of error at most β, this procedure uses L as a subroutine and outputs hypotheses of error at most $g(\beta) < \beta$, for some function $g(\beta)$ that we will specify shortly. To do this, the procedure defines a sequence of three probability distributions on the input space. It then invokes L three times on these three distributions to obtain three hypotheses h_1, h_2 and h_3. These hypotheses are combined into the single function h that takes the majority vote of h_1, h_2 and h_3 and which forms the output of the procedure. The hypothesis h is guaranteed to have error at most $g(\beta)$, which still may be much larger than the desired value ϵ.

In the second and more complex part of the construction, we use this modest boosting procedure repeatedly in a recursive fashion in order to drive the error down to ϵ.

4.3.1   A Modest Accuracy Boosting Procedure

Throughout this section, we shall assume $c \in \mathcal{C}$ is the target concept, $\mathcal{D}$ is the target distribution, and L is an algorithm that with high probability outputs hypotheses with error at most $\beta < 1/2$ when given access to $EX(c, \mathcal{D})$. When there is ambiguity about the distribution, we use $error_{\mathcal{D}}(h)$ to explicitly indicate the error of h with respect to c and $\mathcal{D}$.

Our modest accuracy boosting procedure operates as follows. To begin, algorithm L is invoked on the oracle $EX(c, \mathcal{D})$. We let h_1 denote the hypothesis output by L.

Now we run L again, but this time on a new distribution. Intuitively, this second distribution is designed to extract new information about the target concept — information that was absent in h_1. More precisely, the new distribution $\mathcal{D}_2$ is created by **filtering** $\mathcal{D}$ with respect to the first hypothesis h_1.

Distribution $\mathcal{D}_2$ is defined as follows: to sample from $EX(c, \mathcal{D}_2)$, we first flip a fair coin. If the outcome is heads, we draw labeled examples from $EX(c, \mathcal{D})$ until an example $\langle x, c(x) \rangle$ is drawn such that $h_1(x) = c(x)$ and output $\langle x, c(x) \rangle$. If the outcome is tails, then we draw labeled examples from $EX(c, \mathcal{D})$ until an example $\langle x, c(x) \rangle$ is drawn such that $h_1(x) \neq c(x)$ and output $\langle x, c(x) \rangle$.

Thus, $\mathcal{D}_2$ is essentially $\mathcal{D}$ normalized to give weight exactly $1/2$ to those instances on which h_1 errs; the relative weight of two such instances, however, is unaltered, as is the relative weight of two instances on which h_1 is correct. $\mathcal{D}_2$ is constructed so that h_1 has no advantage over random guessing: that is, $error_{\mathcal{D}_2}(h_1) = 1/2 > \beta$. Thus, invoking L on $EX(c, \mathcal{D}_2)$ yields a hypothesis h_2 which gives us "new information" about c, that is, information not contained in h_1. In particular, we must have $h_1 \neq h_2$.

It is important to note that we can sample from $EX(c, \mathcal{D}_2)$ given access to $EX(c, \mathcal{D})$, and that the expected number of calls we need to $EX(c, \mathcal{D})$ to simulate a single call to $EX(c, \mathcal{D}_2)$ becomes large only if $error_{\mathcal{D}}(h_1) \approx 0$ or $error_{\mathcal{D}}(h_1) \approx 1$. Roughly speaking, neither of these is a major problem since if $error_{\mathcal{D}}(h_1) \approx 0$ then h_1 already has error significantly smaller than β, and $error_{\mathcal{D}}(h_1) \approx 1 > \beta$ cannot happen if L meets its guarantee when run on $EX(c, \mathcal{D})$. However, we shall rigorously handle the issue of the efficiency of filtering later, and for now we simply assume we can sample $EX(c, \mathcal{D}_2)$ in unit time.

For the third simulation of L, we create a third distribution $\mathcal{D}_3$ by again filtering $\mathcal{D}$, this time with respect to both h_1 and h_2. In order to sample from $EX(c, \mathcal{D}_3)$, we draw labeled examples from $EX(c, \mathcal{D})$ until an example $\langle x, c(x) \rangle$ is drawn such that $h_1(x) \neq h_2(x)$, and then output $\langle x, c(x) \rangle$. Invoking L on $EX(c, \mathcal{D}_3)$ yields a hypothesis h_3 which once again gives gives "new information" about c, this time on those inputs such that h_1 and h_2 disagree. We again defer analysis of how efficiently we can sample $EX(c, \mathcal{D}_3)$, and for now we assume we can sample $EX(c, \mathcal{D}_3)$ in unit time.

Finally, the output of the modest accuracy boosting procedure is $h = majority(h_1, h_2, h_3)$; by this we mean that $h(x) = 1$ if and only if at least 2 out of 3 of $h_1(x), h_2(x)$ and $h_3(x)$ are 1. Let us introduce the notation $\beta_1 = error_{\mathcal{D}}(h_1)$, $\beta_2 = error_{\mathcal{D}_2}(h_2)$ and $\beta_3 = error_{\mathcal{D}_3}(h_3)$. Our goal now is to argue that even though β_1, β_2 and β_3 may all be as large as β, $error_{\mathcal{D}}(h)$ is significantly smaller than β.

4.3.2 Error Analysis for the Modest Procedure

Before embarking on the specifics of this argument, it will be helpful to introduce a technical fact that we shall use repeatedly. Throughout the chapter, we will need to map the probability of an event with respect to $\mathcal{D}_2$ back to its probability with respect to $\mathcal{D}$. More precisely, consider any instance x. By the definition of $\mathcal{D}_2$, given the value of $\mathcal{D}_2[x]$ (the weight of x under $\mathcal{D}_2$), the weight $\mathcal{D}[x]$ is completely determined by whether $h_1(x) = c(x)$ or $h_1(x) \neq c(x)$. Thus, if $h_1(x) = c(x)$ then $\mathcal{D}[x] = 2(1 - \beta_1)\mathcal{D}_2[x]$. To see this, note that the transformation of $\mathcal{D}$ to $\mathcal{D}_2$ changes the total weight of the instances where $h_1(x) = c(x)$ from $1 - \beta_1$ to $1/2$, or viewed in reverse, an instance x such that $h_1(x) = c(x)$ and $\mathcal{D}_2[x] = p$ must have had weight $2(1 - \beta_1)p$ under $\mathcal{D}$. Similarly, if $h_1(x) \neq c(x)$ then $\mathcal{D}[x] = 2\beta_1 \mathcal{D}_2[x]$. More generally, for any set $S \subseteq X$ we can write

$$\begin{aligned}
\mathbf{Pr}_{x \in \mathcal{D}}[x \in S] &= 2(1 - \beta_1)\mathbf{Pr}_{x \in \mathcal{D}_2}[h_1(x) = c(x) \wedge x \in S] \\
&+ 2\beta_1 \mathbf{Pr}_{x \in \mathcal{D}_2}[h_1(x) \neq c(x) \wedge x \in S].
\end{aligned} \quad (4.1)$$

In what follows, we will repeatedly obtain expressions for probabilities over $\mathcal{D}$ by first decomposing those probabilities over $\mathcal{D}_2$ into their $h_1 = c$ and $h_1 \neq c$ components, and then obtaining the probability with respect to $\mathcal{D}$ via Equation 4.1.

We now embark on the analysis of the error of the hypothesis found by the modest accuracy boosting procedure. The following lemma gives an upper bound of $g(\beta) = 3\beta^2 - 2\beta^3$ on this error with respect to the original distribution $\mathcal{D}$. The function $g(\beta)$ is important to all of the ensuing analysis, so we pause to note two important facts. First, for any $0 \leq \beta < 1/2$ we have $g(\beta) < \beta$, and $g(1/2) = 1/2$. Second, $g(\beta)$ has a well-defined inverse $g^{-1}(\alpha)$ obeying $g^{-1}(\alpha) > \alpha$ for $0 \leq \alpha < 1/2$.

Lemma 4.1 *Let* $g(\beta) = 3\beta^2 - 2\beta^3$. *Let the distributions* $\mathcal{D}$, $\mathcal{D}_2$ *and* $\mathcal{D}_3$ *be as defined above, and let* h_1, h_2 *and* h_3 *satisfy* $error_{\mathcal{D}}(h_1) \leq \beta$, $error_{\mathcal{D}_2}(h_2) \leq \beta$, *and* $error_{\mathcal{D}_3}(h_3) \leq \beta$. *Then if* $h = majority(h_1, h_2, h_3)$, $error_{\mathcal{D}}(h) \leq g(\beta)$.

Proof: We will show in stages that the error of h is maximized when $\beta_i = \beta$ for all i, that is, when each h_i has the maximum allowed error with respect to its corresponding distribution. The bound of $g(\beta)$ on the error of h with respect to $\mathcal{D}$ will then follow quite easily.

For the purposes of analysis, we will decompose the errors of h into two mutually exclusive types. The first type of error is on those inputs where both h_1 and h_2 already make an error. Note that the output of h_3 is irrelevant in this case, since the majority is already determined by h_1 and h_2, and this majority gives the incorrect label. The second type of error is on those inputs where h_1 and h_2 disagree. In this case, the hypothesis h_3 gets to cast the deciding vote for the majority, and therefore h makes an error if and only if h_3 does. This yields:

$$
\begin{aligned}
error_{\mathcal{D}}(h) &= \mathbf{Pr}_{x \in \mathcal{D}}[h_1(x) \neq c(x) \wedge h_2(x) \neq c(x)] \\
&\quad + \mathbf{Pr}_{x \in \mathcal{D}}[h_3(x) \neq c(x) | h_1(x) \neq h_2(x)]\mathbf{Pr}_{x \in \mathcal{D}}[h_1(x) \neq h_2(x)]
\end{aligned}
$$

$$\begin{aligned} = \; & \mathbf{Pr}_{x \in \mathcal{D}}[h_1(x) \neq c(x) \land h_2(x) \neq c(x)] \\ & + \beta_3 \mathbf{Pr}_{x \in \mathcal{D}}[h_1(x) \neq h_2(x)] \end{aligned} \qquad (4.2)$$

The last equality comes from the fact that choosing randomly from $\mathcal{D}$ conditioned on $h_1(x) \neq h_2(x)$ is the same as choosing from $\mathcal{D}_3$, since this is exactly the definition of $\mathcal{D}_3$.

Our goal now is to use Equation (4.2) to obtain an upper bound on $error_{\mathcal{D}}(h)$ that is first an algebraic expression over the β_i, and eventually over only β. From this expression it will be a simple matter to bound $error_{\mathcal{D}}(h)$ by $g(\beta)$.

To begin with, it is clear from Equation (4.2) that $error_{\mathcal{D}}(h)$ is maximized when $\beta_3 = \beta$, because no other term in the equation depends on $\mathcal{D}_3$ and h_3. This gives

$$\begin{aligned} error_{\mathcal{D}}(h) \; \leq \; & \mathbf{Pr}_{x \in \mathcal{D}}[h_1(x) \neq c(x) \land h_2(x) \neq c(x)] \\ & + \beta \mathbf{Pr}_{x \in \mathcal{D}}[h_1(x) \neq h_2(x)] \end{aligned} \qquad (4.3)$$

It remains to analyze the two probabilities involving h_1 and h_2 in Inequality 4.3. We can represent the distributions $\mathcal{D}$ and $\mathcal{D}_2$ as shown in Figure 4.1. Distribution $\mathcal{D}_2$ can be partitioned into two equal parts as shown: one corresponding to those inputs x where $h_1(x) = c(x)$ and the other corresponding to $h_1(x) \neq c(x)$. As shown, let γ_1 and γ_2 respectively be the error of h_2 on each of these parts, that is,

$$\gamma_1 = \mathbf{Pr}_{x \in \mathcal{D}_2}[h_1(x) = c(x) \land h_2(x) \neq c(x)]$$

and

$$\gamma_2 = \mathbf{Pr}_{x \in \mathcal{D}_2}[h_1(x) \neq c(x) \land h_2(x) \neq c(x)].$$

Clearly we have $\gamma_1 + \gamma_2 = \beta_2$.

Using the expression for γ_1 and using Equation 4.1 to go back to $\mathcal{D}$, we may write

$$\mathbf{Pr}_{x \in \mathcal{D}}[h_1(x) = c(x) \land h_2(x) \neq c(x)] = 2(1 - \beta_1)\gamma_1. \qquad (4.4)$$

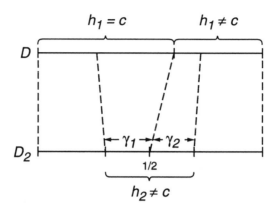

Figure 4.1: *The mapping of distribution $\mathcal{D}$ to distribution $\mathcal{D}_2$. The region $h_1 = c$ "shrinks" from weight $1 - \beta_1 > 1/2$ under $\mathcal{D}$ to weight exactly $1/2$ under $\mathcal{D}_2$, while the region $h_1 \neq c$ "expands" from weight $\beta_1 < 1/2$ under $\mathcal{D}$ to weight exactly $1/2$ under $\mathcal{D}_2$.*

Also note (see Figure 4.1) that

$$\mathbf{Pr}_{x \in \mathcal{D}_2}[h_1(x) \neq c(x) \wedge h_2(x) = c(x)] = 1/2 - \gamma_2$$

and thus by Equation 4.1

$$\mathbf{Pr}_{x \in \mathcal{D}}[h_1(x) \neq c(x) \wedge h_2(x) = c(x)] = 2\beta_1(1/2 - \gamma_2). \qquad (4.5)$$

Using Equations (4.4) and (4.5) and the fact that

$$\begin{aligned} \mathbf{Pr}_{x \in \mathcal{D}}[h_1(x) \neq h_2(x)] = \\ \mathbf{Pr}_{x \in \mathcal{D}}[h_1(x) = c(x) \wedge h_2(x) \neq c(x)] \\ + \mathbf{Pr}_{x \in \mathcal{D}}[h_1(x) \neq c(x) \wedge h_2(x) = c(x)] \end{aligned}$$

we get

$$\mathbf{Pr}_{x \in \mathcal{D}}[h_1(x) \neq h_2(x)] = 2(1 - \beta_1)\gamma_1 + 2\beta_1(1/2 - \gamma_2). \qquad (4.6)$$

Now using the expression for γ_2 and again using Equation 4.1 to go back to $\mathcal{D}$, we may write

$$\mathbf{Pr}_{x \in \mathcal{D}}[h_1(x) \neq c(x) \wedge h_2(x) \neq c(x)] = 2\beta_1\gamma_2. \qquad (4.7)$$

Substituting Equations (4.6) and (4.7) into Inequality (4.3), we get:

$$
\begin{aligned}
error_{\mathcal{D}}(h) &\leq 2\beta_1\gamma_2 + \beta(2(1-\beta_1)\gamma_1 + 2\beta_1(1/2 - \gamma_2)) \\
&= \beta_1\beta(1 - 2\gamma_1) + 2\beta_1\gamma_2(1-\beta) + 2\gamma_1\beta.
\end{aligned}
$$

The last equality can be easily verified algebraically. The coefficient of β_1 in this expression is $\beta(1 - 2\gamma_1) + 2\gamma_2(1 - \beta)$, which is non-negative because $\beta, \gamma_2 \geq 0$ and $\beta, \gamma_1 < 1/2$. Thus the error of h is maximized if $\beta_1 = \beta$, the maximum allowed value for β_1. This, along with some more algebra, allows the expression for the error of h to be further simplified to

$$error_{\mathcal{D}}(h) \leq \beta^2 + 2\beta(1-\beta)(\gamma_1 + \gamma_2).$$

This is maximized if $\gamma_1 + \gamma_2 = \beta_2$ is set to its maximum value β. This yields

$$error_{\mathcal{D}}(h) \leq 3\beta^2 - 2\beta^3$$

as desired. $\square$(Lemma 4.1)

4.3.3   A Recursive Accuracy Boosting Algorithm

So far, we have only given a procedure that drives the error down from β to $g(\beta)$. We now consider the larger problem, where we are given a learning algorithm L with an error bound of only $1/2 - 1/p(n, size(c))$ for some polynomial $p(\cdot, \cdot)$ and we wish to construct a new learning algorithm whose error bound can be made as small as any input ϵ. The basic idea for tackling this problem is quite simple: we will just invoke the modest accuracy boosting mechanism recursively, until the desired error bound is obtained.

Let us be a little more precise. Suppose we are given a desired error bound ϵ. If we had in our possession a learning algorithm L whose hypotheses were guaranteed to have error bounded by $g^{-1}(\epsilon)$ (which is larger than ϵ), then we have already shown how we could make three calls to L using filtered distributions to obtain a hypothesis with error $g(g^{-1}(\epsilon)) = \epsilon$, and we would be done. However, we may not have such an L available. But if we only had an L whose error bound was $g^{-1}(g^{-1}(\epsilon))$, then we could apply our boosting procedure once to improve the error bound to $g(g^{-1}(g^{-1}(\epsilon))) = g^{-1}(\epsilon)$, then again a second time to get the error down to ϵ. Since we regard ϵ as an input parameter, and we must run in time polynomial in $1/\epsilon$, a primary concern with such an approach is how deeply we must nest such recursive calls as a function of ϵ.

The tentative description of the recursive algorithm follows; we will shortly make some small but important modifications. The algorithm takes two arguments as input: a desired error bound α (we discuss the confidence parameter δ momentarily), and an oracle $EX(c, \mathcal{D}')$ for examples. As before, L denotes the assumed weak learning algorithm, and we will use $L(EX(c, \mathcal{D}'))$ to denote the hypothesis returned by an invocation of L using the oracle $EX(c, \mathcal{D}')$.

Algorithm Strong-Learn($\alpha, EX(c, \mathcal{D}')$):

- If $\alpha \geq 1/2 - 1/p(n, size(c))$ then return $L(EX(c, \mathcal{D}'))$. In this case, the error parameter α for this call to **Strong-Learn** can already be achieved by the weak PAC learning algorithm L.

- $\beta \leftarrow g^{-1}(\alpha)$. Here β is the error we require from the level of recursion below us if we are to achieve error α.

- Let $\mathcal{D}'_2$ and $\mathcal{D}'_3$ be obtained by filtering $\mathcal{D}'$ as described in the modest boosting procedure.

- $h_1 \leftarrow$ **Strong-Learn($\beta, EX(c, \mathcal{D}')$)**.

- $h_2 \leftarrow$ **Strong-Learn($\beta, EX(c, \mathcal{D}'_2)$)**.

- $h_3 \leftarrow$ **Strong-Learn**$(\beta, EX(c, \mathcal{D}'_3))$.

- $h \leftarrow majority(h_1, h_2, h_3)$.

- Return h.

Throughout the coming analysis, it will be helpful to think about the execution of this recursive algorithm as a ternary tree. Each node of the tree is labeled by two quantities: a (possibly filtered) oracle for random examples of the target concept, and a desired error bound for this node. The root of the tree is labeled by the oracle $EX(c, \mathcal{D})$ (where c is the target concept and $\mathcal{D}$ is the target distribution) and by the final desired error bound ϵ. Now any node labeled by $EX(c, \mathcal{D}')$ and α has either three children or is a leaf, as we now describe.

If the label $\alpha < 1/2 - 1/p(n, size(c))$ then the desired error bound for this node is still too small to be obtained by invocation of the weak learning algorithm L. In this case, the three children will be labeled by the oracles $EX(c, \mathcal{D}')$, $EX(c, \mathcal{D}'_2)$ and $EX(c, \mathcal{D}'_3)$ as specified by our modest accuracy boosting procedure, and all three children will be labeled by the larger error bound of $\beta = g^{-1}(\alpha)$. This can be interpreted as a request from the parent node to its children for hypotheses of error at most β on the filtered distributions, for if these are supplied by the children then the parent can take the majority and fulfill its desired error bound of α. Thus, these three children correspond to a recursive call by our algorithm.

If, on the other hand, $\alpha \geq 1/2 - 1/p(n, size(c))$ then the desired error bound for this node can be immediately satisfied by a call to the weak learning algorithm L using the oracle $EX(c, \mathcal{D}')$. Then this node will be a leaf, and corresponds to a base case of the recursion.

Note that in this ternary tree, the oracle labeling any node is actually implemented by making calls to the oracle of its parent, which in turn is implemented by making calls to the oracle of its parent, and so on to the root node with oracle $EX(c, \mathcal{D})$.

To simplify the analysis of our recursive algorithm, we will defer until later the issue of the dependence on the confidence parameter. More precisely, in addition to an examples oracle $EX(c, \mathcal{D}')$ and an error parameter α, our algorithm really should also be taking a confidence parameter δ, which is our allowed probability of failing to output a hypothesis of error bounded by α with respect to c and $\mathcal{D}'$. Now in our algorithm, there will many steps at which the algorithm could potentially fail locally, thereby causing a global failure to output a good hypothesis. For instance, if any call to the weak algorithm L fails, or any recursive call of our algorithm fails, we may fail to find a good hypothesis. But for now, we will simply assume that all such steps succeed and analyze the complexity and correctness of the algorithm under this assumption. In other words, for now we will simply ignore the confidence parameter δ. Towards the end of the analysis, it will be easy to reintroduce δ and the possibility of failed steps by giving a bound N on the total number of possible places the algorithm could fail in any execution, and allocating probability at most δ/N to each of these.

We begin the analysis by bounding the maximum depth of the ternary recursion tree induced by the execution of algorithm **Strong-Learn**.

4.3.4   Bounding the Depth of the Recursion

Let $B(\epsilon, p(n, size(c)))$ denote the *depth* (that is, the longest path from the root to a leaf) of the execution tree whose root is labeled by the oracle $EX(c, \mathcal{D})$ and error parameter ϵ when the given weak learning algorithm has a $1/2 - 1/p(n, size(c))$ error bound. Thus, $B(\epsilon, p(n, size(c)))$ is the maximum nesting depth of the recursive calls to the procedure **Strong-Learn**. It is considerably less than the total number of invocations of **Strong-Learn** (which is the total number of nodes in the execution tree), but its analysis will lead to a bound on this total as well.

Lemma 4.2

$$B(\epsilon, p(n, size(c))) = O(\log p(n, size(c)) + \log\log(1/\epsilon)).$$

Proof: To prove this lemma, we first argue that the number of recursive calls to **Strong-Learn** needed to drive the error from its largest value of $1/2 - 1/p(n, size(c))$ down to $1/4$ is $O(\log p(n, size(c)))$. In other words, the depth of any subtree of the execution tree whose error parameter label is $1/4$ or larger is $O(\log p(n, size(c)))$.

To see this, consider any node with a desired error bound of $\beta > 1/4$. The distance of this value to $1/2$ is just $1/2 - \beta$, and the distance to $1/2$ of the desired error bound of the node's parent is the larger value $1/2 - g(\beta)$. We wish to argue that this distance is actually moving away from $1/2$ by a constant multiplicative factor with each invocation of the modest boosting procedure. This is because

$$1/2 - g(\beta) = 1/2 - 3\beta^2 + 2\beta^3 = (1/2 - \beta)(1 + 2\beta - 2\beta^2).$$

It is easy to show using basic calculus that for $\beta \geq 1/4$, the second factor is at least $11/8$. Thus a single invocation of the modest boosting procedure increases the distance of the error bound from $1/2$ by a multiplicative factor of $11/8$. Thus, $\log_{11/8}(p(n, size(c))/4)$ levels of recursion suffice to drive the error bound down to $1/4$.

For $\beta \leq 1/4$, things are even better: the error bound decreases at a doubly exponential rate! To see this, now we simply look at the rate at which the error itself decreases, and we see that in one step β is replaced by $g(\beta) = 3\beta^2 - 2\beta^3 \leq 3\beta^2$. Therefore in k steps the error is at most $(1/3)(3\beta)^{2^k}$. Since $\beta \leq 1/4$, this is at most $(3/4)^{2^k}$. Solving for $(3/4)^{2^k} \leq \epsilon$, we find that $k \geq c_0 \log \log(1/\epsilon)$ suffices for some constant $c_0 > 0$. $\qquad \square$(Lemma 4.2)

4.3.5 Analysis of Filtering Efficiency

We are now ready to tackle one of the main issues we have been avoiding so far: how do we bound the time required to obtain examples from the filtered distributions at each node of the recursion tree given that in reality we have direct access only to the root oracle $EX(c, \mathcal{D})$? It turns out that in order to obtain such a bound, we will need to modify algorithm **Strong-Learn** slightly.

Recall that there were two types of filtering performed at any node in the execution tree labeled by oracle $EX(c, \mathcal{D}')$ and error parameter α: the filtered oracle $EX(c, \mathcal{D}_2')$ was implemented by filtering $\mathcal{D}'$ with respect to the hypothesis h_1 returned by the child labeled by $EX(c, \mathcal{D}')$ and $g^{-1}(\alpha)$. With probability $1/2$, this involved waiting for an example $\langle x, c(x) \rangle$ such that $h_1(x) \neq c(x)$. The expected waiting time is $1/error_{\mathcal{D}'}(h_1)$, which is unacceptably large if $error_{\mathcal{D}'}(h_1)$ is small.

To handle this situation, we simply add a test to make sure that $error_{\mathcal{D}'}(h_1)$ is not "too small" before we attempt to make a recursive call with the filtered oracle $EX(c, \mathcal{D}_2')$. More precisely, after recursively calling **Strong-Learn** on $\beta = g^{-1}(\alpha)$ and $EX(c, \mathcal{D}')$ to obtain h_1, we draw a sufficiently large number m of random examples from $EX(c, \mathcal{D}')$ and use this sample to obtain an empirical estimate $\hat{e}_1$ for $error_{\mathcal{D}'}(h_1)$. The sample size m will be sufficiently large to ensure that

$$error_{\mathcal{D}'}(h_1) - \alpha/3 \leq \hat{e}_1 \leq error_{\mathcal{D}'}(h_1) + \alpha/3.$$

Thus our estimate is accurate within an additive error of $\alpha/3$. Although we shall not compute the required sample size precisely, it is bounded by an inverse polynomial in α, and it is a straightforward exercise to derive it using the Chernoff bounds described in the Appendix in Chapter 9.

Now if $\hat{e}_1 \leq 2\alpha/3$, then we know $error_{\mathcal{D}'}(h_1) \leq \alpha$, and we can already return h_1 without performing the recursive calls. Otherwise, if $\hat{e}_1 > 2\alpha/3$, then we know $error_{\mathcal{D}'}(h_1) \geq \alpha/3$, and therefore the expected number of calls to the oracle $EX(c, \mathcal{D}')$ needed to simulate one call to the filtered oracle $EX(c, \mathcal{D}_2')$ is at most $3/\alpha$.

Bounding the expected number of calls to $EX(c, \mathcal{D}')$ to implement one call to the filtered oracle $EX(c, \mathcal{D}_3')$ is more involved, and again involves a modification to algorithm **Strong-Learn**. Let h_2 denote the hypothesis returned by the recursive call using oracle $EX(c, \mathcal{D}_2')$ and error parameter $\beta = g^{-1}(\alpha)$. Then before making the recursive call to

Strong-Learn with oracle $EX(c, \mathcal{D}_3')$ and error parameter β, we sample from $EX(c, \mathcal{D}')$ to obtain an estimate $\hat{e}_2$ for $error_{\mathcal{D}'}(h_2)$. We take enough examples so that $\hat{e}_2$ is accurate to within additive error τ, where we define $\tau = ((1 - 2\beta)/8) \cdot \alpha$. Again the required sample size can be easily derived using Chernoff bounds, and is bounded by an inverse polynomial in τ.

Now if $\hat{e}_2 \leq \alpha - \tau$ then we know we have already reached our goal of $error_{\mathcal{D}'}(h_2) \leq \alpha$, and we can simply ignore h_1, not make the third recursive call, and return h_2. On the other hand, if $\hat{e}_2 > \alpha - \tau$ then we know $error_{\mathcal{D}'}(h_2) \geq \alpha - 2\tau$, and we will prove below that this (along with the fact that $error_{\mathcal{D}'}(h_1) \geq \alpha/3$) implies $\mathbf{Pr}_{x \in \mathcal{D}'}[h_1(x) \neq h_2(x)] \geq \alpha/24$. Thus the expected number of calls to $EX(c, \mathcal{D}')$ needed to simulate one call to $EX(c, \mathcal{D}_3')$ is at most $24/\alpha$, and we can safely proceed with the recursive call.

Before verifying this claim, we present the modified algorithm just outlined.

Algorithm Strong-Learn$(\alpha, EX(c, \mathcal{D}'))$:

- If $\alpha \geq 1/2 - 1/p(n, size(c))$ then return $L(EX(c, \mathcal{D}'))$.

- $\beta \leftarrow g^{-1}(\alpha)$.

- Let $\mathcal{D}_2'$ and $\mathcal{D}_3'$ be obtained by filtering $\mathcal{D}'$ as described in the modest boosting procedure.

- $h_1 \leftarrow$ **Strong-Learn**$(\beta, EX(c, \mathcal{D}'))$.

- Compute an estimate $\hat{e}_1$ for $error_{\mathcal{D}'}(h_1)$ that is accurate within additive error $\alpha/3$.

- If $\hat{e}_1 \leq 2\alpha/3$ then return h_1.

- $h_2 \leftarrow$ **Strong-Learn**$(\beta, EX(c, \mathcal{D}_2'))$.

- Compute an estimate $\hat{e}_2$ for $error_{\mathcal{D}'}(h_2)$ that is accurate within additive error $\tau = ((1 - 2\beta)/8) \cdot \alpha$.

- If $\hat{e}_2 \leq \alpha - \tau$ then return h_2.

- $h_3 \leftarrow$ **Strong-Learn**$(\beta, EX(c, \mathcal{D}'_3))$.

- $h \leftarrow majority(h_1, h_2, h_3)$.

- Return h.

Lemma 4.3 *Let a node of the execution tree be labeled by oracle $EX(c, \mathcal{D}')$ and error bound α, and let $\beta = g^{-1}(\alpha)$. Let h_1 be the hypothesis returned by the child labeled with $EX(c, \mathcal{D}')$ and β, and let h_2 be the hypothesis returned by the child labeled with $EX(c, \mathcal{D}'_2)$ and β. Let $\tau = ((1 - 2\beta)/8) \cdot \alpha$. Then if $error_{\mathcal{D}'}(h_1) \geq \alpha/3$ and $error_{\mathcal{D}'}(h_2) \geq \alpha - 2\tau$,*

$$\mathbf{Pr}_{x \in \mathcal{D}'}[h_1(x) \neq h_2(x)] \geq \alpha/24.$$

Proof: Let us define

$$\gamma_2 = \mathbf{Pr}_{x \in \mathcal{D}'_2}[h_1(x) \neq c(x) \wedge h_2(x) \neq c(x)] \tag{4.8}$$

as was done in the proof of Lemma 4.1. Note that if we have an upper bound on γ_2 that is strictly less than $1/2$, then we have a lower bound on

$$\mathbf{Pr}_{x \in \mathcal{D}'_2}[h_1(x) \neq c(x) \wedge h_2(x) = c(x)] = 1/2 - \gamma_2$$

that is strictly greater than 0. Furthermore, we can translate this this latter probability back to $\mathcal{D}'$ to obtain a lower bound on

$$\mathbf{Pr}_{x \in \mathcal{D}'}[h_1(x) \neq c(x) \wedge h_2(x) = c(x)]$$

and this finally is a lower bound on $\mathbf{Pr}_{x \in \mathcal{D}'}[h_1(x) \neq h_2(x)]$.

We will now prove that subject to the condition $error_{\mathcal{D}'}(h_2) \geq \alpha - 2\tau$, γ_2 is at most $7/16 < 1/2$. To do this, we maximize γ_2 subject to the condition $error_{\mathcal{D}'}(h_2) \geq \alpha - 2\tau$.

For the purposes of this maximization, we can assume that $error_{\mathcal{D}'}(h_1)$ and $error_{\mathcal{D}'_2}(h_2)$ are as large as possible (which is β, the error parameter given to the recursive calls that compute h_1 and h_2), as shown in Figure 4.2. This is because for any fixed values of $error_{\mathcal{D}'}(h_1)$ and $error_{\mathcal{D}'_2}(h_2)$, if we "added" a region of error to h_1 or h_2 it could only increase the region of their common errors, and thus the value of γ_2.

Thus we set $error_{\mathcal{D}'}(h_1) = error_{\mathcal{D}'_2}(h_2) = \beta$ and hence

$$\mathbf{Pr}_{x \in \mathcal{D}'_2}[h_1(x) = c(x) \wedge h_2(x) \neq c(x)] = \gamma_1 = \beta - \gamma_2. \qquad (4.9)$$

Now by decomposing $error_{\mathcal{D}'}(h_2)$ into its $h_1 = c$ and $h_2 \neq c$ components, and using Equation (4.1) to translate Equations (4.8) and (4.9) back to $\mathcal{D}'$, we write

$$\begin{aligned} error_{\mathcal{D}'}(h_2) &= 2\beta\gamma_2 + 2(1 - \beta)(\beta - \gamma_2) \\ &= 2\gamma_2(2\beta - 1) + 2\beta - 2\beta^2. \end{aligned} \qquad (4.10)$$

Also, under the constraint that $error_{\mathcal{D}'}(h_2) \geq \alpha - 2\tau$ we have

$$\begin{aligned} error_{\mathcal{D}'}(h_2) &\geq \alpha - 2\tau \\ &= \alpha(1 - (1 - 2\beta)/4) \\ &= g(\beta)(1 - (1 - 2\beta)/4) \\ &= (3\beta^2 - 2\beta^3)(3 + 2\beta)/4. \end{aligned} \qquad (4.11)$$

Putting Equations (4.10) and (4.11) together and multiplying both by 4, we obtain

$$8\gamma_2(2\beta - 1) + 8\beta - 8\beta^2 \geq (9\beta^2 - 4\beta^4).$$

Thus

$$8\gamma_2(2\beta - 1) \geq (-8\beta + 17\beta^2 - 4\beta^4) = \beta(2\beta - 1)(8 - \beta - 2\beta^2).$$

Therefore, since $(2\beta - 1) < 0$,

$$\gamma_2 \leq \beta/8(8 - \beta - 2\beta^2).$$

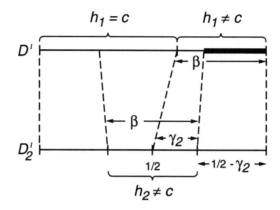

Figure 4.2: *The mapping of distribution $\mathcal{D}'$ to distribution $\mathcal{D}'_2$, with maximum error β for h_1 and h_2. The current goal is to lower bound the shaded region, which is the weight under $\mathcal{D}'$ of the compound event $h_1 \neq c$ and $h_2 = c$ (which implies the desired event $h_1 \neq h_2$).*

Some basic calculus shows that the maximum value of this expression in the range $\beta \in [0, 1/2]$ occurs at $\beta = 1/2$, and is $7/16$. This completes the proof of the claimed bound on γ_2 subject to the constraint $error_{\mathcal{D}'}(h_2) \geq \alpha - 2\tau$.

Now since $\gamma_2 \leq 7/16$, we have that

$$\mathbf{Pr}_{x \in \mathcal{D}'_2}[h_1(x) \neq c(x) \wedge h_2(x) = c(x)] = 1/2 - \gamma_2 \geq 1/16.$$

We now translate this probability back to $\mathcal{D}'$, but must be a little careful in doing so, since the assumption that $\beta_1 = error_{\mathcal{D}'}(h_1)$ was the maximum value β was valid only for the purposes of maximizing γ_2. Thus by Equation 4.1, we write

$$\mathbf{Pr}_{x \in \mathcal{D}'}[h_1(x) \neq c(x) \wedge h_2(x) = c(x)] \geq (2\beta_1)(1/16) = \beta_1/8.$$

Under our assumption $\beta_1 \geq \alpha/3$, we finally obtain

$$\mathbf{Pr}_{x \in \mathcal{D}'}[h_1(x) \neq c(x) \wedge h_2(x) = c(x)] \geq \alpha/24$$

as promised. □(Lemma 4.3)

The following lemma summarizes our bounds on the number of expected calls to $EX(c, \mathcal{D}')$ needed to simulate the two filtered distributions.

Lemma 4.4 *Let a node of the execution tree be labeled by oracle $EX(c, \mathcal{D}')$ and error bound α. Then the expected number of examples that must be drawn from $EX(c, \mathcal{D}')$ to simulate a single draw from $EX(c, \mathcal{D}'_2)$ is at most $3/\alpha$, and the expected number of examples that must be drawn from $EX(c, \mathcal{D}')$ to simulate a single draw from $EX(c, \mathcal{D}'_3)$ is at most $24/\alpha$.*

We now invoke the bounds of Lemma 4.4 repeatedly in order to obtain a bound on how many calls to the root oracle $EX(c, \mathcal{D})$ are required to simulate a single draw from an oracle labeling a node at depth i in the execution tree. To simulate one call to an oracle at the first level of recursion (the children of the root, where the error bound is $g^{-1}(\epsilon)$), we need at most $24/\epsilon$ calls to $EX(c, \mathcal{D})$; to simulate one call to an oracle at the second level of recursion (where the error bound is $g^{-1}(g^{-1}(\epsilon)) = g^{-2}(\epsilon)$), we need at most $24/g^{-1}(\epsilon)$ calls to the first level of recursion, each of which in turn require 24ϵ calls to $EX(c, \mathcal{D})$. By similar reasoning, a call to an oracle at the ith level of the execution tree requires at most

$$\left(\frac{24}{\epsilon}\right)\left(\frac{24}{g^{-1}(\epsilon)}\right)\cdots\left(\frac{24}{g^{-(i-1)}(\epsilon)}\right)$$

calls to $EX(c, \mathcal{D})$ in expectation.

To bound this expression, recall that $g(\beta) = 3\beta^2 - 2\beta^3 \leq 3\beta^2$. We first prove by induction on i that $g^{-i}(\epsilon) \geq (\epsilon^{1/2^i})/3$. For the base case, since $g(x) \leq 3x^2$ we have $x \geq \sqrt{g(x)/3}$, or setting $x = g^{-1}(\epsilon)$, $g^{-1}(\epsilon) \geq \sqrt{\epsilon/3} \geq \sqrt{\epsilon}/3$ as desired. Inductively, we write $g^{-i}(\epsilon) = g^{-1}(g^{-(i-1)}(\epsilon)) \geq g^{-1}(\epsilon^{1/2^{i-1}}/3) \geq ((\epsilon^{1/2^{i-1}}/3)/3)^{1/2} = (\epsilon^{1/2^i})/3$. Therefore

$$\left(\frac{24}{\epsilon}\right)\left(\frac{24}{g^{-1}(\epsilon)}\right)\cdots\left(\frac{24}{g^{-(i-1)}(\epsilon)}\right) \leq \left(\frac{72}{\epsilon}\right)\left(\frac{72}{\epsilon^{1/2}}\right)\left(\frac{72}{\epsilon^{1/4}}\right)\cdots\left(\frac{72}{\epsilon^{1/2^{i-1}}}\right)$$

$$= \frac{72^i}{\epsilon^{1+1/2+1/4+\cdots+1/2^{i-1}}}$$

$$= \frac{72^i \epsilon^{1/2^{i-1}}}{\epsilon^2}$$

$$\leq \frac{72^i (3g^{-(i-1)}(\epsilon))}{\epsilon^2}$$

$$\leq \frac{72^i \cdot 3(3g^{-i}(\epsilon)^2)}{\epsilon^2}$$

$$= \frac{9 \cdot 72^i (g^{-i}(\epsilon))^2}{\epsilon^2}$$

We have shown:

Lemma 4.5 *Let the root of the execution tree be labeled by the oracle*
$EX(c, \mathcal{D})$ and error bound ϵ. Then the expected number of examples that
must be drawn from $EX(c, \mathcal{D})$ to simulate a single draw from an oracle
labeling a node of the execution tree at depth i is bounded by

$$\frac{9 \cdot 72^i (g^{-i}(\epsilon))^2}{\epsilon^2}.$$

4.3.6   Finishing Up

We are now almost ready to bound the sample complexity and running
time of **Strong-Learn**$(\epsilon, EX(c, \mathcal{D}))$, but before doing so must address
one final piece of unfinished business, which is the handling of the confidence parameter δ. Recall that to simplify the analysis so far, we have
assumed that many steps in the algorithm that may in fact have some
probability of failure (such as estimating the error of an intermediate
hypothesis, or a call to the weak learning algorithm, or a recursive call
with some error bound) are always successful. Now we must remove this
assumption, and it is straightforward to do this by "dividing" up our

desired global confidence parameter δ into many small pieces, one for each possible failure. Recall that we have already given a bound on the recursion depth $B = B(\epsilon, p(n, size(c)))$, thus giving a bound of at most 3^B nodes in the execution tree. (Remember that B bounds the recursion depth under the assumption that there are no failures, and therefore does not depend on δ). Now for any node in the execution tree, there are five local steps that may result in a failure we wish to guard against: the estimation of the errors of $error_{\mathcal{D}'}(h_1)$ and $error_{\mathcal{D}'_2}(h_2)$ to sufficient accuracy, and the three recursive calls. Thus, each of these steps will be carried out using confidence parameter $\delta' = \delta/(5 \cdot 3^B)$, resulting in overall probability of failure at most δ.

Throughout the remainder of this section, we will use the shorthand notation $B = B(\epsilon, p(n, size(c)))$ for the execution tree depth which we have already bounded, and let $\delta' = \delta/(5 \cdot 3^B)$. Note that by Lemma 4.2, any quantity that is bounded by an exponential function of B is bounded by $O(p(n, size(c)) \log(1/\epsilon))$.

Let $T(\epsilon, \delta, n, size(c))$ be the expected running time of the invocation of algorithm **Strong-Learn**$(\epsilon, \delta, EX(c, \mathcal{D}))$, let $M(\epsilon, \delta, n, size(c))$ be the expected total number of examples drawn from the oracle $EX(c, \mathcal{D})$ by this invocation, and let $U(\epsilon, \delta, n, size(c))$ be the time required to evaluate the final hypothesis returned by this invocation. Let $t(\delta, n, size(c))$, $m(\delta, n, size(c))$ and $u(\delta, n, size(c))$ be the analogous quantities for the invocation of the weak learning algorithm $L(\delta, EX(c, \mathcal{D}))$.

We start by bounding the time required to evaluate a hypothesis returned by **Strong-Learn**$(\epsilon, \delta, EX(c, \mathcal{D}))$.

Lemma 4.6

$$U(\epsilon, \delta, n, size(c)) = O(3^B \cdot u(\delta', n, size(c)))$$

which is polynomial in $1/\epsilon$, $1/\delta$, n, and $size(c)$.

Proof: The hypothesis returned by **Strong-Learn** exactly mirrors the structure of the execution tree: it is a ternary tree of height B, whose internal nodes are majority functions, and whose leaves are hypotheses returned by calls to the weak learning algorithm L. The total time taken to evaluate all the hypotheses at the leaves is $O(3^B \cdot u(\delta', n, size(c)))$. This is because there are at most 3^B leaves, and each leaf of the execution tree is an invocation of L with confidence parameter δ'. The time taken to evaluate the majorities at the internal nodes is dominated by this bound. □(Lemma 4.6)

We now bound the expected number of examples $M(\epsilon, \delta, n, size(c))$.

Lemma 4.7

$$M(\epsilon, \delta, n, size(c)) = O\left(\frac{216^B}{\epsilon^2}\left(m(\delta', n, size(c)) + p^2(n, size(c)) \log \frac{1}{\delta'}\right)\right)$$

which is polynomial in $1/\epsilon$, $1/\delta$, n, *and* $size(c)$.

Proof: **Strong-Learn**$(\epsilon, \delta, EX(c, \mathcal{D}))$ invokes the weak learning algorithm L at most 3^B times. Each such invocation requires $m(\delta', n, size(c))$ filtered examples, since each time L is called it is with confidence parameter δ'. We have already shown in Lemma 4.5 that to obtain one filtered example at depth B in the execution tree, **Strong-Learn** is expected to draw at most $9 \cdot 72^B(g^{-B}(\epsilon))^2/\epsilon^2 \leq 9 \cdot 72^B/\epsilon^2$ examples from the oracle $EX(c, \mathcal{D})$. Therefore $3^B(9 \cdot 72^B/\epsilon^2)m(\delta', n, size(c)) = O((216^B/\epsilon^2)m(\delta', n, size(c)))$ examples suffice to implement the filtered oracles at the execution tree leaves.

In addition, **Strong-Learn** draws samples at each node of the execution tree in order to estimate the quality of the hypotheses h_1 and h_2. Recall that at the ith level of the execution tree, the desired error bound is $\alpha = g^{-i}(\epsilon)$, and the desired error bound for the $i + 1$st level is $\beta = g^{-1}(\alpha)$. The estimate for the error of h_1 at level i must have additive error bounded by $\alpha/3$, and the estimate for the error of h_2 at level i must have additive error bounded by $\tau = ((1 - 2\beta)/8) \cdot \alpha$. Since $\tau < \alpha/3$, the number of examples required to accurately estimate the error of h_2

dominates the sample size required to estimate the error of h_1, so we will limit our attention to this dominating term.

Note that $\tau \geq (1/(4p(n, size(c))))\alpha$ because

$$1 - 2\beta \geq \left(1 - 2\left(\frac{1}{2} - \frac{1}{p(n, size(c))}\right)\right) = \frac{2}{p(n, size(c))}$$

due to the base case of the recursion. Using Lemma 4.5 and Chernoff bounds, the number of filtered examples required for the tests at level i is thus

$$O\left(\left(\frac{p^2(n, size(c))}{(g^{-i}(\epsilon))^2} \log \frac{1}{\delta'}\right) \frac{72^i(g^{-i}(\epsilon))^2}{\epsilon^2}\right)$$

which is

$$O\left(\left(p^2(n, size(c)) \log \frac{1}{\delta'}\right) \frac{72^B}{\epsilon^2}\right)$$

since $i \leq B$. Since the number of internal nodes is bounded by 3^B, this gives an overall bound for the internal node tests of

$$O\left(\left(p^2(n, size(c)) \log \frac{1}{\delta'}\right) \frac{216^B}{\epsilon^2}\right).$$

Combining the bounds for the leaves and internal nodes gives the stated overall bound. $\qquad\square$(Lemma 4.7)

We now bound $T(\epsilon, \delta, n, size(c))$, the expected running time.

Lemma 4.8

$T(\epsilon, \delta) =$
$$O\left(\frac{648^B}{\epsilon^2}\left(m(\delta', n, size(c)) + \left(p^2(n, size(c)) \log \frac{1}{\delta'}\right) B \cdot u(\delta', n, size(c))\right)\right.$$
$$\left. + 3^B \cdot t(\delta', n, size(c))\right)$$

which is polynomial in $1/\epsilon$, $1/\delta$, n, *and* $size(c)$.

Proof: The running time of **Strong-Learn** may be decomposed into two parts. First, there is time spent at the leaves of the recursion, in the invocations to the weak learning algorithm L. The time for each call to L is at most $t(\delta', n, size(c))$, and the number of such calls is at most 3^B, giving a total of $3^B \cdot t(\delta', n, size(c))$.

The remainder of the running time of can be ascribed to the examples drawn from $EX(c, \mathcal{D})$ and their subsequent passage from the root down to a node in the execution tree. In its passage down the execution tree, an instance may be given as input to at most B hypotheses (one per node passed), where each such hypothesis is being used to implement a filtered distribution.

From the fact that evaluating a hypothesis takes at most time $O(3^B \cdot u(\delta', n, size(c)))$ (the most expensive hypothesis to evaluate is the final root hypothesis), and the fact that the expected total number of examples drawn is

$$
O\left(\frac{216^B}{\epsilon^2} \left(m(\delta', n, size(c)) + p^2(n, size(c)) \log \frac{1}{\delta'} \right) \right)
$$

we obtain the stated total time. $\Box$(Lemma 4.8)

Now it is a simple exercise to show that the polynomial bounds on the expected values of the sample size and running time can instead be expressed as polynomial bounds that hold with high probability, by allotting a fraction of the confidence parameter δ to the small probability that the sample size or running time are excessively large. Combining Lemmas 4.6, 4.7 and 4.8, we obtain our main result:

Theorem 4.9 *Let $\mathcal{C}$ be any concept class and $\mathcal{H}$ any hypothesis class. Then if $\mathcal{C}$ is efficiently weakly PAC learnable using $\mathcal{H}$, $\mathcal{C}$ is efficiently strongly PAC learnable using a hypothesis class of ternary majority trees with leaves from $\mathcal{H}$.*

4.4 Exercises

4.1. Use our transformation of a weak PAC learning algorithm to a strong PAC learning algorithm to show that for any concept class $\mathcal{C}$, if $\mathcal{C}$ is efficiently PAC learnable, then it is efficiently PAC learnable by an algorithm that:

- requires a sample of size at most $1/\epsilon^2 \cdot p_1(n, size(c), \log(1/\epsilon), \log(1/\delta))$;

- runs in time at most $1/\epsilon^2 \cdot p_2(n, size(c), \log(1/\epsilon), \log(1/\delta))$;

- uses memory at most $p_3(n, size(c), \log(1/\epsilon), \log(1/\delta))$;

- outputs hypotheses of size at most $p_4(n, size(c), \log(1/\epsilon))$ that can be evaluated in time at most $p_5(n, size(c), \log(1/\epsilon))$

for some fixed polynomials p_1, p_2, p_3, p_4, p_5.

4.2. Use our transformation of a weak PAC learning algorithm to a strong PAC learning algorithm to show that for any concept class $\mathcal{C}$, if $\mathcal{C}$ is efficiently PAC learnable, then there is an efficient algorithm that, given $0 < \delta \leq 1$ and a sample S of m examples of $c \in \mathcal{C}_n$, outputs with probability at least $1 - \delta$ a hypothesis h that is consistent with S such that $size(h) \leq p(n, size(c), \log m)$ for some polynomial p.

4.3. We say that an algorithm L in the PAC setting is a **group PAC learning algorithm** for $\mathcal{C}$ if there exists a polynomial $p(\cdot, \cdot)$ such for any target concept $c \in \mathcal{C}_n$ and any distribution, when L is given access to $EX(c, \mathcal{D})$ it outputs a hypothesis $h : X^{p(n, size(c))} \to \{0, 1\}$ that with probability $1 - \delta$ satisfies

$$\mathbf{Pr}_{S \in \mathcal{D}^{p(n, size(c))}}[h(S) = 0 | (\forall x \in S)c(x) = 1] \leq \epsilon$$

and

$$\mathbf{Pr}_{S \in \mathcal{D}^{p(n, size(c))}}[h(S) = 1 | (\forall x \in S)c(x) = 0] \leq \epsilon$$

Thus, the hypothesis output by L must be given a large (but still only polynomial size) collection of random examples that are either all positive or all negative, in which case it accurately determines which is the case.

Prove that for any concept class $\mathcal{C}$, $\mathcal{C}$ is efficiently group PAC learnable if and only if it is efficiently weakly PAC learnable.

4.5   Bibliographic Notes

The equivalence of weak and strong learning was proved by Schapire [84, 85], and the proof given in this chapter is due to him. Exercises 4.1 and 4.2 are also due to Schapire, and his paper explores many other fascinating consequences of the construction. Alternative boosting methods have been given by Freund [35, 36]. In Freund's construction, the strong learning algorithm's hypothesis is simply a majority of many hypotheses obtained from filtered runs of the weak learning algorithm.

Experimental results on neural network learning based on boosting ideas are reported by Drucker, Schapire and Simard [30]. Goldman, Kearns and Schapire [42] examine the sample size required for weak learning, showing that it can be considerably less than for strong learning in some cases. Helmbold and Warumth [52] study various properties of the weak learning model and its relationship to sample compression and Occam learning. Boneh and Lipton [24] examine conditions under which boosting can be performed with respect to special distributions, and Decatur and Aslam [12] show that weak learning is still equivalent to strong learning in a restricted version of the PAC model known as statistical query learning, which will be the focus of our study in Chapter 5. Exercise 4.3 is from a paper by Kearns and Valiant [60], which also first introduced the notion of weak learning.

5

Learning in the Presence of Noise

In order to obtain a clean and simple starting point for a theoretical study of learning, many unrealistic assumptions were made in defining the PAC model. One of the most unjustified of these assumptions is that learning algorithms have access to a noise-free oracle for examples of the target concept. In reality, we need learning algorithms with at least some tolerance for the occasional mislabeled example.

In this chapter we investigate a generalization of the PAC model in which the examples received by the learning algorithm are corrupted with *classification noise*. This is *random* and essentially "white" noise affecting only the label of each example. (Learning in the presence of this type of noise implies learning in some slightly more realistic models, and more adversarial error models have also been examined in the literature; see the Bibliographic Notes at the end of the chapter.) In this setting we will see that much of the theory developed so far is preserved even in the presence of such noise. For instance, all of the classes we have shown to be efficiently PAC learnable remain so even with a classification noise rate approaching the information-theoretic barrier of $1/2$.

To show this, we will actually introduce another new model, called *learning from statistical queries*. This model is a specialization of the PAC model in which we restrict the learning algorithm to form its hypothesis solely on the basis of estimates of probabilities. We will then give a theorem stating that any class efficiently learnable from statistical queries can be efficiently learned in the presence of classification noise. While we show that conjunctions of literals can be efficiently learned from statistical queries (and thus in the presence of classification noise), we leave it to the reader (in the exercises) to verify that all of the other efficient PAC learning algorithms we have given have efficient statistical query analogues.

5.1 The Classification Noise Model

In the classification noise model, a PAC learning algorithm will now be given access to a modified and noisy oracle for examples, denoted $EX^{\eta}_{CN}(c, \mathcal{D})$. Here $c \in \mathcal{C}$ and $\mathcal{D}$ are the target concept and distribution, and $0 \le \eta < 1/2$ is a new parameter called the **classification noise rate**. This new oracle behaves in the following manner: as with $EX(c, \mathcal{D})$, a random input $x \in X$ is drawn according to the distribution $\mathcal{D}$. Then with probability $1 - \eta$, the labeled example $\langle x, c(x) \rangle$ is returned to the learning algorithm, but with probability η, the (incorrectly) labeled example $\langle x, \neg c(x) \rangle$ is returned, where $\neg c(x)$ is the complement of the binary value $c(x)$. Despite the classification noise in the examples received, the goal of the learner remains that of finding a good approximation h to the target concept c with respect to the distribution $\mathcal{D}$. Thus, on inputs ϵ and δ and given access to $EX^{\eta}_{CN}(c, \mathcal{D})$, the learning algorithm is said to succeed if with probability at least $1 - \delta$ it outputs a hypothesis h satisfying $error(h) \equiv \mathbf{Pr}_{x \in \mathcal{D}}[c(x) \ne h(x)] \le \epsilon$.

Although the criterion for success remains unchanged in the noisy model, we do need to modify the definition of efficient learning. Note that if we allow the noise rate η to equal $1/2$, then PAC learning becomes impossible in any amount of computation time, because every label seen by the algorithm is the outcome of an unbiased coin flip, and conveys no information about the target concept. Similarly, as the noise rate *approaches* $1/2$, the labels provided by the noisy oracle are providing less and less information about the target concept. Thus we see there is a need to allow the learning algorithm more oracle calls and more computation time as the noise rate approaches $1/2$.

We also need to specify what knowledge the learning algorithm has, if any, about the value of the noise rate η. For simplicity we will assume that the learning algorithm is provided with an upper bound $1/2 > \eta_0 \geq \eta$ on the noise rate. (This assumption can in fact be removed; see Exercise 5.4.) The new notion of efficiency can then be formalized by allowing the learning algorithm's running time to depend on the quantify $1/(1 - 2\eta_0)$, which increases as the upper bound η_0 approaches $1/2$. (Making rigorous the informal arguments used here to argue that this dependence is needed is the topic of Exercise 5.5.)

Definition 13 *(PAC Learning in the Presence of Classification Noise) Let C be a concept class and let $\mathcal{H}$ be a representation class over X. We say that C is **PAC learnable using $\mathcal{H}$ in the presence of classification noise** if there exists an algorithm L with the following property: for any concept $c \in C$, any distribution $\mathcal{D}$ on X, any $0 \leq \eta < 1/2$, and any $0 < \epsilon < 1$, $0 < \delta < 1$, and η_0 (where $\eta \leq \eta_0 < 1/2$), if L is given access to $EX_{CN}^{\eta}(c, \mathcal{D})$ and inputs ϵ, δ and η_0, then with probability at least $1 - \delta$, L outputs a hypothesis concept $h \in \mathcal{H}$ satisfying error$(h) \leq \epsilon$. This probability is taken over the randomization in the calls to $EX_{CN}^{\eta}(c, \mathcal{D})$, and any internal randomization of L.*

*If L runs in time polynomial in n, $1/\epsilon$, $1/\delta$ and $1/(1 - 2\eta_0)$ we say that C is **efficiently PAC learnable using $\mathcal{H}$ in the presence of classification noise**.*

Before proceeding further, let us convince ourselves with some concrete examples that learning in this apparently more difficult model really does require some new ideas. Recall that one of the first PAC learning algorithms we gave in Chapter 1 was for the class of boolean conjunctions of literals. The algorithm initializes the hypothesis to be the conjunction of all $2n$ literals over $x_1, \ldots, x_n$, and deletes any literal that appears negated in a positive example of the target conjunction (the negative examples received are ignored). The problem with using this same algorithm in the classification noise setting is obvious and fatal. With the noisy oracle, the algorithm may actually be given a negative example of the target conjunction as a positively labeled example, resulting in unwarranted and costly deletions of literals. For instance, suppose that the target conjunction c contains at least one unnegated literal, say x_1. Then the vector of all 0's is a negative example of the target. However, if this single vector has significant weight under $\mathcal{D}$, say weight γ, then there is probability $\gamma\eta$ that the learning algorithm will receive the vector of all 0's as a *negatively* labeled example from $EX_{CN}^{\eta}(c, \mathcal{D})$, causing the deletion of all unnegated literals from the hypothesis.

Similarly, consider our algorithm from Chapter 1 for PAC learning axis-aligned rectangles in the real plane. This algorithm takes a sufficiently large sample of random examples of the target rectangle, and chooses as its hypothesis the most specific (smallest area) rectangle that includes all of the positive examples but none of the negative examples. But such a rectangle may not even exist for a sample from the noisy oracle $EX_{CN}^{\eta}(c, \mathcal{D})$.

5.2   An Algorithm for Learning Conjunctions from Statistics

Intuitively, the problem with our conjunctions learning algorithm in the classification noise setting is that the algorithm will make drastic and irreversible changes to the hypothesis on the basis of a single example. In the noisy setting, where every individual example received from $EX_{CN}^{\eta}(c, \mathcal{D})$ is suspect since its label could be the result of an error, it seems natural to seek algorithms that instead form their hypotheses based on the properties of large samples, or that learn from *statistics*.

As an example, consider the following rather different algorithm for

PAC learning boolean conjunctions (still in the original noise-free setting). For each literal z over the boolean input variables $x_1, \ldots, x_n$, denote by $p_0(z)$ the probability that z is set to 0 in a random instance drawn according to the distribution $\mathcal{D}$. If $p_0(z)$ is extremely small, then we can intuitively "ignore" z, since it is almost always set to 1 (satisfied) with respect to $\mathcal{D}$. We define $p_{01}(z)$ to be the probability that a random instance from $\mathcal{D}$ fails to satisfy z, but does satisfy (that is, is a positive example of) the target conjunction c. Note that for any literal appearing in c, $p_{01}(z) = 0$. If $p_{01}(z)$ is large, then we would like to avoid including z in our hypothesis conjunction, since there is a reasonable chance of drawing a positive example of c in which z is 0. We say that z is *significant* if $p_0(z) \geq \epsilon/8n$ and *harmful* if $p_{01}(z) \geq \epsilon/8n$. Note that since we always have $p_{01}(z) \leq p_0(z)$, any harmful literal is also significant.

We now argue that if h is the conjunction of all the significant literals that are not harmful, then h has error less than ϵ with respect to c and $\mathcal{D}$. First we consider $\mathbf{Pr}_{a \in \mathcal{D}}[c(a) = 0 \wedge h(a) = 1]$. Note that the event $c(a) = 0 \wedge h(a) = 1$ occurs only when there is some literal z appearing in c that does not appear in h, and z is set to 0 in a. Since h contains all the significant literals that are not harmful, and c contains no harmful literals, any such literal z must not be significant. Then we have that $\mathbf{Pr}_{a \in \mathcal{D}}[c(a) = 0 \wedge h(a) = 1]$ is at most the probability that some insignificant literal is 0 in a, which by the union bound is at most $2n(\epsilon/8n) = \epsilon/4$. To bound $\mathbf{Pr}_{a \in \mathcal{D}}[c(a) = 1 \wedge h(a) = 0]$, we simply observe that the event $c(a) = 1 \wedge h(a) = 0$ occurs only when there is some literal z not appearing in c but appearing in h, and z is set to 0 in a. Since h contains no harmful literals, we have that $\mathbf{Pr}_{a \in \mathcal{D}}[c(a) = 1 \wedge h(a) = 0]$ is bounded by the probability that some harmful literal is set to 0 in a but $c(a) = 1$, which by the union bound is at most $2n(\epsilon/8n) = \epsilon/4$. Thus $error(h) \leq \epsilon/4 + \epsilon/4 = \epsilon/2$.

The above analysis immediately suggests an efficient algorithm for PAC learning conjunctions (in our original noise-free model). The probabilities $p_0(z)$ for each literal z can be estimated using $EX(c, \mathcal{D})$ by drawing a sufficiently large set of examples and computing the fraction of inputs on which z is set to 0. Similarly, the probabilities $p_{01}(z)$ can be estimated by drawing a sufficiently large set of examples and computing the fraction on which z is set to 0 and the label is 1. Note that while we cannot exactly determine which literals are harmful and which are significant (since we can only estimate the $p_0(z)$ and $p_{01}(z)$), we have left enough room to maneuver in the preceding analysis that accurate estimates are sufficient. For instance, it can be verified using Chernoff bounds (see the Appendix in Chapter 9) that if our algorithm takes a sufficiently large (but still only polynomial in n, $1/\epsilon$ and $1/\delta$) sample for its estimates, and chooses as its hypothesis h the conjunction of all literals z such that the resulting estimate $\hat{p}_0(z)$ for $p_0(z)$ satifies $\hat{p}_0(z) \geq \epsilon/8n$, but the estimate $\hat{p}_{01}(z)$ for $p_{01}(z)$ satifies $\hat{p}_{01}(z) \leq \epsilon/2n$, and the sample size is sufficient to make our estimates $\hat{p}_0(z)$ and $\hat{p}_{01}(z)$ within an additive error of $\epsilon/8n$ of their true values, then with probability $1 - \delta$, h will satisfy $error(h) \leq \epsilon$.

A nice property of this new algorithm is that it forms its hypothesis solely on the basis of estimates of a small number of probabilities (namely, the $p_0(z)$ and $p_{01}(z)$). Of course, at this point all we have shown is another efficient algorithm for PAC learning conjunctions. The feeling that this algorithm is somehow more robust to classification noise than our original algorithm is nothing more than an intuition. We now generalize and formalize the notion of PAC learning solely on the basis of probability estimates. This is most easily done by introducing yet another model of learning. We then proceed to verify our intuition by showing that efficient learning in the new model automatically implies efficient PAC learning in the presence of classification noise.

5.3   The Statistical Query Learning Model

Our new learning model can be viewed as placing a *restriction* on the way in which a PAC learning algorithm can use the random examples it receives from the oracle $EX(c, \mathcal{D})$. Let $\mathcal{C}$ be a concept class over X. In the statistical query model, if $c \in \mathcal{C}$ is the target concept and $\mathcal{D}$ is the target distribution, then we replace the usual PAC oracle $EX(c, \mathcal{D})$ with an oracle $STAT(c, \mathcal{D})$ that accepts **statistical queries** of the form (χ, τ). Here χ is a mapping $\chi : X \times \{0, 1\} \rightarrow \{0, 1\}$ and $0 < \tau \leq 1$. We think of χ as a function that maps a labeled example $\langle x, c(x) \rangle$ of the target concept to 0 or 1, indicating either the presence or absence of some property in $\langle x, c(x) \rangle$. For instance, in our new algorithm for PAC learning conjunctions we took a large random sample, and for each $\langle a, c(a) \rangle$ in the sample we computed the predicate $\chi_z(a, c(a))$ that is 1 if and only if the literal z is 0 in a but $c(a) = 0$. This predicate corresponds to the probability $p_{01}(z)$, that is, $p_{01}(z) = \mathbf{Pr}_{a \in \mathcal{D}}[\chi_z(a, c(a)) = 1]$.

In general, for a fixed target concept $c \in \mathcal{C}$ and distribution $\mathcal{D}$, let us define

$$P_\chi = \mathbf{Pr}_{x \in \mathcal{D}}[\chi(x, c(x)) = 1].$$

We interpret a statistical query (χ, τ) as a request for the value P_χ. However, on input (χ, τ) the oracle $STAT(c, \mathcal{D})$ will not return exactly P_χ, but only an approximation. More precisely, the output of $STAT(c, \mathcal{D})$ on input query (χ, τ) is allowed to be *any* value $\hat{P}_\chi$ satisfying $P_\chi - \tau \leq \hat{P}_\chi \leq P_\chi + \tau$. Thus, the output of $STAT(c, \mathcal{D})$ is simply any estimate of P_χ that is accurate within additive error τ. We assume that each query to $STAT(c, \mathcal{D})$ takes unit time.

We call τ the **tolerance** of the statistical query, and the choice of both χ and τ are left to the learning algorithm (modulo some important restrictions discussed momentarily). For instance, in our conjunctions example, recall that by the analysis of the last section it suffices to estimate the probabilities $p_{01}(z) = P_{\chi_z}$ to within tolerance $\tau = \epsilon/8n$.

At this point, it should be clear that given access to the oracle $EX(c, \mathcal{D})$, it is a simple matter to simulate the behavior of the oracle $STAT(c, \mathcal{D})$ on a query (χ, τ) with probability at least $1 - \delta$. We just draw from $EX(c, \mathcal{D})$ a sufficient number of random labeled examples $\langle x, c(x) \rangle$, and use the fraction of the examples for which $\chi(x, c(x)) = 1$ as our estimate $\hat{P}_\chi$ of

P_χ. Now by Chernoff bounds, the number of calls to $EX(c, \mathcal{D})$ required will be polynomial in $1/\tau$ and $\log(1/\delta)$, and the time required will be polynomial in the time required to evaluate χ, and in $1/\tau$ and $\log(1/\delta)$. To ensure that efficient algorithms for learning using $STAT(c, \mathcal{D})$ can be efficiently simulated using $EX(c, \mathcal{D})$, we must place some natural restrictions on τ (namely, that it is an inverse polynomial in the learning problem parameters) and on χ (namely, that it can be evaluated in polynomial time). Thus we require that algorithms only ask $STAT(c, \mathcal{D})$ for estimates of sufficiently "simple" probabilities, with sufficiently coarse tolerance. This is done in the following definition, which formalizes the model of learning from statistical queries. The intuition that algorithms with access to $STAT(c, \mathcal{D})$ can be efficiently simulated given access to $EX(c, \mathcal{D})$ is then formalized in greater detail as Theorem 5.1 below.

Definition 14 *(The Statistical Query Model) Let $\mathcal{C}$ be a concept class and let $\mathcal{H}$ be a representation class over X. We say that $\mathcal{C}$ is **efficiently learnable from statistical queries using** $\mathcal{H}$ if there exists a learning algorithm L and polynomials $p(\cdot, \cdot, \cdot)$, $q(\cdot, \cdot, \cdot)$ and $r(\cdot, \cdot, \cdot)$ with the following property: for any $c \in \mathcal{C}$, for any distribution $\mathcal{D}$ over X, and for any $0 < \epsilon < 1/2$, if L is given access to $STAT(c, \mathcal{D})$ and input ϵ, then*

- *For every query (χ, τ) made by L, the predicate χ can be evaluated in time $q(1/\epsilon, n, size(c))$, and $1/\tau$ is bounded by $r(1/\epsilon, n, size(c))$.*

- *L will halt in time bounded by $p(1/\epsilon, n, size(c))$.*

- *L will output a hypothesis $h \in \mathcal{H}$ that satisfies $error(h) \leq \epsilon$.*

Notice that the confidence parameter δ has disappeared from this definition. Recall that this parameter guarded against the small but nonzero probability that an extremely unrepresentative sample is drawn from $EX(c, \mathcal{D})$ in the PAC learning model. Since $EX(c, \mathcal{D})$ has now been replaced by the oracle $STAT(c, \mathcal{D})$, whose behavior is completely determined modulo the query tolerance τ, there is no need for δ. Of course, we could allow a certain failure probability for the case of randomized learning algorithms, but choose not to for the sake of simplicity, since we will only examine deterministic algorithms.

The following theorem verifies that we have defined the statistical query model in a way that ensures efficient simulation in the PAC model. Its proof is the subject of Exercise 5.6. Thus, we have found a model that specializes the PAC model in a way that allows learning algorithms to estimate probabilities, but to do nothing else.

Theorem 5.1 *Let C be a concept class and $\mathcal{H}$ be a representation class over X. Then if C is efficiently learnable from statistical queries using $\mathcal{H}$, C is efficiently PAC learnable using $\mathcal{H}$.*

In the following section we will show a much more interesting and useful result: any class that is efficiently learnable from statistical queries is in fact efficiently PAC learnable even in the presence of classification noise. Before this, however, we pause to note that by the analysis of Section 5.2, we already have our first positive result in the statistical query model:

Theorem 5.2 *The representation class of conjunctions of literals is efficiently learnable from statistical queries.*

5.4 Simulating Statistical Queries in the Presence of Noise

Let us fix the target concept $c \in C$ and the distribution $\mathcal{D}$, and suppose we are given a statistical query (χ, τ). We now give an efficient method for obtaining an accurate estimate of

$$P_\chi = \mathbf{Pr}_{x \in \mathcal{D}}[\chi(x, c(x)) = 1]$$

given access only to the noisy examples oracle $EX^\eta_{CN}(c, \mathcal{D})$. We will then show how this method can be used to efficiently simulate any statistical query learning algorithm in the presence of classification noise.

5.4.1 A Nice Decomposition of P_χ

The key idea behind obtaining the desired expression for P_χ is to define a partition of the input space X into two disjoint regions X_1 and X_2 as follows: X_1 consists of all those points $x \in X$ such that $\chi(x, 0) \neq \chi(x, 1)$, and X_2 consists of all those points $x \in X$ such that $\chi(x, 0) = \chi(x, 1)$. Thus, X_1 is the set of all inputs such that the label "matters" in determining the value of χ, and X_2 is the set of all inputs such that the label is irrelevant in determining the value of χ. Note that X_1 and X_2 are disjoint and $X_1 \cup X_2 = X$.

Having defined the regions X_1 and X_2, we can now define the *induced distributions* on these regions. Thus, we let $p_1 = \mathbf{Pr}_{x \in \mathcal{D}}[x \in X_1]$ and $p_2 = \mathbf{Pr}_{x \in \mathcal{D}}[x \in X_2]$ (note that $p_1 + p_2 = 1$), and we define $\mathcal{D}_1$ over X_1 by letting

$$\mathbf{Pr}_{x \in \mathcal{D}_1}[x \in S] = \frac{\mathbf{Pr}_{x \in \mathcal{D}}[x \in S]}{p_1}$$

for any subset $S \subseteq X_1$. Thus, $\mathcal{D}_1$ is just $\mathcal{D}$ restricted to X_1. Similarly, we define $\mathcal{D}_2$ over X_2 by letting

$$\mathbf{Pr}_{x \in \mathcal{D}_2}[x \in S] = \frac{\mathbf{Pr}_{x \in \mathcal{D}}[x \in S]}{p_2}$$

for any subset $S \subseteq X_2$.

For convenience, let us introduce the shorthand notation $\mathbf{Pr}_{EX(c,\mathcal{D})}[\cdot]$ and $\mathbf{Pr}_{EX^\eta_{CN}(c,\mathcal{D})}[\cdot]$ to denote probabilities over pairs $\langle x, b \rangle \in X \times \{0, 1\}$ drawn from the subscripting oracle. We will now derive an expression for $P_\chi = \mathbf{Pr}_{EX(c,\mathcal{D})}[\chi = 1]$ (we have omitted the arguments x, b to χ for brevity) involving only the quantities

$$\eta, p_1, \mathbf{Pr}_{EX^\eta_{CN}(c,\mathcal{D}_1)}[\chi = 1], \mathbf{Pr}_{EX^\eta_{CN}(c,\mathcal{D})}[(\chi = 1) \wedge (x \in X_2)].$$

Looking ahead, we will then show that an accurate guess for η can be made and verified given only the upper bound η_0, and that the latter three probabilities can in fact be estimated from the *noisy* oracle $EX_{CN}^{\eta}(c, \mathcal{D})$.

To derive the desired expression for P_{χ}, we may write:

$$
\begin{aligned}
P_{\chi} &= \mathbf{Pr}_{EX(c,\mathcal{D})}[\chi = 1] \\
&= \mathbf{Pr}_{EX(c,\mathcal{D})}[(\chi = 1) \wedge (x \in X_1)] + \mathbf{Pr}_{EX(c,\mathcal{D})}[(\chi = 1) \wedge (x \in X_2)] \\
&= \mathbf{Pr}_{EX(c,\mathcal{D})}[x \in X_1]\mathbf{Pr}_{EX(c,\mathcal{D})}[\chi = 1 | x \in X_1] \\
&\quad + \mathbf{Pr}_{EX(c,\mathcal{D})}[(\chi = 1) \wedge (x \in X_2)] \\
&= p_1\mathbf{Pr}_{EX(c,\mathcal{D}_1)}[\chi = 1] + \mathbf{Pr}_{EX_{CN}^{\eta}(c,\mathcal{D})}[(\chi = 1) \wedge (x \in X_2)] \qquad (5.1)
\end{aligned}
$$

where to obtain the final equality we have used the fact that for $x \in X_2$, we may replace the correct label by a noisy label without changing the probability that $\chi = 1$.

Note that since χ is always dependent on the label in region X_1, we also have:

$$
\begin{aligned}
\mathbf{Pr}_{EX_{CN}^{\eta}(c,\mathcal{D}_1)}[\chi = 1] &= (1 - \eta)\mathbf{Pr}_{EX(c,\mathcal{D}_1)}[\chi = 1] + \eta\mathbf{Pr}_{EX(c,\mathcal{D}_1)}[\chi = 0] \\
&= (1 - \eta)\mathbf{Pr}_{EX(c,\mathcal{D}_1)}[\chi = 1] \\
&\quad + \eta(1 - \mathbf{Pr}_{EX(c,\mathcal{D}_1)}[\chi = 1]) \\
&= \eta + (1 - 2\eta)\mathbf{Pr}_{EX(c,\mathcal{D}_1)}[\chi = 1].
\end{aligned}
$$

Solving for $\mathbf{Pr}_{EX(c,\mathcal{D}_1)}[\chi = 1]$ and substituting into Equation 5.1, we obtain:

$$
P_{\chi} = p_1\frac{\mathbf{Pr}_{EX_{CN}^{\eta}(c,\mathcal{D}_1)}[\chi = 1] - \eta}{1 - 2\eta} + \mathbf{Pr}_{EX_{CN}^{\eta}(c,\mathcal{D})}[(\chi = 1) \wedge (x \in X_2)] \quad (5.2)
$$

As promised, we now show that the probabilities

$$
p_1, \mathbf{Pr}_{EX_{CN}^{\eta}(c,\mathcal{D}_1)}[\chi = 1], \mathbf{Pr}_{EX_{CN}^{\eta}(c,\mathcal{D})}[(\chi = 1) \wedge (x \in X_2)]
$$

appearing in Equation (5.2) can in fact be estimated from the noisy oracle $EX_{CN}^{\eta}(c, \mathcal{D})$. In a later section we return to the issue of estimating the noise rate.

First, note that it is easy to estimate p_1 using only calls to $EX^\eta_{CN}(c, \mathcal{D})$: we simply take many noisy examples $\langle x, b \rangle$ from $EX^\eta_{CN}(c, \mathcal{D})$, ignore the provided label b, and test whether $\chi(x, 0) \neq \chi(x, 1)$. If so, then $x \in X_1$, otherwise $x \in X_2$. Thus for a large enough sample, the fraction of the x falling in X_1 will be a good estimate for p_1 by Chernoff bounds. The fact that the labels are noisy does not bother us, since membership in X_1 is a property of the input x alone.

Next, $\mathbf{Pr}_{EX^\eta_{CN}(c, \mathcal{D}_1)}[\chi = 1]$ can be estimated from $EX^\eta_{CN}(c, \mathcal{D})$. Note that we do not have direct access to the subscripting oracle, since it is defined with respect to $\mathcal{D}_1$ and not $\mathcal{D}$. Instead, we simply sample pairs $\langle x, b \rangle$ returned by $EX^\eta_{CN}(c, \mathcal{D})$ and use only those inputs x that fall in X_1 (using the membership test $\chi(x, 0) \neq \chi(x, 1)$). For such x, we compute $\chi(x, b)$ (using the noisy label b given with x) and use the fraction of times $\chi(x, b) = 1$ as our estimate.

Finally, note that we can estimate $\mathbf{Pr}_{EX^\eta_{CN}(c, \mathcal{D})}[(\chi = 1) \wedge (x \in X_2)]$ from $EX^\eta_{CN}(c, \mathcal{D})$ because we have a membership test for X_2, and this probability is already defined directly with repsect to the noisy oracle.

5.4.2   Solving for an Estimate of P_χ

Equation (5.2) has the desired form, being a simple algebraic expression for P_χ in terms of η and the probabilities that we have already argued can be accurately and efficiently estimated from $EX^\eta_{CN}(c, \mathcal{D})$. Assuming that we have "sufficiently accurate" estimates for all of the quantities on the right hand side of Equation (5.2), we can use the estimates to solve for an accurate estimate of P_χ.

Of course, in order to use this method to obtain an estimate of P_χ that is accurate within the desired additive error τ, we may need to estimate the probabilities on the right hand side of Equation (5.2) with an additive accuracy τ' that is slightly smaller than τ. For instance, for any $A, B \in [0, 1]$ and $\hat{A}, \hat{B} \in [0, 1]$ that satisfy $A - \tau' \leq \hat{A} \leq A + \tau'$ and

$B - \tau' \leq \hat{B} \leq B + \tau'$ for some $\tau' \in [0, 1]$, we have $AB - 2\tau' \leq \hat{A}\hat{B} \leq AB + 3\tau'$. Thus if we are using the product of the estimates $\hat{A}$ and $\hat{B}$ to estimate the product AB within additive error τ, then $\tau' = \tau/3$ suffices. However, Equation (5.2) is more complex than a single product, and thus we need to make τ' even smaller to prevent the accumulation of too much error when solving for P_χ. It turns out that the choice $\tau' = \tau/27$ will suffices; this comes from the fact that the right hand side of Equation (5.2) can be multiplied out to obtain a sum of three terms, with each term being a product of at most three factors. Thus if every estimated factor has additive error at most $\tau/27$, then each estimated product will have error at most $3(3\tau/27) = \tau/3$, and the estimated sum will have error at most τ, as desired. As we shall now see, however, we need to guess η with even greater accuracy.

5.4.3 Guessing and Verifying the Noise Rate

The main issue that remains unresolved is that when estimating the right hand side of Equation (5.2) to solve for P_χ, we do not know the exact value of η, but have only the upper bound η_0. This is handled by simulating the statistical query algorithm (let us denote this algorithm by L) $\lceil 1/2\Delta \rceil$ times, where $\Delta \in [0, 1]$ is a quantity in our control that will be determined by the analysis. The ith time L is simulated (for $i = 0, 1, 2, \ldots, \lceil 1/2\Delta \rceil - 1$), we substitute the guess $\hat{\eta} = i\Delta$ for η whenever solving for a probability P_χ using Equation (5.2). Eventually we will choose the best of the $1/2\Delta$ hypotheses output by L on these many simulations as our final hypothesis.

Note that for some value of i, the guess $\hat{\eta} = i\Delta$ satisfies

$$\eta - \Delta \leq \hat{\eta} \leq \eta + \Delta.$$

We would now like to derive conditions on Δ that will ensure that for this i we have

$$\frac{1}{1 - 2\eta} - \tau_{\min} \leq \frac{1}{1 - 2\hat{\eta}} \leq \frac{1}{1 - 2\eta} + \tau_{\min}. \tag{5.3}$$

Here $\tau_{\min}$ will be a quantity smaller than any of the tolerances τ needed by L (but still an inverse polynomial in the learning problem parameters). Like the estimates for the probabilities discussed in the last section, this will ensure that on this ith run of L, our guess $1/(1 - 2\hat{\eta})$ for the factor $1/(1 - 2\eta)$ in Equation (5.2) will be sufficiently close to let us solve for P_χ within the desired τ.

Now we know

$$\frac{1}{1 - 2(\eta - \Delta)} \leq \frac{1}{1 - 2\hat{\eta}} \leq \frac{1}{1 - 2(\eta + \Delta)}.$$

Taking the leftmost inequality of this equation, we see that the leftmost inequality of Equation (5.3) will be satisfied if we have

$$\frac{1}{1 - 2\eta} - \tau_{\min} \leq \frac{1}{1 - 2(\eta - \Delta)}.$$

Solving for constraints on Δ gives:

$$1 - 2\eta + 2\Delta \leq \frac{1}{\frac{1}{1 - 2\eta} - \tau_{\min}}$$

or

$$2\Delta \leq \frac{1}{\frac{1}{1 - 2\eta} - \tau_{\min}} - (1 - 2\eta).$$

If we set $x = 1/(1 - 2\eta)$ we obtain

$$2\Delta \leq \frac{1}{x - \tau_{\min}} - \frac{1}{x}$$

or, if we further define $f(x) = 1/x$,

$$2\Delta \leq f(x - \tau_{\min}) - f(x).$$

The right hand side of this inequality suggests analysis via the derivative of f. Now $f'(x) = -1/x^2$ and we may write $f(x - \tau_{\min}) \geq f(x) + c_0\tau_{\min}/x^2$ for some constant $c_0 > 0$, giving

$$\Delta \leq \frac{c_0\tau_{\min}}{2x^2} = \frac{c_0\tau_{\min}}{2}(1 - 2\eta)^2.$$

An identical analysis gives a similar bound on Δ for achieving the rightmost inequality in Equation (5.3). Thus we see that to ensure that our additive error in guessing the value of the factor $1/(1 - 2\eta)$ in Equation (5.2) is smaller than $\tau_{\min}$, we should make sure that the "resolution" Δ of our successive guesses for η is smaller than $c_0\tau_{\min}/(2(1-2\eta)^2)$. Since we only have the upper bound η_0, we will instead use the smaller value $\Delta = c_0\tau_{\min}/(2(1 - 2\eta_0)^2)$.

The preceding analysis shows that when Δ is properly chosen then on one of the simulations L our guess $\hat{\eta}$ will be sufficiently close to η, and on this run L must output a hypothesis h such that $error(h) \leq \epsilon$. We must still give some way of verifying which simulation was the good one. This is a straightforward matter. Let $h_0, \ldots, h_{\lceil 1/2\Delta \rceil - 1}$ be the hypotheses output by L on the $\lceil 1/2\Delta \rceil$ simulations. If we define $\gamma_i = \mathbf{Pr}_{EX^\eta_{CN}(c,\mathcal{D})}[h_i(x) \neq b]$ (this is the probability h_i disagrees with the label provided by the noisy oracle), then $\gamma_i = (1 - \eta)error(h_i) + \eta(1 - error(h_i)) = \eta + (1 - 2\eta)error(h_i)$, and $\gamma_i - \gamma_j = (1 - 2\eta)(error(h_i) - error(h_j))$. This shows that if we estimate all of the γ_i to within an additive error of $\epsilon/(2(1-2\eta))$ (which is easily done, since γ_i is defined with respect to the noisy oracle) and choose as our final hypothesis that h_i whose associated estimate $\hat{\gamma}_i$ is smallest, then $error(h) \leq \epsilon$ with high probability. Again, having only the upper bound η_0 we can instead use the smaller additive error of $\epsilon/(1 - 2\eta_0)$.

5.4.4   Description of the Simulation Algorithm

We are finally ready to give a detailed outline of the overall simulation, followed by the main result of this chapter.

Algorithm Simulate-SQ$(\epsilon, \delta, \eta_0)$:

- $\tau_{\min} \leftarrow 1/(4r(1/\epsilon, n, size(c)))$, where $r(1/\epsilon, n, size(c))$ is the polynomial bound on the inverse tolerance for all queries of the statistical query algorithm L.

- $\Delta \leftarrow c_0 \tau_{\min} / (2(1 - 2\eta_0)^2)$.

- For $i = 0$ to $\lceil 1/2\Delta \rceil - 1$:

    - $\hat{\eta} \leftarrow i\Delta$.

    - Simulate the statistical query algorithm L with accuracy parameter ϵ and using $\hat{\eta}$ as the guessed noise rate. More precisely, for every statistical query (χ, τ) made by L:

        * Randomly sample from the noisy oracle $EX^{\eta}_{CN}(c, \mathcal{D})$ to compute estimates $\hat{p}_1$ for $p_1 = \mathbf{Pr}_{EX(c,\mathcal{D})}[x \in X_1]$, $\hat{q}$ for $q = \mathbf{Pr}_{EX^{\eta}_{CN}(c,\mathcal{D}_1)}[\chi = 1]$ and $\hat{r}$ for

        $$r = \mathbf{Pr}_{EX^{\eta}_{CN}(c,\mathcal{D})}[(\chi = 1) \wedge (x \in X_2)].$$

        Here X_1, X_2 is the partition of X defined by χ. These estimates should be accurate (with high probability) within an additive error of $\tau' = \tau/27$.

        * $\hat{P}_{\chi} \leftarrow \hat{p}_1(\hat{q} - \hat{\eta})/(1 - 2\hat{\eta}) + \hat{r}$. This is the estimated solution of Equation (5.2).

        * Return $\hat{P}_{\chi}$ to L.

    - Let h_i be the hypothesis returned by the ith simulation of L.

- For $i = 0$ to $\lceil 1/2\Delta \rceil - 1$, let $\gamma_i = \mathbf{Pr}_{EX^{\eta}_{CN}(c,\mathcal{D})}[h_i(x) \neq b]$. Randomly sample from $EX^{\eta}_{CN}(c, \mathcal{D})$ to obtain estimates $\hat{\gamma}_i$ that are accurate within additive error $\epsilon/(2(1 - 2\eta_0))$, and output the h_i with the smallest $\hat{\gamma}_i$.

The only details missing from our analysis of this simulation is its dependence on the confidence parameter δ, and of course, a precise bound on the number of examples from $EX^{\eta}_{CN}(c, \mathcal{D})$ required by the simulation. The handling of δ is the standard one used in Section 4.3.6 when proving the equivalence of weak and strong learning. Namely, in any execution of **Simulate-SQ** there are many places in which we need to randomly sample to accurately estimate some probability, and there is always some small probability that we fail to get an accurate estimate. If N is the number of such estimates, we can simply allocate probability of failure δ/N to each and apply the union bound to bound our total probability of failure, and we can always use the running time of L as a crude bound on N. Finally, although we have been careful to argue that for every estimate we can tolerate an additive error that is polynomial in ϵ, $\tau_{\min}$ and $(1 - 2\eta_0)$ (and thus that a polynomial sample suffices by Chernoff bounds), we leave it to the reader (Exercise 5.7) to give precise bounds, and to in fact improve the simulation sample bounds in certain natural cases by drawing a *single* initial sample from $EX^{\eta}_{CN}(c, \mathcal{D})$ from which all probabilities can be estimated throughout the simulation.

The statement of our main result follows.

Theorem 5.3 *Let C be a concept class and let $\mathcal{H}$ be a representation class over X. Then if C is efficiently learnable from statistical queries using $\mathcal{H}$, C is efficiently PAC learnable using $\mathcal{H}$ in the presence of classification noise.*

From Theorems 5.2 and 5.3, we have:

Corollary 5.4 *The representation class of conjunctions of literals is efficiently PAC learnable in the presence of classification noise.*

We leave it to the reader in the exercises to verify that the other classes for which we have provided PAC learning algorithms also have statistical query algorithms, and thus are learnable in the presence of classification noise.

5.5 Exercises

5.1. Show that the representation class of decision lists is efficiently learnable from statistical queries.

5.2. Show that there is a statistical query model analogue to the efficient algorithm given in Section 2.3 for learning conjunctions with few relevant literals. Show that this statistical query algorithm can be efficiently simulated in the classification noise model using a number of calls to $EX^{\eta}_{CN}(c, \mathcal{D})$ whose dependence on the number of literals $size(c)$ is polynomial, but whose dependence on the total number of variables n is only logarithmic.

5.3. Consider the variant of the statistical query model in which the learning algorithm, in addition to the oracle $STAT(c, \mathcal{D})$, is also given access to *unlabeled* random draws from the target distribution $\mathcal{D}$. Argue that Theorem 5.3 still holds for this variant, then show that the concept class of axis-aligned rectangles in $\Re^n$ can be efficiently learned in this variant (and thus is efficiently PAC learnable in the presence of classification noise).

5.4. Show that if there is an efficient algorithm for PAC learning in the presence of classification noise by an algorithm that is given a noise rate upper bound η_0 $(1/2 > \eta_0 \geq \eta \geq 0)$ and whose running time depends polynomially on $1/(1 - 2\eta_0)$, then there is an an efficient algorithm that is given no information about the noise rate and whose running time depends polynomially on $1/(1 - 2\eta)$.

5.5. Give the weakest conditions you can on a concept class $\mathcal{C}$ that imply that any algorithm for PAC learning $\mathcal{C}$ in the presence of classification noise must have a sample complexity that depends at least linearly on $1/(1 - 2\eta)$.

5.6. Prove Theorem 5.1.

5.7. Give the best sample size bounds you can for the simulation of a statistical query algorithm in the presence of classification noise given in Section 5.4.4. Now suppose further that the statistical query algorithm always chooses its queries χ from some restricted class $\mathcal{Q}$ of functions from $X \times \{0, 1\}$ to $\{0, 1\}$. Give a modified simulation with improved sample size bounds that depend on $\log |\mathcal{Q}|$ (in the case of finite $\mathcal{Q}$) and

$VCD(\mathcal{Q})$.

5.6 Bibliographic Notes

The classification noise variant of the PAC model was introduced by Angluin and Laird [10], who proved that boolean conjunctions are efficiently PAC learnable in the presence of classification noise. Their paper also contains several useful and general results on learning with noise, as does the book of Laird [63]. Prior to the introduction of the statistical query model, algorithms for PAC learning with classification noise were given by Sakakibara [82] and Kearns and Schapire [61, 85], who examine a model of learning *probabilistic concepts*, in which the noise rate can be regarded as dependent on the instance.

The statistical query model and the theorems given for it in this chapter are due to Kearns [56], who also establishes that the statistical query model is strictly weaker than the PAC model, and gives lower bounds on the number of statistical queries that must be made in terms of the VC dimension. The paper also examines some apparently less benign noise models in which the statistical query results given here still hold. Exercises 5.1, 5.2, 5.3, 5.6 and 5.7 are also from the paper of Kearns. The relationship between the statistical query model and other models of robust learning is examined by Decatur [28], and Decatur and Aslam [12] establish the equivalence of weak and strong learning in the statistical query model. A recent paper has given a complete characterization of the number of queries required for learning in the statistical query model (Blum et al. [18]).

In addition to the classification noise model, several other variants of the PAC model have been introduced to model errors in the data. These include PAC learning in the presence of *malicious errors* (Valiant [93]; Kearns and Li [57]),and a model of errors in which there is noise in the inputs but not in the labels (Shackelford and Volper [87]); Goldman and

Sloan [41]; Sloan [88]). The book of Laird [63] contains a nice overview of several error models. Littlestone examines a model of errors in on-line learning [67].

6

Inherent Unpredictability

6.1 Representation Dependent and Independent Hardness

Recall that in Chapter 1, we proved that some particular concept classes are hard to PAC learn if we place certain restrictions on the hypothesis class used by the learning algorithm. More precisely, it was shown that if $RP \neq NP$, then there is no polynomial-time algorithm for PAC learning k-term DNF using k-term DNF. However, we then went on to show that k-term DNF is efficiently PAC learnable if the algorithm is allowed to output a hypothesis from the more expressive class of kCNF formulae.

These results raise an interesting and fundamental question regarding the PAC learning model: are there classes of concepts that are hard to PAC learn, not because of hypothesis class restrictions, but because of the inherent computational difficulty of prediction — that is, regardless of the hypothesis class $\mathcal{H}$ used by a learning algorithm? More precisely, we are interested in the existence of concept classes $\mathcal{C}$ in which the VC dimension of $\mathcal{C}_n$ is polynomial in n (and thus by the results of Chapter 3, there is no *information-theoretic* barrier to fast learning — a sample of polynomial size is sufficient to determine a good hypothesis), yet $\mathcal{C}$ is not efficiently PAC learnable using any polynomially evaluatable hypothesis class $\mathcal{H}$. In fact, by the equivalence of weak and strong learning proved in Chapter 1, we may as well strengthen this last condition and ask that $\mathcal{C}$ be not even weakly learnable using any polynomially evaluatable hypothesis class. We shall informally refer to a class $\mathcal{C}$ meeting these conditions as **inherently unpredictable**, since despite the fact that a small sample contains sufficient information to determine a good hypothesis, a polynomial time algorithm cannot even find a hypothesis beating a fair coin. Such a class would be hard to learn for different and arguably more meaningful reasons than the class of k-term DNF, for which the hardness results of Chapter 1 are essentially the consequence of a perhaps artificial syntactic restriction on the hypothesis representation.

In this chapter and the next, we will prove not only that inherently unpredictable classes exist, but furthermore that several rather natural classes of concepts are inherently unpredictable. These results will also demonstrate an interesting connection between hardness results for PAC learning and constructions in the field of public-key cryptography, where the necessary tools for our results were first developed.

6.2   The Discrete Cube Root Problem

Our proofs of inherent unpredictability will rely on some unproven computational assumptions that have become widely accepted as standard working assumptions in cryptography and computational complexity. In fact, since the $P = NP$ question is a fundamental unresolved problem in complexity theory, we cannot hope to prove inherent unpredictability for any polynomially evaluatable class without some complexity assumption. This is because for any polynomially evaluatable class $\mathcal{H}$, the problem of determining, on input any labeled sample S, whether there is a hypothesis $h \in \mathcal{H}$ consistent with S is in NP (because given any witness $h \in \mathcal{H}$ we can *verify* consistency with S in polynomial time). If $P = NP$, then such a consistent hypothesis can be computed in polynomial time, and thus by

Occam's Razor (Theorem 2.1) the concept class is PAC learnable. Thus, in the same way that the hardness of PAC learning k-term DNF using k-term DNF relied on the complexity-theoretic assumption $RP \neq NP$, and therefore on the assumed intractability of particular computational problems such as graph coloring, we must expect any theorem stating that a concept class is inherently unpredictable to rely on the assumed intractability of some specific computational problem. We now propose a candidate problem for our purposes, which will require a brief digression into number theory.

Let $N = pq$ be the product of two prime natural numbers p and q of approximately equal length. Factoring numbers of this form is widely believed to be computationally intractable, even in the case where the primes p and q are chosen randomly and we only ask the factoring algorithm to succeed with some non-negligible probability. Let $f_N(x) = x^3 \ mod \ N$, and consider the problem of inverting $f_N(x)$ — that is, the problem of computing x on inputs N and $f_N(x)$ (but not given p and q!).

In order to make this problem well-defined, we first need to arrange things so that $f_N(x)$ is in fact a bijection (permutation). Before doing so let us review some elementary number theory. The natural numbers in $\{1, \cdots, N-1\}$ that are relatively prime with N (two natural numbers are **relatively prime** if their greatest common divisor is 1) form a group under the operation of multiplication modulo N. This group is denoted by Z_N^*, and the **order** of this group, which we denote by $\varphi(N) = |Z_N^*|$, is $\varphi(N) = (p-1)(q-1)$. Returning to the question of whether $f_N(x)$ is a bijection: we claim that if 3 does not divide $\varphi(N)$, then $f_N(x)$ is a permutation of Z_N^*.

To see this, let d satisfy $3d = 1 \ mod \ \varphi(N)$. Such a d exists because the greatest common divisor of 3 and $\varphi(N)$ is 1, and so by Euclid's theorem there are integers c and d such that $\varphi(N)c + 3d = 1$. In fact, d can be efficiently computed using Euclid's extended greatest common divisor algorithm. Now we claim that the inverse function $f_N^{-1}(y)$ of $f_N(x)$ is simply the mapping $f_N^{-1}(y) = y^d \ mod \ N$: since $3d = 1 \ mod \ \varphi(N)$ means

$3d = k\varphi(N) + 1$ for some natural number k, we have

$$
\begin{aligned}
(f_N(x))^d \bmod N \;&=\; (x^3 \bmod N)^d \bmod N \\
&=\; x^{3d} \bmod N \\
&=\; x^{k \cdot \varphi(N)+1} \bmod N \\
&=\; (x^{\varphi(N)})^k x \bmod N.
\end{aligned}
$$

But a well-known theorem of Euler states that any element of a group raised to the order of the group is equal to the group's identity element, giving $(x^{\varphi(N)})^k = 1^k \bmod N = 1 \bmod N$ and thus $(f_N(x))^d = x \bmod N$ as desired. In the sequel we will refer to d as the **inverting exponent** for N. The existence of this inverse mapping $f_N^{-1}(y)$ establishes that $f_N(x)$ is indeed a bijection.

We can now formally define our problem.

Discrete Cube Root Problem. Two primes p and q are chosen such that 3 does not divide $\varphi(N) = (p-1)(q-1)$, where $N = p \cdot q$. Then $x \in Z_N^*$ is chosen. An algorithm for the Discrete Cube Root Problem is given as input both N and $y = f_N(x)$, and must output x.

Note that the length of the input to this problem is $O(\log N)$ — not N. So a polynomial time algorithm for this problem must run in time polynomial in $\log N$. We now discuss the computational difficulty of the Discrete Cube Root Problem, leading to a formal assumption about its intractability that is widely believed.

6.2.1   The Difficulty of Discrete Cube Roots

Notice that the Discrete Cube Root Problem would be easy to solve in polynomial time if the prime factors p and q of N were also provided as part of the input along with N and y. We could simply compute the inverting exponent d for N from p and q using Euclid's algorithm, and then compute $f_N^{-1}(y) = y^d \bmod N = x \bmod N$. We would have to be a little careful in computing $y^d \bmod N$ efficiently, since we have time only polynomial in $\log N$, whereas d is of the order of N. There is a standard trick for computing $y^d \bmod N$ by repeatedly squaring y modulo N which we will describe in detail in Section 6.3. One consequence of this observation is that for each fixed N of length n bits there is a boolean circuit of size polynomial in n that computes cube roots modulo N — the circuit simply has the inverting exponent d for N "hard-wired", and then performs the required exponentiation on the input y.

How hard is computing cube roots when the prime factors of N are not part of the input, which is the way we have defined the Discrete Cube Root Problem? The obvious method — namely, to first factor N to obtain p and q, compute d from p and q using Euclid's algorithm, and then efficiently compute cube roots via exponentiation as outlined above — runs into the widely known and computationally difficult problem of factoring integers. Although computing cube roots has not been proved to be as hard as factoring, the security of the well-known RSA public key cryptosystem is based on the assumption that the Discrete Cube Root Problem is intractable.

We now formally state our intracability assumption for the Discrete Cube Root Problem, which is an assumption on the average-case difficulty:

The **Discrete Cube Root Assumption** states that for every polynomial $p(\cdot)$, there is no algorithm that runs in time $p(n)$, and that on input N and $y = f_N(x)$ (where N is an n-bit number that is the product of two randomly chosen primes p and q such that 3 does not divide $\varphi(N) = (p-1)(q-1)$, and x is chosen randomly in Z_N^*) outputs x with probability exceeding $1/p(n)$. The probability is taken over the random draws of p and q and x, and any internal randomization of the algorithm.

The fact that extensive efforts have not yielded any efficient algorithm or even a heuristic for computing discrete cube roots means that any PAC learning problem that is proved intractable under the Discrete Cube Root Assumption is, at least for all practical purposes, not learnable given our current understanding of number-theoretic computation.

6.2.2   Discrete Cube Roots as a Learning Problem

Suppose we are given a random N, and $y = f_N(x)$ for a random $x \in Z_N^*$, and we want to compute x from these inputs. The Discrete Cube Root Assumption asserts that this is a difficult problem. But now suppose that in addition to these two inputs, we had access to many already solved "examples" for the given N. That is, suppose we are also given a sample

$$\langle y_1, f_N^{-1}(y_1) \rangle, \ldots, \langle y_k, f_N^{-1}(y_k) \rangle$$

where each $y_i \in Z_N^*$ is chosen randomly. Then does the problem of computing x become any easier?

The answer to this question is no, because since we are already given N, we can generate such random pairs efficiently ourselves by picking a random $x_i \in Z_N^*$ and obtaining the pair $\langle f_N(x_i), x_i \rangle$. By setting $y_i = f_N(x_i)$ (and thus $x_i = f_N^{-1}(y_i)$), and remembering that f_N is a bijection on Z_N^*, we see that these pairs have the same distribution as those $\langle y_i, f_N^{-1}(y_i) \rangle$ generated by first picking a random number $y_i \in Z_N^*$ and then computing $f_N^{-1}(y_i)$.

In our study so far, we have viewed the learning problem as that of using a training sample of random examples to find a hypothesis that has small error with respect to the target function and distribution. An equivalent view of the learning problem is that of using the training sample to predict the target function's output on a new randomly chosen input from the domain. If we choose our target function to be f_N^{-1} for some N, the input domain to be Z_N^*, the input distribution to be uniform on Z_N^*, then under the Discrete Cube Root Assumption we have a computationally hard learning problem.

Before we cast this hard learning problem in the PAC model, let us first formalize it a little further. For every natural number n, let the class $\mathcal{F}_n$ consist of all the inverse functions f_N^{-1} for the functions $f_N(x) = x^3 \mod N$, where $N = pq$ is n bits long and is the product of two primes p and q such that 3 is relatively prime with $\varphi(N) = (p-1)(q-1)$. Let $f_N^{-1} \in \mathcal{F}_n$ be the target function, and let the learning algorithm be given access to a source of random input-output pairs of f_N^{-1}, where the input distribution is uniform on Z_N^*. (Note that this hard distribution depends on the target function f_N^{-1}; in particular, it is not same as the uniform distribution on $\{0,1\}^n$.) The goal of the learning algorithm is to discover in time polynomial in n a hypothesis function h that agrees with f_N^{-1} even on only $1/p(n)$ of the distribution for some fixed polynomial $p(\cdot)$. If an algorithm A exists for this problem, it is easy to see that the Discrete Cube Root Assumption is false: given N and y as input, we first set y aside and use N to generate examples of f_N^{-1} with respect to the uniform distribution on Z_N^* as described above. We use these examples to simulate algorithm A, and then use the hypothesis h output by A to compute $f_N^{-1}(y)$. Then for a random input y, we get the correct value for $f_N^{-1}(y)$ with probability at least $1/p(n)$, thus contradicting the Discrete Cube Root Assumption.

We have already informally argued (and again, we will provide details in Section 6.3) that each function in $\mathcal{F}_n$ can be computed by a boolean circuit whose size polynomial in n. On the other hand, $\mathcal{F}$ is hard to learn in this PAC-like setting for multivalued functions (under the Discrete Cube Root Assumption). We emphasize that this negative result does not place any restriction on the form of the hypothesis h output by the learning algorithm — the only requirement is that the hypothesis can be evaluated in polynomial time. This requirement is obviously necessary in the argument just given, since the last step in using the learning algorithm to solve an instance y of the Discrete Cube Root Problem is to evaluate the hypothesis on y.

The only aspect of our learning problem that keeps it from sitting squarely in the PAC model is that our function class $\mathcal{F}$ is a class of multivalued functions, not a class of boolean functions. Indeed, it is easy to see that we could not hope for such a strong negative result for a boolean function class, since for any boolean function we can always find a hypothesis whose error is bounded by $1/2$ with respect to any input distribution (by simply using the randomized hypothesis that flips a fair coin to predict each label), whereas the Discrete Cube Root Assumption implies that for $\mathcal{F}$, even achieving error bounded by $1 - 1/p(n)$ for any polynomial $p(\cdot)$ is intractable.

However, there is an easy fix that yields a true PAC learning problem. The idea is simple: we regard each output bit of the function f_N^{-1} as a concept (boolean function). If there is an algorithm that can be used to learn each of these output bits with high accuracy, then we can reconstruct all of the output bits with high accuracy.

More precisely, for each multivalued function f_N^{-1}, we define n boolean functions $f_{N,i}^{-1}$, $1 \leq i \leq n$, where for any $y \in Z_N^*$, $f_{N,i}^{-1}(y)$ is defined to be the ith bit of $f_N^{-1}(y)$. Now we let $\mathcal{C}_n$ be the boolean function class obtained by including $f_{N,i}^{-1}$ in $\mathcal{C}_n$ for all $f_N^{-1} \in \mathcal{F}_n$ and all $1 \leq i \leq n$.

Theorem 6.1 *Under the Discrete Cube Root Assumption, the concept class $\mathcal{C}$ is not efficiently PAC learnable (using any polynomially evaluatable hypothesis class).*

Proof: Suppose for contradiction that $\mathcal{C}$ was PAC learnable in polynomial time by algorithm A. Then given Discrete Cube Root Problem inputs N and y, as before we can efficiently generate random examples for each of the n functions $f_{N,i}^{-1}$ by choosing x' randomly from Z_N^*, setting $y' = f_N(x')$, letting the example for $f_{N,i}^{-1}$ be (y', x_i'), where x_i' denotes the ith bit of x'. We thus run n separate simulations of A, one for each $f_{N,i}^{-1}$, setting the error parameter ϵ to be $1/n^2$ in each simulation. Now we can use the n hypotheses output by A to reconstruct all the bits of $f_N^{-1}(y)$ and by the union bound, the probability that all the bits are correct is at least $1 - 1/n$, contradicting the Discrete Cube Root Assumption. $\square$(Theorem 6.1)

6.3 Small Boolean Circuits Are Inherently Unpredictable

One of the basic goals of learning theory is to understand how the computational effort required to learn a concept class scales with the computational effort required to evaluate the functions in the concept class. Thus we are not simply interested in whether there exist inherently unpredictable concept classes (and by Theorem 6.1, we now know that under there do, at least under the Discrete Cube Root Assumption), but in how "computationally simple" such classes could be. Obviously there are limits to how simple a hard-to-learn concept class can be. For instance, we already know that if every concept in a class can be computed by a 3-term DNF formula, then that class cannot be inherently unpredictable, because we can use the hypothesis class of 3CNF, for which there is a cubic time PAC learning algorithm.

Therefore, to further understand the implications of the inherent unpredictability result for the concept class $\mathcal{C}$ in Theorem 6.1, we must provide an upper bound on the resources required to evaluate a concept in $\mathcal{C}$. We have already argued briefly that polynomial size boolean circuits suffice, but we now describe these circuits more precisely in order to pave the way to a refined construction and a considerably stronger hardness result in the next section.

Let us first rigorously define what we mean by a boolean circuit. A boolean circuit over $\{0,1\}^n$ is a directed acyclic graph in which each vertex has indegree (or **fan-in**) either 0,1, or 2, and unbounded outdegree (or **fan-out**). Each vertex of indegree 0 is labeled with one of the input variables $x_1, \ldots, x_n$. Each vertex of indegree 1 is labeled by the symbol $\neg$, and each vertex of indegree 2 is labeled by one of the symbols $\vee$ and $\wedge$. There is a single designated **output vertex** of outdegree 0. When the n input vertices are assigned boolean values, the graph computes a boolean function on $\{0,1\}^n$ in the obvious way. When we refer to the class of **polynomial size boolean circuits**, we mean the concept class

$\mathcal{C}$ in which each concept $c \in \mathcal{C}_n$ is computed by a boolean circuit with at most $p(n)$ vertices, for some fixed polynomial $p(\cdot)$. In the following analysis, we are implicitly choosing the polynomial $p(\cdot)$ large enough to perform the required computations.

The circuit to compute the multivalued function $f_N^{-1} \in \mathcal{F}_n$ (from which we can easily extract circuits for the boolean functions $f_{N,i}^{-1} \in \mathcal{C}_n$) will have the inverting exponent d for N "hard-wired". Therefore, the circuit only needs to compute $y^d \bmod N$. The trick for doing this efficiently (since d may be as large as n bits long, and we have already observed that we do not have time to multiply y by itself d times), is to first generate large powers of y by repeated squaring modulo N, and then combine these to obtain $y^d \bmod N$.

The repeated squaring of $y \bmod N$ yields the sequence of $\lfloor \log d \rfloor + 1$ numbers

$$y \bmod N, y^2 \bmod N, y^4 \bmod N, y^8 \bmod N, y^{16} \bmod N, \ldots, y^{2^{\lfloor \log d \rfloor}} \bmod N$$

using $\lfloor \log d \rfloor + 1$ sequential multiplications of n bit numbers. It is important to take the result so far *mod N* at each step to prevent the numbers from becoming too long.

Now the appropriate elements of this sequence — exactly those corresponding to the 1's in the binary representation of d — can be multiplied together modulo N to obtain $y^d \bmod N$. This takes at most an additional $\lfloor \log d \rfloor + 1$ sequential multiplications. Since the multiplication of two $O(n)$-bit numbers can be implemented using circuits whose size is polynomial in n, and we need to perform only $O(\lfloor \log d \rfloor) = O(n)$ multiplications, the entire circuit for computing $y^d \bmod N$ has size polynomial in n.

Since we have just shown that the class of polynomial size circuits contains our hard class $\mathcal{C}$, we immediately obtain the following result.

Theorem 6.2 *Under the Discrete Cube Root Assumption, the representation class of polynomial size boolean circuits is not efficiently PAC* *learnable (using any polynomially evaluatable hypothesis class).*

6.4 Reducing the Depth of Inherently Unpredictable Circuits

Theorem 6.2 gives us our first hardness result for PAC learning a natural concept class that does not rely on artificial restrictions on the learning algorithm's hypothesis class. However, there is a sense in which it is the weakest such hardness result possible — after all, we cannot really hope to learn a class more powerful than polynomial size circuits in polynomial time.

In this section we will refine our construction of circuits that are hard to PAC learn in order to show that even very simple concept classes, such as the class of all boolean functions computed by *shallow* (that is, log-depth) polynomial size circuits, are inherently unpredictable. Furthermore, in Chapter 7, we will develop a notion of reducibility among learning problems that, combined with our refined hardness result for log-depth circuits, allows us to prove the inherent unpredictability of other important concept classes, such as the class of all concepts computed by deterministic finite automata.

Let us begin by analyzing the depth of the circuit we have proposed for computing the function $f_N^{-1} \in \mathcal{F}_n$. The circuit used the trick of repeated squaring $\lfloor \log d \rfloor + 1 = \Theta(n)$ times, and therefore the depth of the circuit is $\Theta(n)$. Furthermore, no shallower circuit for computing $y^d \bmod N$ from the input y is known.

Our goal is to prove that even circuits whose size is polynomial in n but whose depth (longest path from an input vertex to the output vertex) is at most $O(\log n)$ are hard to learn. More precisely, the class of **log-depth, polynomial size boolean circuits** is the concept class $\mathcal{C}$ in which each concept $c \in \mathcal{C}_n$ is computed by a boolean circuit with at most $p(n)$ vertices and depth at most $k \log n$, for some fixed constant k (independent of n) and some fixed polynomial $p(\cdot)$. In the following analysis, we are implicitly choosing the constant k and the polynomial $p(\cdot)$ large enough to perform the required computations.

While the restriction to log-depth circuits may at first seem somewhat arbitrary, it is well-known that the class of log-depth, polynomial size circuits computes essentially the same functions as the rather natural class of polynomial size **boolean formulae**. (By this we mean that there exists a polynomial $p(\cdot)$ such that every log-depth circuit of size s can be represented as a boolean formula of size at most $p(s)$, and every boolean formula of size s can be represented by a log-depth circuit of size at most $p(s)$; see Exercise 6.2.) A boolean formula over $\{0,1\}^n$ is simply a well-formed expression over a logical language containing symbols for the usual boolean connectives $\vee, \wedge, \neg$, the symbols "(" and ")" for indicating order of evaluation, and symbols for the boolean input variables $x_1, \ldots, x_n$. Such an expression computes a boolean function over $\{0,1\}^n$ in the obvious way. A convenient alternative representation for a boolean formula is a boolean circuit in which the underlying graph must be a tree: at the root (output) node of this tree, we place the outermost connective of the boolean formula; inductively, the left and right subtrees of the root are the trees for the left and right subexpressions joined by the outermost connective in the formula. Figure 6.1 shows an example formula and the corresponding tree.

When we refer to the class of polynomial size boolean formulae, we actually mean the family in which each formula over $\{0,1\}^n$ is an expression of at most $p(n)$ symbols for some fixed polynomial $p(\cdot)$, where again we will implicitly choose the polynomial $p(\cdot)$ large enough to perform the required computations.

Intuitively, one primary difference between boolean formulae (log-depth circuits) and general boolean circuits is that if the same logical subexpression $E(x_1, \ldots, x_n)$ is needed many times, in a formula we may have to duplicate the expression with each use, while in a circuit we may simply increase the fan-out of the subcircuit computing $E(x_1, \ldots, x_n)$

$$f = (((\bar{x}_1 \vee x_5) \wedge x_2) \vee \bar{x}_3) \wedge x_4$$

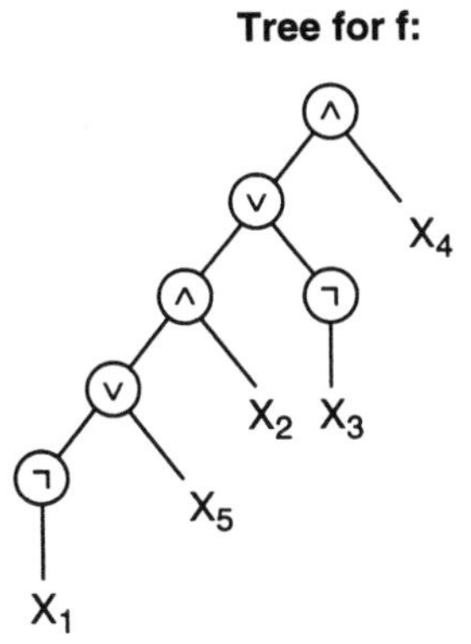

Tree for f:

Figure 6.1: *A boolean formula and its tree circuit representation.*

and get the repetition for free. Thus, there may be some functions that can be computed by a small boolean circuit, but require a much larger boolean formula (although the existence of such functions remains an important open question), and we might wonder if it is these functions that cause the inherent unpredictability of small boolean circuits. We now show a negative answer to this question.

6.4.1 Expanding the Input

To show that shallow circuits are hard to learn, we shall modify each function $f_N^{-1} \in \mathcal{F}_n$ by providing additional inputs that make the computation of $f_N^{-1}(y) = y^d \bmod N$ possible using a shallow circuit, but that do not alter the difficulty of learning. In order to argue that learning remains hard, we will have to choose different hard input distributions.

The motivating idea behind the modification is actually quite simple. Suppose that knowing only the product N and a value y, we are watching someone who also knows the decrypting exponent d for N perform the computation of $y^d \ mod \ N$ by the trick of repeated squaring of y, followed by multiplication of the appropriate square powers. If the entire computation is performed before us, then we can in fact learn the value of d from this computation, since the square powers of y multiplied together to obtain $y^d \ mod \ N$ correspond exactly to the binary representation of d, and we will have learned something we cannot obviously compute efficiently ourselves. However, if the party knowing d only computes the square powers in front of us, and then multiplies the appropriate powers together privately, then we have definitely *not* learned anything new: we could have efficiently computed these square powers of y ourselves. In this way, the party knowing d can reduce the amount of private computation to the bare minimum, without compromising the secrecy of d. In the following analysis, it is this private computation that corresponds to the circuit complexity of the target functions, which is reduced by this trick.

More precisely, for each f_N^{-1} with inverting exponent d, let us define a new function g_N^{-1} that is a mapping from $(Z_N^*)^{\lfloor \log d \rfloor + 1}$ to Z_N^*. For any $y \in Z_N^*$ we define

$$g_N^{-1}(y \ mod \ N, y^2 \ mod \ N, \ldots, y^{2^{\lfloor \log d \rfloor}} \ mod \ N) = y^d \ mod \ N = f_N^{-1}(y).$$

Thus, g_N^{-1} is essentially the same function as f_N^{-1} with one important difference: g_N^{-1} is provided with an "expanded input" in which the successive square powers of the original input y are already computed. Note that the length of the inputs to g_N^{-1} is $O(\log^2 N) = O(n^2)$ bits rather than the $O(\log N) = O(n)$ bits of input for f_N^{-1}, but is still polynomial in n. Furthermore, g_N^{-1} is simply the inverse of the vector-valued function

$$g_N(x) = (x^3 \ mod \ N, x^6 \ mod \ N, \ldots, x^{3 \cdot 2^{\lfloor \log d \rfloor}} \ mod \ N)$$

Thus, vectors in $(Z_N^*)^{\lfloor \log d \rfloor + 1}$ that are not of the successive square form are not in the range of g_N, and therefore g_N^{-1} will be defined to be the special value $*$ on such vectors.

The first important property we need of g_N^{-1} is that, like f_N^{-1}, it is hard to compute g_N^{-1} if the inverting exponent d for N is unknown. More precisely, if we let N be the product of two randomly chosen $n/2$-bit primes p and q such that 3 does not divide $\varphi(N) = (p-1)(q-1)$, and we choose y randomly in Z_N^*, then under the Discrete Cube Root Assumption it is hard to compute $g_N^{-1}(y \bmod N, y^2 \bmod N, \ldots, y^{2^{\lfloor \log d \rfloor}} \bmod N)$ on inputs N and

$$(y \bmod N, y^2 \bmod N, \ldots y^{2^{\lfloor \log d \rfloor}} \bmod N).$$

Otherwise, given inputs N and $y \in Z_N^*$ for the Discrete Cube Root Problem, a polynomial time procedure could compute the required powers of y modulo N by repeated squaring, thus obtaining the expanded input required for g_N^{-1}, and then invoke the procedure for computing g_N^{-1} to compute $f_N^{-1}(y)$. This would violate the Discrete Cube Root Assumption.

The second important property is that, *unlike f_N^{-1}*,

$$g_N^{-1}(y \bmod N, y^2 \bmod N, \ldots y^{2^{\lfloor \log d \rfloor}} \bmod N)$$

can be computed by a shallow circuit that has d hard-wired. This circuit simply multiplies together the appropriate powers of y that are provided in the input sequence. Again, the numbers to be multiplied together are those powers $y^{2^i} \bmod N$ such that the ith bit of d is 1, as in the circuit for f_N^{-1}).

The problem of multiplying at most n numbers modulo N is a well-studied one and is known as the problem of **iterated products**. A naive implementation would multiply the desired numbers in pairs, and then the results in pairs, and so on, to get a circuit that is binary tree in which each internal node is a multiplication and each of the at most n leaves is one of the numbers to be multiplied. The depth of this tree is at most $\log n$. Unfortunately, since each internal node of the tree must be implemented by a multiplication circuit for two n-bit numbers, and this in itself requires circuit depth $\Omega(\log n)$, the final depth of this proposed circuit would be $O(\log^2 n)$ rather than $O(\log n)$. However, there is a sophisticated circuit construction due to Beame, Cook and Hoover (see the Bibliographic Notes at the end of the chapter) that is beyond the scope of our investigation, but that provides circuits for iterated product of total depth only $O(\log n)$, as desired.

As with the functions f_N^{-1}, the functions g_N^{-1} are not boolean but multivalued. The definition of the associated boolean function (concept) class $\mathcal{C}'$ is completely analogous to the definition of the concept class $\mathcal{C}$ for the f_N^{-1}: for each function g_N^{-1} and each $1 \leq i \leq n$, we define the concept $g_{N,i}^{-1} \in \mathcal{C}_{n^2}$ to be the ith output bit of g_N^{-1}.

Now given Discrete Cube Root Problem inputs N and y, in the same way that a PAC learning algorithm for $\mathcal{C}$ could be used to obtain accurate approximations for all the output bits of f_N^{-1}, a PAC learning algorithm A for $\mathcal{C}'$ can be used to obtain accurate approximations for all the output bits of g_N^{-1}: we can set aside y and first generate random examples of g_N^{-1} by choosing x' randomly in Z_N^*, setting $y' = f_N(x')$, and computing the successive square powers. Setting

$$ z' = (y' \bmod N, (y')^2 \bmod N, \ldots, (y')^{2^{\lfloor \log d \rfloor}} \bmod N) $$

we can compute the random example $\langle z', g_N^{-1}(z') \rangle$. The bits of x' are the boolean labels for the n functions $g_{N,i}^{-1}$ on the expanded input and can be used in n separate simulations of A. As with the argument for the $f_{N,i}^{-1}$, the n hypotheses output by A can then be used to compute $f_N^{-1}(y)$, contradicting the Discrete Cube Root Assumption. Notice that the hard distribution for the function $g_{N,i}^{-1}$ is not the uniform distribution over the input space $(Z_N^*)^{\lfloor \log d \rfloor + 1}$ but uniform over only those inputs that have the appropriate successive square form.

Since we have argued above that the concepts in $\mathcal{C}'$ are contained in the class of log-depth circuits, we have proved the following theorem:

Theorem 6.3 *Under the Discrete Cube Root Assumption, the representation class of polynomial size, log-depth boolean circuits (or equivalently, the class of polynomial size boolean formulae) is not efficiently PAC learnable (using any polynomially evaluatable hypothesis class).*

6.5 A General Method and Its Application to Neural Networks

We conclude this chapter by observing that en route to proving that the class of polynomial size boolean formulae is not efficiently PAC learnable, we in fact identified a general property of representation classes that renders them inherently unpredictable. In particular, the only special property we required of boolean formulae was their ability to efficiently compute the iterated product of a list of numbers. By formalizing this ability as a general property of representation classes, we will also be able to prove the inherent unpredictability of polynomial size neural networks.

Definition 15 *Let C be a representation class. We say that C **computes iterated products** if there exists a fixed polynomial $p(\cdot)$ such that for any natural number N of n bits and any $1 \leq i \leq n$, there is a concept $c \in C_{n^2}$ (thus, c has n^2 inputs) such that $size(c) \leq p(n)$, and for any $z_1, \ldots, z_n \in Z_N^*$, $c(z_1, \ldots, z_n)$ is the ith bit in the binary representation of the product $z_1 \cdots z_n \bmod N$.*

Armed with this definition, by arguments identical to those used to derive Theorem 6.3, we obtain:

Theorem 6.4 *Let C be any representation class that computes iterated products. Then under the Discrete Cube Root Assumption, C is not efficiently PAC learnable (using any polynomially evaluatable hypothesis class).*

Recall that in Section 3.7 we demonstrated that the number of examples required to PAC learn any class of neural networks scaled only polynomially with the number of parameters required to specify the networks. This result ignored computational considerations, and concentrated just on the sample complexity of PAC learning. We now apply Theorem 6.4 to show that the computational considerations are rather formidable. Our result relies on the following lemma due to J. Reif, whose proof is beyond the scope of our investigation (see the Bibliographic Notes at the end of the chapter).

Lemma 6.5 *(Reif) There is fixed polynomial $p(\cdot)$ and an infinite family of directed acyclic graphs (architectures) $G = \{G_{n^2}\}_{n \geq 1}$ such that each G_{n^2} has n^2 boolean inputs and at most $p(n)$ nodes, and for any natural number N of n bits there is an assignment of linear threshold functions to each node in G_{n^2} such that the resulting neural network computes iterated products modulo N. Furthermore, the depth of G_{n^2} is a fixed constant independent of n.*

In fact, Reif shows that Lemma 6.5 holds even when we are constrained to choose only weights in $\{0, 1\}$ for the linear threshold function at each node. From this lemma and Theorem 6.4, we immediately obtain:

Theorem 6.6 *Under the Discrete Cube Root Assumption, there is fixed polynomial $p(\cdot)$ and an infinite family of directed acyclic graphs (architectures) $G = \{G_{n^2}\}_{n \geq 1}$ such that each G_{n^2} has n^2 boolean inputs and at most $p(n)$ nodes, the depth of G_{n^2} is a fixed constant independent of n, but the representation class $\mathcal{C}_G = \cup_{n \geq 1} \mathcal{C}_{G_{n^2}}$ (where $\mathcal{C}_{G_{n^2}}$ is the class of all neural networks over $\Re^{n^2}$ with underlying architecture G_{n^2}) is not efficiently PAC learnable (using any polynomially evaluatable hypothesis class). This holds even if we restrict the networks in $\mathcal{C}_{G_{n^2}}$ to have only binary weights.*

6.6 Exercises

6.1. In this problem we consider the problem of computing discrete *square roots* rather than cube roots.

First, show that if $N = pq$ is the product of two primes p and q, and $a = x^2 \bmod N$ for some $x \in Z_N^*$, then there is a $y \in Z_N^*$ such that $a = y^2 \bmod N$ and $y \neq x \bmod N$ and $y \neq -x \bmod N$ (Hint: use the Chinese Remainder Theorem). Thus, any square a modulo N has two "different" square roots.

Now consider the **Discrete Square Root Problem**: given N that is the product of two $n/2$-bit primes, and an integer a that is the square modulo N of an element of Z_N^*, find an $x \in Z_N^*$ satisfying $a = x^2 \bmod N$. Show that if there is an efficient algorithm for the Discrete Square Root Problem, then there is an efficient algorithm for factoring integers, and vice-versa.

Thus the Discrete Square Root Problem is actually equivalent to factoring. With some mild additional assumptions on the numbers to be factored, this equivalence can be preserved by the techniques of this chapter to show that PAC learning the classes considered is as hard as a factoring problem; we chose to use discrete cube roots primarily for technical convenience.

6.2. Show that there is a fixed polynomial $p(\cdot)$ such that every log-depth boolean circuit of size s can be represented as a boolean formula of size $p(s)$, and every boolean formula of size s can be represented as a log-depth boolean circuit of size $p(s)$. Thus, within polynomial factors of size, these classes have equivalent computational power.

6.7   Bibliographic Notes

The first representation-independent hardness results for PAC learning follow from the influential paper of Goldreich, Goldwasser and Micali [43]. In this paper, it is shown (under a cryptographic construction) that polynomial-size boolean circuits are not efficiently PAC learnable, even if the input distribution is uniform, we only require weak learning, and membership queries are available (see Chapter 8).

The results of this chapter are due to Kearns and Valiant [60]. The Discrete Cube Root Problem was first proposed as the basis for the RSA public-key cryptosystem, named after its inventors Rivest, Shamir and Adelman [81]. The log-depth implementation of iterated products is due to Beame, Cook and Hoover [14]. Lemma 6.5 is due to Reif [76].

The Kearns and Valiant results were improved by Kharitonov [62], who showed that boolean formulae remain hard to PAC learn even if the input distribution is uniform, and membership queries are available. The Kharitonov results also apply to the class of constant-depth circuits of $\wedge$ and $\vee$ gates of unbounded fan-in. Interestingly (under an appropriately strong but still plausible assumption), these hardness results match the upper bound given for this class by an elegant learning algorithm due to Linial, Mansour and Nisan [64]. Angluin and Kharitonov [9] use cryptographic assumptions to demonstrate that membership queries cannot help for learning general DNF formulae.

The use of cryptographic tools and assumptions to obtain intractability results for learning is now fairly common in computational learning theory. In the reverse direction, a recent paper (Blum et al. [19]) demonstrates how certain assumptions on the difficulty of PAC learning problems can be used to obtain cryptographic primitives such as private-key cryptosystems and pseudo-random bit generators.

7

Reducibility in PAC Learning

From the positive results of Chapters 1 and 2 and the hardness results of Chapter 6, we now have examples, for natural and nontrivial concept classes, of both efficient PAC learning and inherent unpredictability. Although we have certainly identified some powerful methods for obtaining both kinds of results — for instance, the method of finding an Occam algorithm for a concept class in order to show that it is efficiently PAC learnable, and the method of showing that a concept class can compute iterated products in order to demonstrate its inherent unpredictability — we still lack a framework that allows us to compare the relative complexity of PAC learning concept classes whose actual status in the PAC model is uncertain.

In this chapter, we develop a notion of *reducibility* for learning in the PAC model. In order to choose a notion of reducibility that is meaningful we must first state our goals. Informally, we are of course interested in a notion of reducibility that preserves efficient PAC learnability. Thus if a concept class C "reduces" to a concept class C', and C' is efficiently PAC learnable, then it should follow that C is also efficiently PAC learnable.

There will be at least three uses for the reducibility we develop. First, if C reduces to C', and we already have an efficient learning algorithm for C', then the reduction immediately yields an efficient learning algorithm for $\mathcal{C}$. Recall that it was exactly this method that provided an efficient algorithm for learning kCNF from our efficient algorithm for learning boolean conjunctions (1CNF) in Chapter 1. Second, we can give evidence for the intractability of learning a concept class $\mathcal{C}'$ by showing that another concept class $\mathcal{C}$, believed to be hard to learn, reduces to $\mathcal{C}'$. Third, if $\mathcal{C} \supset \mathcal{C}'$, but we do not know if either of $\mathcal{C}$ and $\mathcal{C}'$ is efficiently PAC learnable, a reduction of $\mathcal{C}$ to $\mathcal{C}'$ at least proves that learning the subclass $\mathcal{C}'$ is no easier than learning $\mathcal{C}$.

We begin with a motivating example falling in the final category. While the PAC learnability of general disjunctive normal form (DNF) formulae remains unresolved so far, we use a simple reduction to demonstrate that the monotone version of the problem is not easier than the unrestricted version.

7.1   Reducing DNF to Monotone DNF

We have informally discussed DNF formulae at many points throughout our studies. Formally, a general **disjunctive normal form (DNF) formula** over $\{0, 1\}^n$ is an expression of the form $c = T_1 \vee T_2 \vee \cdots \vee T_m$, where each term T_i is a conjunction of literals over the boolean variables $x_1, \ldots, x_n$. Since each term can be represented using at most $O(n)$ bits, we define $size(c) = mn$. Because a learning algorithm is always allowed time polynomial in n, it is fair to think of the dependence on $size(c)$ as allowing the learning algorithm to also have time polynomial in the number of terms m.

If we let $\mathcal{C}_n$ be the class of all DNF formulae over $\{0, 1\}^n$, note that $\mathcal{C}_n$ actually contains a representation of every possible boolean function over $\{0, 1\}^n$; however, the PAC learning problem is nevertheless "fair" in principle, because we measure the complexity of a function by its DNF representation size. Thus the learning algorithm is provided with more computation for more complex target functions.

Recall that in Chapter 1 we studied the severely restricted subclass of DNF formulae in which the number of terms was bounded by a fixed constant k (thus, $size(c) = kn$). We called such a formula a k-term DNF formula, and we proved that PAC learning such formulae is hard if the hypothesis class used is also k-term DNF formulae, but can be done efficiently if k-CNF formulae is used as the hypothesis class. However, since this solution required time exponential in k, it is inapplicable to the general problem, where the number of terms is a parameter. On the other hand, the inherent unpredictability methods of Chapter 6 also seem inapplicable, since DNF formulae do not appear up to the task of efficiently computing iterated products. In short, the efficient PAC learnability of general DNF formulae remains one of the most important open problems in the PAC model. Our modest goal here is to use a reduction to dismiss one possible source for the apparent difficulty of this problem — namely, the fact that the target formulae are allowed to have both negated and unnegated variables.

A **monotone DNF formula** over $\{0,1\}^n$ is simply a disjunction $c' = T_1 \vee T_2 \vee \cdots \vee T_m$ in which each T_i is a conjunction over the boolean variables $x_1, \ldots, x_n$ (but *not* their negations). Thus, the difference between monotone DNF and general DNF is that we forbid negated variables in the monotone case. Obviously, unlike for general DNF, it is not the case that every boolean function over $\{0,1\}^n$ can be represented as a monotone DNF formula. Could it be the case that there is an efficient PAC learning algorithm for monotone DNF formulae, yet general DNF formulae are inherently unpredictable?

The answer is no. Suppose we had an efficient learning algorithm L' for PAC learning monotone DNF formulae using some polynomially evaluatable hypothesis class $\mathcal{H}'$. We now show that L' can actually be used as a subroutine in an efficient PAC learning algorithm L for general DNF formulae.

Let us consider a small example. Suppose that we have a general DNF formula over the variables $x_1, \ldots, x_6$, say $c = (x_1 \wedge \overline{x}_5 \wedge x_6) \vee (\overline{x}_1 \wedge x_2 \wedge x_4)$. By introducing "new" variables $y_1, \ldots, y_6$ but always assigning $y_i = \overline{x}_i$, we may also write c as $(x_1 \wedge y_5 \wedge x_6) \vee (y_1 \wedge x_2 \wedge x_4)$. Now this is a monotone formula over the expanded variable set $x_1, \ldots, x_6, y_1, \ldots, y_6$; let us use c' to denote this monotone representation of c. Note that $size(c')$ is not too much larger than $size(c)$.

Suppose now we are given the positive example $\langle 010110, 1 \rangle$ of c over the original variables x_i. Then the *expanded instance* 010110 101001, which is the original instance followed by its bitwise complement, is a positive example of the monotone formula c' over the expanded variable set consisting of the x_i and the y_i. More generally, it is easy to verify that if $\langle a, c(a) \rangle$ is any example of c, then $\langle a \cdot comp(a), c(a) \rangle$ is always a correct example of c', where $comp(a)$ is the bitwise complement of a and $\cdot$ denotes string concatenation. It is crucial to note that this transformation of the instances $a \rightarrow a \cdot comp(a)$ is independent of the actual target formula c, and can be efficiently computed from a.

Now given access to the examples oracle $EX(c, \mathcal{D})$ for a target general DNF formula c over $\{0, 1\}^n$, our algorithm L will simply simulate the algorithm L' for the monotone case. Each time L' requests a random example, L will take a random labeled example $\langle a, c(a) \rangle$ of c from $EX(c, \mathcal{D})$, and give the transformed example $\langle a \cdot comp(a), c(a) \rangle$ of length $2n$ to L'. Since the examples given to L' are perfectly consistent with the monotone formula c', algorithm L' will then produce some polynomially evaluatable boolean function h' over the $2n$ variables $x_1, \ldots, x_n, y_1, \ldots, y_n$ that is accurate with respect to the distribution $\mathcal{D}'$ induced on the transformed examples by the simulation. Note that $\mathcal{D}'$ may be quite different from $\mathcal{D}$. For instance, if $\mathcal{D}$ was the uniform distribution on $\{0, 1\}^n$, $\mathcal{D}'$ will not be the uniform distribution on $\{0, 1\}^{2n}$, but the uniform distribution on pairs $a \cdot a' \in \{0, 1\}^{2n}$ where $a, a' \in \{0, 1\}^n$ and $a' = comp(a)$.

The hypothesis h of L will then be given by $h(a) = h'(a \cdot comp(a))$. It is easy to see that $error_{\mathcal{D}}(h) = error_{\mathcal{D}'}(h')$, because $h(a) \neq c(a)$ if and only if $h'(a \cdot comp(a)) \neq c'(a \cdot comp(a))$, and a has exactly the same weight under $\mathcal{D}$ that $a \cdot comp(a)$ has under $\mathcal{D}'$. Also, since L' runs in time polynomial in $size(c')$, and we have already pointed out that $size(c')$ is not much larger than $size(c)$, L runs in time polynomial in $size(c)$, and also in time polynomial in $2n$.

We have shown:

Theorem 7.1 *If the representation class of general DNF formulae is efficiently PAC learnable, then the representation class of monotone DNF formulae is efficiently PAC learnable.*

7.2 A General Method for Reducibility

We have just given a simple example of a reduction of one learning problem to another. We now give a general definition of this notion.

Definition 16 *We say that the concept class $\mathcal{C}$ over instance space X* **PAC-reduces** *to the concept class $\mathcal{C}'$ over instance space X' if the following conditions are met:*

- *(Efficient Instance Transformation) There exists a mapping $G : X \to X'$ and a polynomial $p(\cdot)$ such that for every n and every $x \in X_n$, $G(x) \in X'_{p(n)}$, and G is computable in polynomial time. Thus, G maps instances in X of length n to instances in X' of length $p(n)$, and can be efficiently computed.*

- *(Existence of Image Concept) There exists a polynomial $q(\cdot)$ such that for every concept $c \in \mathcal{C}_n$, there is a concept $c' \in \mathcal{C}'_{p(n)}$ with the property that $size(c') \leq q(size(c))$, and for all $x \in X_n$, $c(x) = 1$ if and only if $c'(G(x)) = 1$. Thus, for any concept $c \in \mathcal{C}$ there is a concept $c' \in \mathcal{C}'$ that is not much larger than c, and whose behavior on the transformed instances exactly mirrors that of c on the original instances.*

Note that while we insist the instance transformation be efficiently computable, there is no such demand on the mapping from c to c'; we only ask for its existence. Thus, it may be intractable (or even impossible) to compute the representation of c' from the representation of c.

Under this formalization, our reduction of DNF to monotone DNF was $G(a) = a \cdot comp(a)$ (thus, instances of length n were mapped to instances of length $2n$), and c' was just the monotone DNF formula obtained by replacing each occurrence of $\overline{x}_i$ in c with the variable y_i.

The basic property we require of our reducibility is established by the following theorem.

Theorem 7.2 *Let C and C' be concept classes. Then if C PAC-reduces to C', and C' is efficiently PAC learnable, C is efficiently PAC learnable.*

Proof: Given a learning algorithm L' for C', we use L' to learn C in the obvious way: given a random example $\langle x, c(x) \rangle$ of an unknown target concept $c \in C$, we compute the labeled example $\langle G(x), c(x) \rangle$ and give it to L'. If the instances $x \in X$ are drawn according to $\mathcal{D}$, then the instances $G(x) \in X'$ are drawn according to some induced distribution $\mathcal{D}'$. Although we do not know the target concept c, our definition of reduction guarantees that the computed examples $\langle G(x), c(x) \rangle$ are consistent with some $c' \in C'$, and thus L' will output a hypothesis h' in time polynomial in $size(c')$ (and thus polynomial in $size(c)$) that has error at most ϵ with respect to $\mathcal{D}'$. Our hypothesis for c becomes $h(x) = h'(G(x))$, which is easily seen to have at most ϵ error with respect to $\mathcal{D}$. $\square$(Theorem 7.2)

Another useful way of stating Theorem 7.2 is to say that if C PAC-reduces to C', and C is inherently unpredictable then C' is inherently unpredictable. It is this view of our reducibility we use in the next section.

7.3 Reducing Boolean Formulae to Finite Automata

In this section, we derive the main result of this chapter, which is that the class of boolean formulae PAC-reduces to the class of deterministic finite automata. We shall show this in two parts. First, we show that the class of log-space Turing machines PAC-reduces to finite automata. Then we show that the class of boolean formulae PAC-reduces to log-space Turing machines. The main result then follows from the transitivity of our reducibility, which is established in Exercise 7.1.

There is a minor technicality involved with defining concept classes represented by finite automata and Turing machines, because we normally think of these devices as accepting strings of a possibly infinite number of different lengths, while we have been thinking of a concept as being defined only over instances of some fixed length n. For the purposes of this chapter, however, it will suffice to define our concept classes by restricting our attention to the behavior of a finite automaton or Turing machine on inputs of a single common length.

Thus, consider the concept class $\mathcal{C}$ in which there is a constant k (we will implicitly choose k as large as necessary in our analysis) such that every concept $c \in \mathcal{C}_n$ over $\{0,1\}^n$ can be evaluated by a Turing machine T_c that uses only $k \log n$ work space (thus, we assume that T_c has a read-only input tape and a separate read/write work tape). Thus, for every $c \in \mathcal{C}_n$ and every $a \in \{0,1\}^n$, $T_c(a) = c(a)$. We call this the representation class of **log-space Turing machines**, and we define $size(c)$ to be the number of states in the finite control of T_c. Similarly, let $\mathcal{C}'$ be the concept class in which each $c' \in \mathcal{C}'_n$ over $\{0,1\}^n$ can be evaluated by a deterministic finite automata $M_{c'}$; thus for any $a \in \{0,1\}^n$, $c'(a) = 1$ if and only if $M_{c'}$ accepts a. We call this the representation class of **deterministic finite automata**, and we define $size(c')$ to be the number of states in $M_{c'}$. We now show that $\mathcal{C}$ PAC-reduces to $\mathcal{C}'$.

Theorem 7.3 *The class of log-space Turing machines PAC-reduces to the class of deterministic finite automata.*

Proof: We describe for each $k \log n$-space Turing machine $T = T_c$ (computing some concept c in $\mathcal{C}_n$) a small DFA $M = M_c$ that will simulate T on appropriately transformed instances $G(a)$. Intuitively (and we will flesh out the details momentarily), M must overcome two handicaps in order to simulate T. The first is that T has logarithmic work space but a DFA has no explicit memory. This is easily compensated for by encoding all the $2^{k \log n} = n^k$ possible work tape contents of T in the state diagram of M, and can be done using only n^k additional size overhead in M. The second handicap is that T can move its read-only input head either right or left on the input tape, while a DFA must proceed forward (to the right) through its input at every transition. This can be overcome with the help of the instance transformation G. For any input $a \in \{0,1\}^n$ to T, $G(a)$ will simply replicate a many times: thus $G(a) = aa \cdots a$. If at any point T moves left on the input a, then M will simply move $n - 1$ symbols forward on $G(a)$, arriving in the next copy of a but one symbol to the left of its position in the former copy, thus affecting a move to the left. This requires a $\log n$ bit counter, which can also be encoded in the state diagram of M using only polynomially many states. The number of copies $p(n)$ of a that must be given in $G(a)$ is clearly bounded by the running time of T (since this bounds the number of possible input head moves by T), which is polynomial.

To see this is more detail, consider constructing a directed graph G_T based on the description of T. Each node of G_T is labeled by a tuple (s, σ, i) where s is a state of the finite control of T, σ is a binary string of length $k \log n$, which we interpret as the work tape contents of T, and $1 \le i \le n$ is interpreted as an index indicating the head position of T on the input tape. Then we draw a directed edge, labeled by the bit $b \in \{0,1\}$, from the node (s, σ, i) to the node $(s', \sigma', i + 1)$ if and only if T, when in state s with work tape contents σ and input head position i, on reading a b from the input would move the input head right and go to state s' with work tape contents σ'. (Note that this can only happen if σ and σ' differ only in the single bit at the head position.) We will additionally label this directed edge by an R to indicate a move to the right on the input. Similarly, we will label an edge from a node with input head index i to a node with input head index $i-1$ by an L.

Now G_T is "almost" a DFA simulating T, if we allow the traversal of a transition labeled R or L to move the input head of G_T right or left, respectively. But it is easy to see that we can replace each R transition by a finite automata that simply reads through the next $n+1$ input bits of $G(a)$, and each L transition by a one that reads through the next $n-1$ bits of $G(a)$. The resulting graph is exactly a finite automata whose behavior on $G(a)$ is the same as T on a. Note that the size of this automata is polynomial in n and polynomial in the number of states in the finite control of T. $\qquad\square$(Theorem 7.3)

We now reduce boolean formulae to log-space Turing machines to complete the sequence of reductions.

Theorem 7.4 *The class of boolean formulae PAC-reduces to the class of log-space Turing machines.*

Proof: We show that for any boolean formula f over $\{0,1\}^n$, there is a log-space Turing machine T_f, with a number of finite control states that is polynomial in $size(f)$, that on input a computes $f(a)$ (thus, the instance transformation $G(a)$ is simply the identity transformation). We will actually prove the stronger result that there is a single log-space Turing machine T that takes as input a boolean formula f and an assignment a, and computes $f(a)$; the desired machine T_f can be obtained by fixing the formula input of T to be f. (Thus, T is universal for the class of boolean formulae.)

Recall that a boolean formula can be thought of as a circuit whose underlying graph is a tree (see Figure 6.1 in Chapter 6 and the accompanying text). Let us label each node in this tree with a unique natural number that we call the *name* of the node. Assume without loss of generality that the formula f that is input to T is encoded as a list of items representing the tree circuit for f. Each item consists of a label indicating the name of a node in the binary tree for computing f (this label requires at most $O(\log size(f))$ bits, where $size(f)$ is the number of gates in the tree for f), a couple of bits indicating the gate type ($\wedge$, $\vee$ or $\neg$), and the labels of the left and right children of this gate. Now to compute $f(a)$, T conducts a depth-first search of the tree using the item list. To keep track of the search, T only needs to store the label of the current gate, and a few bits indicating the current "direction" of the search (that is, whether we arrived at the current gate g from the parent of g, the left child of g, or the right child of g). We also only ever need to store a single bit v indicating the value of the computation so far. For instance, if we are currently at an $\vee$ gate that we arrived at from the left child, and the value of the subfunction computed by the subtree rooted at the left child was $v = 1$, then there is no need to explore the right child of this gate; we can simply continue back up the tree and maintain the value $v = 1$. On the other hand, if $v = 0$ then we must explore the right subtree but we can overwrite the value of v, since the left subtree evaluated to 0 and thus cannot make the current $\vee$ evaluate to 1. The value of v returned from the right subtree will become the value for the current $\vee$ node. Similarly, if the current gate is an $\wedge$ gate and we returned from the left child with $v = 0$, we can simply continue up the tree with this value, bypassing the right subtree. Otherwise, we explore the right subtree and overwrite v.

$\square$(Theorem 7.4)

From Theorems 7.3 and 7.4 and the transitivity of our reducibility (see Exercise 7.1), we immediately obtain:

Corollary 7.5 *The class of boolean formulae PAC-reduces to the class of deterministic finite automata.*

Thus, drawing on the results of Chapter 6, we obtain:

Theorem 7.6 *Under the discrete cube root assumption, the representation class of deterministic finite automata is inherently unpredictable.*

In light of this negative result, in the next chapter we will investigate a natural model of learning that provides the learner more power than in the PAC model, and obtain an efficient learning algorithm for finite automata.

7.4 Exercises

7.1. Prove that our reducibility for PAC learning is transitive. Thus, for any concept classes C_1, C_2 and C_2, if C_1 PAC-reduces to C_2 and C_2 PAC-reduces to C_3, then C_1 PAC-reduces to C_3.

7.2. The concept class of **halfspaces** in $\Re^n$ is defined as follows: each concept is defined by a vector $\vec{u} \in \Re^n$ of unit length. An input $\vec{x} \in \Re^n$ is a positive example of $\vec{u}$ if and only if $\vec{u} \cdot \vec{x} \equiv \sum_{i=1}^{n} u_i \cdot x_i \geq 0$. In the the concept class of **exclusive-or of two halfspaces**, each concept is defined by a pair $(\vec{u}, \vec{v})$ of unit vectors in $\Re^n$. An input $\vec{x} \in \Re^n$ is a positive example of $(\vec{u}, \vec{v})$ if either $\vec{u} \cdot \vec{x} \geq 0$ and $\vec{v} \cdot \vec{x} < 0$, or $\vec{u} \cdot \vec{x} < 0$ and $\vec{v} \cdot \vec{x} \geq 0$; otherwise, $\vec{x}$ is a negative example.

Show that the class of exclusive-or of halfspaces PAC-reduces to the the class of halfspaces.

7.3. A **read-once DNF formulae** over $\{0, 1\}^n$ is a disjunction $c = T_1 \vee T_2 \vee \cdots \vee T_m$ (where each T_i is a conjunction of literals over the boolean variables $x_1, \ldots, x_n$) in which every variable is restricted to appear at most once (whether negated or unnegated). Show that the representation class of general DNF formulae in which each formula over $\{0, 1\}^n$ has at most $p(n)$ terms, for some fixed polynomial $p(\cdot)$, PAC-reduces to the representation class of read-once DNF formulae.

7.5   Bibliographic Notes

The general definition of PAC-reducibility was developed by Pitt and Warmuth [73], who also give the reduction of boolean formulae to finite automata and many other interesting reductions. The reduction of general DNF to monotone DNF is due to Kearns et al. [58]. Such reductions are now a standard tool of computational learning theory; the paper of Long and Warmuth [68] gives examples for geometric concept classes. Exercise 7.2 is due to M. Warmuth and L.G. Valiant.

8

Learning Finite Automata by Experimentation

8.1   Active and Passive Learning

Although our early investigation of PAC learning revealed a number of natural but simple classes (such as boolean conjunctions, decision lists, and some geometric concepts) that are efficiently PAC learnable, the results given in Chapters 6 and 7 present rather daunting negative evidence regarding the efficient learnability of more complex classes such as boolean formula and finite automata. These intractability results must lead us to question, at least in some of its details, the model of learning under consideration. For instance, are there sources of information about the target concept that are more powerful than random examples but are still somehow natural, and that we should make available to the learning algorithm? Might our failure to model such sources partially account for the chasm between the hope that efficient learning should be possible and the intractability results we have derived?

Perhaps the most obvious source of information that we have failed to model is *experimentation*. The PAC model is a passive model of learning, in the sense that the learning algorithm has absolutely no control over the sample of labeled examples drawn. However, it is easy to imagine that the ability to experiment with the target concept might be extremely helpful to the learner. This is what we shall demonstrate in this chapter. We model experimentation by giving the learner the ability to make *membership queries*: the learner, when learning the target concept c, is given access to an oracle that on any input x returns the correct target label $c(x)$. Thus the learning algorithm may choose particular inputs and see their target classification rather than only passively receiving random labeled inputs.

One setting where membership queries are natural is when the learner is assisted by a teacher. Nature, as modeled by the target distribution in the PAC model, is indifferent to the learner and provides only random examples of the target concept. Particular questions that the learner may have are answered only insofar as the random training sample happens to answer them. The teacher, on the other hand, knows the target concept (or perhaps has already learned an accurate approximation to it), and is sufficiently patient to classify inputs of the learner's choice as positive or negative examples of the target.

In this chapter we show that allowing membership queries can have a significant impact on the complexity of learning problems. In particular, we show we can learn deterministic finite automata in polynomial time in the augmented PAC model where the learning algorithm is given access to an oracle for membership queries in addition to the usual oracle for random examples. This result will in fact follow from an efficient algorithm for learning finite automata in a more demanding model: *exact learning from membership and equivalence queries*, which we define in the next section. Combining this positive result with the hardness results of Chapters 6 and 7, we conclude under the Discrete Cube Root Assumption, membership queries provably make the difference between intractability and efficient learning for finite automata.

In the latter part of the chapter, we generalize our learning algorithm for finite automata to solve another natural learning problem. Imagine that the learner is actually a robot wandering in an unknown environment which consists of s distinct sites. At each step the robot can move from its current site to a neighboring site by performing one of a small set of primitive operations (for example, by moving one step forward, or to the left). Suppose that each site contains some information that can help the robot orient itself in the environment. An example of such information could be the color of the current site. We can actually assume without loss of generality that there is only a single bit of information at each site, because we can modify an arbitrary environment into an equivalent binary environment by replacing each site of the original environment by a "corridor" of binary-valued sites in the new environment that encode the value at the original site.

The robot's goal is to derive a complete model of the observable behavior of its environment. More precisely, the model should predict the exact sequence of bits the robot would observe on any sequence of moves starting from its current position. A natural model of the environment is that of a deterministic finite state automaton. The states of the automaton correspond to the sites in the environment, and transitions correspond to the primitive moves. Each state of the automaton has a single bit of information associated with it (namely, whether it is an accepting state or a rejecting state). This bit represents the bit of information at the corresponding site in the environment.

We give an efficient algorithm for creating an exact model of any such deterministic finite state environment. The algorithm is a refinement of the algorithm for learning finite automata from membership queries. Let us briefly sketch the essential difference between these two automata learning problems. While the robot can actively experiment with its environment (the target automaton), it cannot reset the automaton to a definite state (like the start state). However, this is precisely the ability that is conferred upon the learner by membership queries, since a membership query may be regarded as a reset to the start state followed by an execution of the query string. To prove the robot learning result we show how to simulate a weak reset that is effective enough to help us simulate the previous learning algorithm.

8.2   Exact Learning Using Queries

We now introduce a model of learning called **exact learning from membership and equivalence queries.** As usual, the learning algorithm is attempting to learn an unknown target concept chosen from some known concept class $\mathcal{C}$. Unlike in the PAC model, where we were satisfied with a close approximation to the target concept, we will insist that the learning algorithm output the representation of a concept that is exactly equivalent to the target concept. Instead of random examples as in the PAC model, however, the learner now has access to oracles answering the following two types of queries:

- **Membership Queries:** On a membership query, the learning algorithm may select any instance x and receive the correct classification $c(x)$.

- **Equivalence Queries:** On an equivalence query, the learning algorithm submits a hypothesis concept $h \in \mathcal{C}$. If $h(x) = c(x)$ for all x then the learner has succeeded in exactly identifying the target. Otherwise, in response to the query the learner receives an instance x such that $h(x) \neq c(x)$. Such an instance is called a **counterexample**. We make no assumptions on the process generating the counterexamples. For instance, they may be chosen in a manner designed to be confusing to the learning algorithm.

Definition 17 *We say that the representation class $\mathcal{C}$ is* **efficiently exactly learnable from membership and equivalence queries** *if there is a fixed polynomial $p(\cdot, \cdot)$ and an algorithm L with access to membership and equivalence query oracles such that for any target concept $c \in \mathcal{C}_n$, L outputs in time $p(size(c), n)$ a concept $h \in \mathcal{C}$ such that $h(x) = c(x)$ for all instances x.*

Note that we have assumed that concepts are defined only over instances of a single common length n (such as in the case of boolean formulae over $\{0,1\}^n$). This is clearly not the case for a finite automaton, which may accept strings of any length. To apply the definition of exact learning from queries to finite automata, we could simply restrict our attention to finite automata accepting strings of only a single length, as was done in deriving the hardness results in Chapter 7 (such a restriction only makes the hardness result stronger). But it turns out we can give an efficient algorithm without this restriction, provided we make a minor but necessary modification to the definition. For finite automata, if the counterexamples given by the equivalence oracle can be arbitrarily long, it is natural that for our new definition should allow the running time of the learning algorithm to depend on the length of these counterexamples (since we certainly should give the algorithm enough time to read the counterexamples). Thus, to generalize our definition to handle the exact learning of finite automata, in Definition 17 we simply assume that rather than being the exact length of all examples, the parameter n is a given a priori bound on the length of the *longest* counterexample that will be given to L in response to any equivalence query. (In Exercise 8.2 we show that for any equivalence query there always exists a counterexample whose length is at most polynomial in the number of states of the target automaton, and moreover the shortest counterexample can be efficiently computed given the target automaton. Thus, by providing sufficiently short counterexamples, a cooperative teacher can induce the exact learning algorithm for finite automata to run in time polynomial in the number of target states.)

At first glance, it might appear that equivalence queries are an unrealistically strong source of information to provide to the learner. However, it can be shown (see Exercise 8.1) that any representation class that is efficiently exactly learnable from membership and equivalence queries is also **efficiently PAC learnable with membership queries**. By this we mean that it is efficiently learnable in the PAC model, provided the learning algorithm is provided with membership queries in addition to the usual oracle $EX(c, \mathcal{D})$ for random examples. All other aspects of the PAC model, including the success criterion of finding a hypothesis with error less than ϵ with respect to the target concept and distribution, remain intact.

8.3   Exact Learning of Finite Automata

Over the next several sections, we will gradually develop and analyze an algorithm for efficiently exactly learning deterministic finite automata from membership and equivalence queries. We will keep the development at a fairly high level to emphasize the intuition behind the algorithm, but will eventually provide a complete and precise description of the algorithm in Section 8.3.5.

Let M be the target automaton, and assume without loss of generality that M is minimized (that is, it has the fewest states among all automata accepting the same language). We define $size(M)$ to be the number of states of M.

The key idea of the algorithm is to attempt to continually discover new states of M. By new states we mean states exhibiting behavior that is demonstrably different from the states discovered so far. The algorithm runs in phases. In each phase, the algorithm constructs a tentative hypothesis automaton $\hat{M}$ whose states are the currently discovered states of M. It then makes an equivalence query on $\hat{M}$. The counterexample from this equivalence query allows the algorithm to use membership queries to discover a new state of M. When all the states of M have been discovered, we will have $\hat{M} = M$.

8.3.1   Access Strings and Distinguishing Strings

How can the learning algorithm discover information about the states of M? The algorithm will maintain a set S consisting of at most $size(M)$ **state access strings**, and a set D of **distinguishing strings**:

- (*Access*) Each string $s \in S$, when executed from the start state of M, leads to a unique state of M that we denote $M[s]$.

- (*Distinguishability*) For each pair of strings $s, s' \in S$ such that $s \neq s'$, there is a distinguishing string $d \in D$ such that one of sd and $s'd$ reaches an accepting state of M, and the other reaches a rejecting state of M. (That is, exactly one of $M[sd]$ and $M[s'd]$ is an accepting state.)

We shall refer to the states $\{M[s] : s \in S\}$ as the *known* states of M, since we know how to access them from the start state. Notice that all these known states must be distinct. This is because for each pair of strings $s, s' \in S$, there is a string d in D that witnesses the fact that starting from states $M[s]$ and $M[s']$ and executing d leads to different final states. The goal of the learning algorithm is to discover all the states of M by finding $size(M)$ access strings, together a with distinguishing string for every pair of access strings. The task of reconstructing the actual transitions of M from this information is quite straightforward (as we shall see).

In the algorithm, the current sets S and D of access and distinguishing strings will be maintained in a convenient data structure, a binary **classification tree**. Each internal node is labeled by a string in D, and each leaf is labeled by a string in S. The tree is constructed by placing at the root any string d from D that distinguishes two strings in S, and placing in the left subtree of the root all strings $s \in S$ such that sd is rejected by M, and in the right subtree all $s \in S$ such that sd is accepted. This induces a nontrivial partition of S (since d distinguishes some pair of strings in S), and we simply recurse at each subtree until each string in S is at its own leaf. Then any pair of access strings $s, s' \in S$ are distinguished by the string labeling their least common ancestor in the classification tree. Our algorithm will dynamically maintain a classification tree representation of S and D.

Our algorithm will make sure that the distinguishing string that labels the root of the classification tree is always the empty string λ. This will

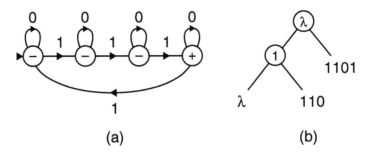

(a)   (b)

Figure 8.1: (a) *Finite automaton counting the number of* 1*'s in the input* 3 *mod* 4. (b) *A classification tree for this automaton.*

ensure that all the access strings to accepting states will lie in the right subtree and the access strings to rejecting states in the left subtree. The algorithm will also arrange that λ is one of the access strings. This ensures that we can access the start state of the automaton.

Figure 8.1(a) shows a finite automaton that will form the basis of a running example. This automaton accepts an input string if and only if the number of 1's in the string is 3 modulo 4. Figure 8.1(b) shows a classification tree for this automaton, with access strings $\{\lambda, 110, 1101\}$ and distinguishing strings $\{\lambda, 1\}$.

8.3.2 An Efficiently Computable State Partition

Now suppose we are given a new string s' that is not in the current access string set S, but that $M[s'] = M[s]$ for some access string $s \in S$. Then we can efficiently determine s from s' by **sifting** s' down our classification tree using membership queries: starting at the root, if we are at an internal node labeled by the distinguishing string d, we make a membership query on the string $s'd$ and go to the left or right subtree as indicated by the query answer (left on reject, right on accept). We continue in this manner to reach a leaf, which must be labeled by s.

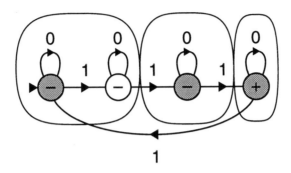

Figure 8.2: *Partition induced by the classification tree in Figure 8.1.*

More importantly, even if $M[s'] \neq M[s]$ for all $s \in S$, sifting s' down the classification tree still defines a path to a leaf, and this path depends only on $M[s']$. In other words, for any strings s' and s'', if $M[s'] = M[s'']$ then sifting s' and s'' defines exactly the same path down the classification tree. Thus, the classification tree induces a partition on the states of M, and each equivalence class of this partition contains exactly one state $M[s]$ such that $s \in S$, which we will consider the representative element for the equivalence class.

Sifting can be efficiently implemented, and the number of membership queries for a sift operation is bounded by the depth of the classification tree.

Figure 8.2 shows the partition of the automaton of Figure 8.1(a) that is induced by the classification tree of Figure 8.1(b). The known or representative state in each equivalence class has been shaded. Note that the access string for a known state may not be the shortest string reaching that state. For example, in Figures 8.1 and 8.2, we have the access string 110 even though the shorter string 11 accesses the same state.

8.3.3 The Tentative Hypothesis $\hat{M}$

We are now in a position to describe the construction of a hypothesis automaton $\hat{M}$, whose states can be thought of as the known states of M (that is, states for which there are access strings in the leaves of the current classification tree). If all the states of M have been discovered then it will turn out that $\hat{M} = M$. Otherwise, the counterexample from the equivalence query on $\hat{M}$ will be used to discover a new state (that is, access string) of M.

We first define $\hat{M}$ algorithmically and then provide some insight into its structure. Given the classification tree, it is easy to construct $\hat{M}$ using equivalence queries. We identify (label) the states of $\hat{M}$ with the access strings in the classification tree. For each access string (state) s and symbol b, the destination state of the b-transition out of state s is just the access string that results from sifting sb down the classification tree.

$\hat{M}$ can be thought of as an automaton whose states are a subset of the states of M, but with transitions that are possibly quite different than those of M. Imagine a state diagram of M in which the transitions are represented by dashed lines, and the states are grouped by the equivalence classes defined by the current classification tree. (See Figure 8.3(a), in which M is the four-state automaton shown, with its transitions represented by dashed lines. The states of M are partitioned into two classes of two states each.) Now let us shade each known state $M[s]$ for $s \in S$. (The shaded states of M in Figure 8.3(a) are the known states.) Then $\hat{M}$ will be defined only on those states of M that are shaded, and each equivalence class of M has exactly one such shaded state. The transitions of $\hat{M}$, which will be represented by bold lines, are defined as follows: for $b \in \{0, 1\}$, the bold b-transition leaving the shaded state $M[s]$ is obtained simply by taking M's dashed b-transition leaving $M[s]$ and redirecting it from its current destination state to the unique shaded state of the equivalence class of the destination state in M. (See Figure 8.3(a).) For example, in Figure 8.3(a), the dashed 0-transition of the left

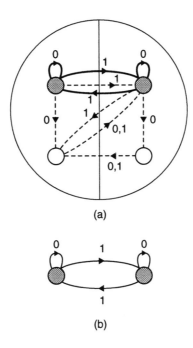

(a)

(b)

Figure 8.3: (a) *Embedded hypothesis defined by a partition of a target automaton into two equivalence classes. Transitions of the target automaton M are dashed, transitions of the hypothesis $\hat{M}$ defined by the partition and the shaded known states are bold.* (b) *The resulting hypothesis $\hat{M}$ extracted.*

shaded state stays in the same equivalence class of states; thus, the bold 0-transition of the left shaded state becomes a self-loop. Similarly, the dashed 1-transition of the right shaded state goes to the left equivalence class; thus, the bold 1-transition of the right shaded state also goes to the left equivalence class, but is redirected to the left shaded state. Notice that in the case when all the states of M are shaded, $\hat{M} = M$.

We should point out a common point of confusion about $\hat{M}$: $\hat{M}$ might look very different from M and it might accept a totally different language than that accepted by M. So it is a mistake to think of $\hat{M}$ as an approximation to the target automaton M (unless they have the same number of states, in which case $M = \hat{M}$). A related point is that the learning algorithm makes progress by increasing the number of access strings or leaves in the classification tree. The tentative hypothesis automaton $\hat{M}$ facilitates this increase in the number of leaves in the classification tree.

8.3.4   Using a Counterexample

We now show how we can use a string γ that is a counterexample to the equivalence of M and $\hat{M}$ in order to discover a new state of M, thus allowing the classification tree to be updated. The conceptual idea is to simulate the behavior of both M and $\hat{M}$ in parallel on the string γ (that is, follow both the dashed trajectory and the bold trajectory dictated by γ) in order to discover the first point at which the two trajectories diverge to different equivalence classes of states. At this point of divergence, the dashed and bold transitions must take place from two different states in the same equivalence class, thus providing us with access to a new state in this equivalence class.

To make this precise, we first recall our assumption that the root of the classification tree is labeled by the empty string λ, and that one of the access strings is λ (both of these conditions will be easily arranged by our algorithm in its initialization step). The first condition implies that no equivalence class of M contains both an accepting and a rejecting state. The second condition implies that in the embedding of $\hat{M}$ in M, the start states of the two automata coincide, and thus the machines are "synchronized" at the start of any string. So the dashed and bold trajectories determined by the counterexample γ begin in a common equivalence class (in fact, in the same state) and end up in different equivalence classes (since exactly one of M and $\hat{M}$ accepts γ).

Let $\hat{M}[s]$ denote the state reached by following the transitions of $\hat{M}$ on string s; this is just the final destination of the bold trajectory determined by s. Let γ_i denote the ith symbol of γ and let $\gamma[i]$ denote the prefix of γ

of length i, that is $\gamma[i] = \gamma_1 \cdots \gamma_i$. Let $1 \leq j \leq |\gamma|$ be the first index such that the equivalence class of $M[\gamma[j]]$ differs from that of $\hat{M}[\gamma[j]]$ (thus, the two trajectories have diverged for the first time). See Figure 8.4.

By the choice of j, we know that $M[\gamma[j-1]]$ and $\hat{M}[\gamma[j-1]]$ are in the same equivalence class, yet the dashed transition from $M[\gamma[j-1]]$ and the bold transition from $\hat{M}[\gamma[j-1]]$ on the symbol γ_j led to different equivalence classes. This means that $M[\gamma[j-1]]$ and $\hat{M}[\gamma[j-1]]$ are actually different states in the same equivalence class. Since the only shaded (known) state in this class is $\hat{M}[\gamma[j-1]]$, and recalling that the access strings discovered so far reach only the shaded states, $M[\gamma[j-1]]$ is a new state with access string $\gamma[j-1]$.

To distinguish $M[\gamma[j-1]]$ from all previously discovered states (that is, to place this state in its own equivalence class), we only need to distinguish $M[\gamma[j-1]]$ and $\hat{M}[\gamma[j-1]]$ from each other (that is, to "split" the current equivalence class to which they both belong). The correct distinguishing string simply expresses the fact that the γ_j transitions from $M[\gamma[j-1]]$ in M and from $\hat{M}[\gamma[j-1]]$ in $\hat{M}$ lead to different equivalence classes, namely, the equivalence classes of $M[\gamma[j]]$ and $\hat{M}[\gamma[j]]$. If d is the string distinguishing the equivalence classes of $M[\gamma[j]]$ and $\hat{M}[\gamma[j]]$, then the correct distinguishing string for $M[\gamma[j-1]]$ and $\hat{M}[\gamma[j-1]]$ is $\gamma_j d$.

It should be clear that the task of updating the classification tree by processing a counterexample string can be carried out efficiently using membership queries. This involves determining the equivalence class of each prefix of the counterexample string by sifting it down the current classification tree, as well as tracing its path in the hypothesis automaton $\hat{M}$, which is known explicitly.

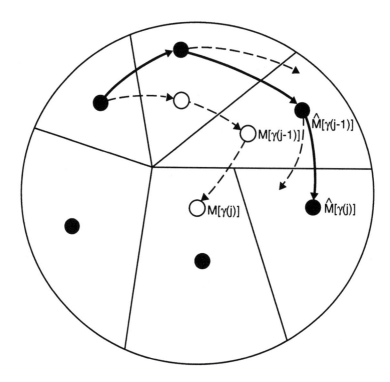

Figure 8.4: *The trajectories in the target automaton (dashed transitions, unshaded states) and the hypothesis automaton (bold transitions, shaded states) traced by a counterexample. From each shaded state on the bold trajectory, the dashed transition of the target automaton (which may be different from the bold transition) is shown for completeness.*

   To sum up, as long as the number of leaves of the classification tree is smaller than $size(M)$, the hypothesis automaton $\hat{M}$ is necessarily different from M. Therefore an equivalence query must return some counterexample string γ which we can use to update the classification tree by adding a new leaf node. Eventually the classification tree will have $size(M)$ leaf nodes, each accessing a different state of M, and at this point $\hat{M} = M$.

8.3.5 The Algorithm for Learning Finite Automata

We can now describe our algorithm for learning finite automata in some detail. We start by describing the subroutine **Sift**. This subroutine takes as input a string s and the current classification tree T, and outputs the access string in T of the equivalence class of $M[s]$, the state of M accessed by s.

Procedure Sift(s, T):

- Initialization: set the current node to be the root node of T.

- Main Loop:

    - Let d be the distinguishing string at the current node in the tree.

    - Make a membership query on sd. If sd is accepted by M, update the current node to be the right child of the current node. Otherwise, update the current node to be the left child of the current node.

    - If the current node is a leaf node, then return the access string stored at this leaf. Otherwise, repeat the Main Loop.

Next, we describe the procedure for constructing the hypothesis automaton $\hat{M}$ that is defined by the current classification tree T.

Procedure Tentative-Hypothesis(T):

- For each access string (leaf) of T, create a state in $\hat{M}$ that is labeled by that access string. Let the start state of $\hat{M}$ be the state λ.

- For each access state s of $\hat{M}$ and each $b \in \{0, 1\}$, compute the b-transition out of state s in $\hat{M}$ as follows:

    – $s' \leftarrow \textbf{Sift}(sb, T)$.

    – Direct the b-transition out of state s to state s'.

- Return $\hat{M}$.

Next we describe the procedure **Update-Tree**, which takes as arguments the current classification tree T and a counterexample string γ to the hypothesis automaton $\hat{M}$ defined by T. The procedure finds a new access string, and updates T by adding a new leaf node labeled with the new access string.

Procedure Update-Tree(γ, T):

- For each prefix $\gamma[i]$ of γ:

    – $s_i \leftarrow \textbf{Sift}(\gamma[i], T)$.
    – Let $\hat{s}_i = \hat{M}[\gamma[i]]$.

- Let j be the least i such that $s_i \neq \hat{s}_i$.

- Replace the node labeled with the access string s_{j-1} in T with an internal node with two leaf nodes. One leaf node is labeled with the access string s_{j-1} and the other with the new access string $\gamma[j-1]$. The newly created internal node is labeled with the distinguishing string $\gamma_j d$, where d is the correct distinguishing string for s_j and $\hat{s}_j$ (d can be obtained from T).

We are now ready to describe the overall algorithm for learning finite automata:

Algorithm Learn-Automaton:

- Initialization:

    – Do a membership query on the string λ to determine whether the start state of M is accepting or rejecting.

- Construct a hypothesis automaton that consists simply of this single (accepting or rejecting) state with self-loops for both the 0 and 1 transitions.

- Perform an equivalence query on this automaton; let the counterexample string be γ.

- Initialize the classification tree T to have a root labeled with the distinguishing string λ and two leaves labeled with access strings λ and γ.

- Main Loop:

  - Let T be the current classification tree.

  - $\hat{M} \leftarrow$ **Tentative-Hypothesis**(T).

  - Make an equivalence query on $\hat{M}$. If it is equivalent to the target then output $\hat{M}$ and halt. Otherwise, let γ be the counterexample string.

  - **Update-Tree**(T, γ).

  - Repeat Main Loop.

In Figure 8.5, we show the evolution of the hypothesis $\hat{M}$ and the classification tree as the algorithm is executed on the target automaton first shown in Figure 8.1.

8.3.6 Running Time Analysis

The number of times the Main Loop of algorithm **Learn-Automaton** is executed is exactly $size(M)$. This is because, as we have already argued, each iteration discovers a new state of M in the form of an access string, and when all states are discovered then $\hat{M} = M$. Each execution of the Main Loop of **Learn-Automaton** makes a call to procedure **Tentative-Hypothesis** to compute $\hat{M}$, and each such call invokes $O(size(M))$ sifting operations. Also, each execution of the Main Loop of

Learn-Automaton requires the processing of a single counterexample by procedure **Update-Tree**. A counterexample of length n requires at most n sifting operations. Therefore, we have $size(M)$ Main Loop executions, each of which requires $O(size(M) + n)$ sifting operations, where n is the length of the longest counterexample. It is easy to see that the running time of our algorithm is dominated by the sifting operations, and that sifting is a $O(size(M))$ operation. We have thus derived the first of the two main results of this chapter:

Theorem 8.1 *The representation class of deterministic finite automata is efficiently exactly learnable from membership and equivalence queries.*

It is worth noting that as a corollary to our analysis of the learning algorithm, we can give an alternative derivation of the well-known Myhill-Nerode theorem, which states that for any regular language L there is a unique automaton of minimum size accepting L. First observe that the learning algorithm only gets information about the language L accepted by the target automaton M, and so if two different target automata M_1 and M_2 accept the same language L then the learning algorithm must produce the same output automaton $\hat{M}$. On the other hand, we showed that output automaton $\hat{M}$ is identical to the target automaton, *assuming only* that the target automaton is a minimum state automaton. It follows that the minimum state automaton accepting L is unique.

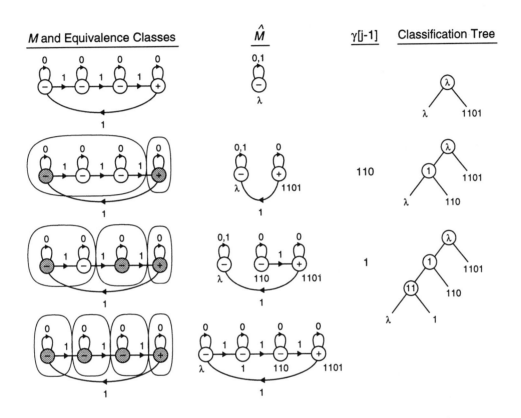

Figure 8.5: *Sample execution of algorithm* **Learn-Automaton** *on the 3 mod 4 counter target automaton. In the first column, we show the target automaton with the partition defined by the classification tree of the previous row, along with the shaded known states. The second column shows the hypothesis $\hat{M}$ defined by the partition to its left; the states of $\hat{M}$ are also labeled by their access string. Every equivalence query on $\hat{M}$ is answered by the same repeated counterexample $\langle 1101, 1 \rangle$ until $\hat{M} = M$. The third column shows the prefix $\gamma[j-1]$ of $\gamma = 1101$ on which a difference of equivalence classes is first detected, and the fourth column shows the classification tree at each step.*

8.4   Learning without a Reset

In this section, we strengthen the result from the previous section and give an efficient algorithm for learning deterministic finite automata from equivalence queries and membership queries **without resets**. By this we mean that the membership oracle does not reset M to its start state before each membership query; instead it simply starts processing the next query string from its current state. Thus the answer to the query string γ^i which follows a sequence of queries $\gamma^1, \ldots, \gamma^{i-1}$ indicates whether $M[\gamma^1 \cdots \gamma^{i-1}\gamma^i]$ is an accepting or rejecting state. As stated in the introduction, we will assume without loss of generality that each of the query strings γ_i is only a single-bit query.

We need to be a little careful in specifying the goal of the learner in this new setting. The problem arises from the fact that the target automaton M may contain components from which the learning algorithm can never escape once they are entered, and thus might not be able to explore the rest of the automaton. For simplicity, we shall finesse this problem by simply assuming that M is **strongly connected**: that is, there is a directed path between every pair of states in M. In the more general case, the automaton would eventually get trapped in a strongly connected component. In this case the learning algorithm would end up with an accurate model of this strongly connected component.

In keeping with the idea that the learner's goal is to model its environment from its current position, we shall also modify the oracle for equivalence queries. Whenever the learning algorithm makes an equivalence query on hypothesis automaton $\hat{M}$, this query is interpreted from the learning algorithm's current position. This means that if $\hat{M}$ is equivalent to M when we define the start state of M to be the current position of the learning algorithm in M, then learning is complete, and if $\hat{M}$ is not equivalent to M from the current position, a counterexample from the current position is provided. Thus, a counterexample to $\hat{M}$ provides the learning algorithm with a sequence of moves γ such that if we execute γ from the current position in M, and if we execute γ from the start state of $\hat{M}$, different outputs are obtained. For brevity, we shall refer to this learning model for finite automata with the modified membership and equivalence queries as the **no-reset model** of exactly learning deterministic finite automata from membership and equivalence queries, and to the original model as the **reset model**. Note that the no-reset model only makes sense in the context of learning the particular representation class of finite automata, whereas the original model is of more general interest.

It is not difficult to see that a learning algorithm in the no-reset model can be simulated by an algorithm in the reset model, by making a membership query for each prefix of the string describing the movements of the no-reset learner. On the other hand, the no-reset learner does not seem to have the power of membership queries with resets, since it may not know how to return to the start state from its current position in the target automaton.

We will use the notion of *homing sequences* to effect a kind of simulation of resets in the no-reset model, and this will allow us to modify our algorithm **Learn-Automaton** for the reset model into an efficient *randomized* algorithm for learning automata in the no-reset model. The overview of the development is as follows. We begin in Section 8.4.1 by defining a homing sequence, and showing how we can learn in the no-reset model if we are given a short homing sequence for the target automaton. In Section 8.4.2 we prove the existence of short homing sequences, and we analyze the key idea of our new algorithm: simulating many copies of our algorithm **Learn-Automaton** using a possibly faulty homing sequence. We show that the failure of such a simulation allows us to improve our proposed homing sequence and restart the entire simulation. In Section 8.4.3 we give a detailed description of our algorithm and its analysis, and in Section 8.4.4 we return to address an assumption made during the development about the many simulated copies of **Learn-Automaton**.

8.4.1   Using a Homing Sequence to Learn

Let M be the target automaton. As before we will assume that M is a minimum state automaton, and let $size(M)$ be the number of states of M. To begin with, without loss of generality we will assume that our learning algorithm knows the value of $size(M)$; it is a simple exercise to eliminate this assumption.

For any string h, we denote by $output(q, h)$ the output (that is, the complete sequence of accept/reject bits) observed by executing h from state q of M, and by $state(q, h)$ the state of M reached by executing h from q. For any sequence h, we define

$$output(h) = \{output(q, h) : q \in M\}.$$

This is just the set of all possible outputs observed by executing h as we range over all possible starting states q of M. Notice that if M has $size(M)$ states, $|output(h)| \leq size(M)$ for any sequence h.

A **homing sequence** for a finite automaton M is a sequence h such that for any state q of M, $output(q, h)$ uniquely determines $state(q, h)$: that is, if $output(q, h) = output(q', h)$ then $state(q, h) = state(q', h)$. Note that we do not demand that $q = q'$; a homing sequence simply ensures that identical output sequences imply the same destination state, not the same origin.

Let us first show the existence of short homing sequences for any automaton, and how a homing sequence can be used to learn in the no-reset model, and defer the problem of finding such a sequence in the no-reset model to Section 8.4.2. The main idea is that any sequence h that is not already a homing sequence can be extended to a sequence hx such that $|output(hx)| > |output(h)|$ for some string x of length at most $size(M)$. Since $|output(h)| \leq size(M)$ for every string h, we will have the desired homing sequence after at most $size(M)$ such extensions.

First note that for any h and any x, $|output(hx)| \geq |output(h)|$. Now if h is not a homing sequence, there exist two different states q

and q' of M such that $output(q, h) = output(q', h)$, but $state(q, h) \neq state(q', h)$. However, there must be a distinguishing sequence d for the destination states $state(q, h)$ and $state(q', h)$. So now we get two distinct output sequences $output(q, hd) \neq output(q', hd)$ in place of the single output sequence $output(q, h) = output(q', h)$, and thus $|output(hx)| > |output(h)|$.

Returning to our learning problem, note that a homing sequence h provides a kind of "weak" reset for M. Although executing h does not always return us to the same fixed state of M, it does "orient" us within M, in the sense that the output observed upon executing h uniquely determines the resulting state. Given the homing sequence h, we can imagine simulating our learning algorithm **Learn-Automaton** for the reset model in the following way: each time **Learn-Automaton** requests a reset (that is, makes a membership query), we temporarily suspend its execution and repeatedly execute h until some execution results in the specific output sequence σ. We then resume simulation of **Learn-Automaton** and in this way, before every membership query of **Learn-Automaton** we return to the same fixed state of M, which we may consider the "start state".

Unfortunately, we have no way of bounding the amount of time we may have to wait before executing h gives rise to the specific output sequence σ. This will be addressed by simulating many copies L_σ of **Learn-Automation**, one for each output sequence σ that we have observed upon executing h (that is, one for each $\sigma \in output(h)$ that we have seen so far). At any time, at most one copy L_σ will be awake. When this copy makes a membership query, we suspend its execution, execute h and obtain some output σ', and then awaken (that is, resume execution of) the copy $L_{\sigma'}$. There are at most $|output(h)| \leq size(M)$ copies, and any copy that terminates has exactly learned M. Each copy does at most as much computation as an execution of **Learn-Automaton** in the reset model, and thus the total amount of computation performed is at most $size(M)$ times that of **Learn-Automaton** (plus a small overhead cost for the executions of h). Thus we have shown:

Lemma 8.2 *There is an efficient algorithm for exactly learning deterministic finite automata in the no-reset model of membership and equivalence queries, provided the algorithm is also given a homing sequence for the target automaton as input.*

The main difficulty with the above proposal is that we must first somehow find a homing sequence. We now address this issue.

8.4.2   Building a Homing Sequence Using Oversized Generalized Classification Trees

The overall idea for finding a homing sequence will be to run the multi-copy simulation suggested above using a sequence h which in fact may not be a homing sequence. If this simulation fails to learn M, we will be able to extend h to a sequence hx that is "closer" to being a homing sequence.

For any sequence h, let us denote by $reset(h, \sigma)$ the set of possible states of M we could be in if the string σ has just been observed as the output while executing the string h. Thus,

$$reset(h, \sigma) = \{r \in M : (\exists q \in M) state(q, h) = r, output(q, h) = \sigma\}.$$

Suppose that we use a sequence h which is not a homing sequence, and awaken the copy L_σ only when we have just executed h and observed the ouput sequence σ. Then every time that L_σ is awakened, M will be in some state in $reset(h, \sigma)$.

As we have mentioned, our hope is to iteratively update h from failed attempts to learn M using the copies L_σ, until we end up with a homing sequence, at which point we have already argued the correctness of our multi-copy simulation (Lemma 8.2). The correctness of this scheme will rely on the following important property of each L_σ, whose proof we shall defer until a later section: if we use a sequence h which is not a homing sequence to run the copies L_σ, then each L_σ either halts and outputs an automaton equivalent to M, or it successively constructs a series of larger and larger *generalized classification trees*.

Structurally, a generalized classification tree looks just like the classification tree of algorithm **Learn-Automaton** in the reset model. The key property of a generalized classification tree T is that for any access string (leaf) of T, and any distinguishing string (internal node) d of T that is on the path from the root to s, there is some state $q \in reset(h, \sigma)$ that "witnesses" the claimed behavior of M on these strings. More precisely, we say that T is a **generalized classification tree** with respect to h and σ if and only if for any access string s and distinguishing string d on the path from the root to s in T, if s is in the right (left, respectively) subtree of d, there is a $q \in reset(h, \sigma)$ such that $state(q, sd)$ is accepting (rejecting, respectively). Note that a classification tree is just a generalized classification tree in which $|reset(h, \sigma)| = 1$.

Assuming for now that each copy L_σ can only either halt with a correct hypothesis automaton or construct successively larger generalized classification trees, the only way in which our simulation can fail when using an h that is not a homing sequence is that some copy L_σ constructs a generalized classification tree T_σ with $size(M) + 1$ leaves. We now propose and analyze a randomized scheme for using such an oversized T_σ to find a string x such that hx is closer to being a homing sequence, in the sense that $|output(hx)| > |output(h)|$.

Let $r \in reset(h, \sigma)$. Thus r is one of perhaps many states that M could be in when L_σ is restarted when using the sequence h. Since M has only $size(M)$ states and T_σ contains $size(M)+1$ access strings, there must exist access strings s_i and s_j of T_σ such that $state(r, s_i) = state(r, s_j)$ by the Pigeonhole Principle. Let d be the distinguishing string for s_i and s_j in T_σ. Then since s_i and s_j lead to the same state of M from r, we must also have $state(r, s_i d) = state(r, s_j d)$; assume without loss of generality that this is an accepting state. On the other hand, since d is a distinguishing string for s_i and s_j in T_σ, there must also exist states $r_i, r_j \in reset(h, \sigma)$ such that exactly one of $state(r_i, s_i d)$ and $state(r_j, s_j d)$

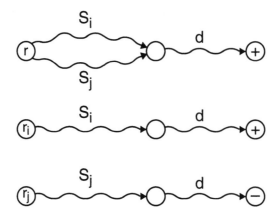

Figure 8.6: *Homing sequence update.*

is an accepting state, say $state(r_i, s_i d)$. Now $hs_j d$ is closer to being a homing sequence than h, because on output σ, h might have led us to either of r and r_j, but now $s_j d$ distinguishes between r and r_j (see Figure 8.6).

Of course, we have no way of determining just by looking at T_σ which access strings s_i and s_j have the above property. Instead, we use a randomized scheme that chooses two leaves s_i and s_j of T_σ at random, and updates the proposed homing sequence h to be $hs_j d$, where d is the distinguishing string (least common ancestor) for s_i and s_j in T_σ. We then restart the entire multi-copy simulation of algorithm **Learn-Automaton**.

Since we know that there is some pair s_i and s_j in T_σ that can be used to improve h, the probability that we actually make an improvement is at least $1/(size(M))^2$. Note that even if we fail to make an improvement to h, we certainly cannot make it worse because we always have $|output(hs_j d)| \geq |output(h)|$.

8.4.3 The No-Reset Algorithm

We are now prepared to give a detailed description of our algorithm for the no-reset model. We then provide its analysis under the assumption that all copies L_σ of **Learn-Automaton** always maintain a generalized classification tree, and then return to validate this assumption in the following section.

Algorithm No-Reset-Learn-Automaton:

- $h \leftarrow \lambda$.

- Main Loop:

  - Execute (that is, make a membership query on) the current proposed homing sequence h, and let σ be the output sequence observed.

  - If the output sequence σ has not previously been observed after executing the current h, initialize a copy L_σ of algorithm **Learn-Automaton**.

  - Awaken copy L_σ and simulate its next membership query and all subsequent computation up to (but not including) the next membership query:

    * Any time L_σ makes a equivalence query $\hat{M}$, give this query to the equivalence query oracle. If it is successful, halt and output $\hat{M}$ (learning is complete). If it is unsuccessful return the counterexample γ to L_σ.

    * If the generalized classification tree T_σ of copy L_σ ever has size of $size(M) + 1$ leaves, then choose leaves s_i and s_j of T_σ at random, and perform the update $h \leftarrow hs_jd$, where d is the least common ancestor of s_i and s_j in T_σ. Delete all copies of algorithm **Learn-Automaton** and restart the entire simulation by returning to the Main Loop.

For the analysis, note that **No-Reset-Learn-Automaton** halts only if learning is complete. Thus we only need to bound the running time. First, we observe that the number of times the tentative homing sequence can be improved is at most $size(M)$; this is because as we already argued, each improvement increases the size of the set $output(h)$ up to a maximum of $size(M)$. Improvements in the tentative homing sequence happen with probability at least $1/(size(M))^2$ each time the algorithm discovers an oversized classification tree. Since the simulation is simply restarted after each such modification to the tentative homing sequence, the running time of the algorithm is bounded by $size(M)^3$ multiplied by the time required to build an oversized tree starting with a new tentative homing sequence. From Section 8.4.1, the latter quantity is at most $(size(M))$ times the running time of **Learn-Automaton** in the reset model. Therefore the expected running time of the new algorithm is at most $(size(M))^4$ times the running time of **Learn-Automaton** in the reset model.

8.4.4   Making Sure L_σ Builds Generalized Classification Trees

We now must return to an issue that we had deferred earlier: we still need to show that each copy L_σ has the property that even if it is awakened when we observe output σ upon executing a string h that is not a homing sequence, L_σ either halts and outputs an automaton equivalent to M, or it successively constructs a series of larger and larger generalized classification trees T_σ. The issue here is that if h is not a homing sequence then each reset of L_σ puts M in an arbitrary state $q \in reset(h, \sigma)$.

First, let us assume that the lack of a consistent reset state does not ever cause the copy L_σ to abort. We will momentarily come back and address this assumption. In this case, the only way L_σ halts is if it made a successful equivalence query, and therefore discovered an automaton equivalent to M. On the other hand, if it does not halt, then it works in phases, and in each phase it adds a new leaf node to its current tree T_σ, which we now argue is a generalized classification tree.

We thus have to verify that if d is a distinguishing string on the path from the root to the leaf s in the current tree T_σ, then if s is in the right subtree of d there is some reset state $q \in reset(h, \sigma)$ such that the $state(q, sd)$ is an accepting state, and if s is in the left subtree of d there is some reset state $q \in reset(h, \sigma)$ such that the $state(q, sd)$ is a rejecting state. This fact is established by proving that for every such (s, d) pair there is a *witness* in the membership query history of L_σ — that is, L_σ must have at some point performed the membership query sd, and that the current tree T_σ is consistent with the answer given to that membership query.

Recall that T_σ is modified only by a call to **Update-Tree**(T_σ, γ) for some counterexample string γ. Let us denote the updated tree by T'_σ. We will show that if all (s, d) pairs of T_σ were witnessed, then this continues to be true of T'_σ. Since we update T_σ by adding a single access string $\gamma[j - 1]$ and a single distinguishing string $\gamma_j d$, we must only verify that there are witnesses for pairs that involve one of these two strings.

There are only two access strings in T'_σ whose path from the root passes through the new internal node labeled $\gamma_j d$ — namely, $\gamma[j-1]$ and s, where s is the access string reached by sifting $\gamma[j-1]$ down T_σ (see Section 8.3.4). Of these, the pair $(\gamma[j-1], \gamma_j d)$ was witnessed by the membership query $\gamma[j-1]\gamma_j d = \gamma[j]d$ which was made while doing a sift operation on the string $\gamma[j]$ (while processing the counterexample γ). The pair $(s, \gamma_j d)$ was witnessed by the membership query $s\gamma_j d$ which was performed to determine the destination state for the γ_j-transition out of the state s in the tentative hypothesis automaton $\hat{M}$. To see this more clearly, recall that determining this transition involved sifting $s\gamma_j$ down T_σ, and that d is one of the distinguishing strings on the path from the root to access string s in T_σ.

Lastly, we must witness every remaining new pair $(\gamma[j-1], d')$ of T'_σ for all of the distinguishing strings $d' \neq \gamma - jd$ on the path from the root to $\gamma[j-1]$. Note that all such d' were present in the tree T_σ. All these pairs were witnessed while sifting the string $\gamma[j-1]$ down T_σ to determine its equivalence class.

As our final detail, we have to consider the possibility that L_σ may abort since the answers to the membership queries can be inconsistent because there is no consistent reset state. We will show that (with one small exception which is easily fixed) L_σ never checks the answers to membership queries for consistency. First observe that L_σ makes membership queries in two places: one is to fill in the transitions of the hypothesis automaton $\hat{M}$. Notice that even if the answers to all these queries were arbitrary, they would not cause L_σ to abort, they would just result in incorrect transitions for $\hat{M}$. The other place where the algorithm makes membership queries is while processing the counterexample string γ. Once again incorrect answers to membership queries do not cause the algorithm to abort, with one small exception. Let the length of the counterexample string γ be m. Suppose that all the prefixes of γ up to $\gamma[m-1]$ reveal no difference between the equivalence class in $\hat{M}$ and the equivalence class in M. When the algorithm goes on to compute the equivalence class of $\gamma[m] = \gamma$ in M (using membership queries), it must not turn out to be equal to the equivalence class of γ in $\hat{M}$, otherwise the algorithm as stated would abort. This situation is easily fixed by changing the algorithm so that if it gets this far it does not try to compute the equivalence class of γ, but instead uses the information that γ was a counterexample to directly update the generalized classification tree as follows: the new access string is $\gamma[m-1]$ and the new distinguishing string is γ_m. The correctness of the generalized classification tree is unchanged except for the fact that the correctness of the pair $s = \gamma[m-1]$ and $d = \gamma_m$ relies on the fact γ was a counterexample string after a reset operation, and therefore there must be some reset state $q \in reset(h, \sigma)$ such that $state(q, \gamma)$ is an accepting or rejecting string as claimed by the counterexample.

We have finally shown:

Theorem 8.3 *There is a randomized algorithm that halts in expected polynomial time and exactly learns the representation class of deterministic finite automata in the no-reset learning model.*

It is easy to argue that we can alternatively state this result by saying that there is a randomized algorithm that takes as input $0 < \delta \leq 1$, and that with probability at least $1 - \delta$, exactly learns any deterministic finite automata c in the no-reset model in time polynomial in $\log(1/\delta)$, n and $size(c)$. Here n is again a bound on the length of the longest counterexample to any equivalence query.

8.5 Exercises

8.1. Show that for any representation class $\mathcal{C}$, if $\mathcal{C}$ is efficiently exactly learnable from membership and equivalence queries, then $\mathcal{C}$ is efficiently learnable in the PAC model with membership queries.

8.2. Show that properties of the classification trees constructed by our algorithm for learning finite automata in the reset model imply that any two inequivalent states in any deterministic finite automata M of s states have a distinguishing string of length at most s. Show that for any equivalence query $\hat{M}$ of our algorithm, if $\hat{M} \neq M$ then there is a counterexample of length $2s$ which can be found efficiently on input $\hat{M}$ and M.

8.3. Let $\mathcal{C}_n$ be the class of monotone DNF formulae over $x_1, \ldots, x_n$, and let $\mathcal{C} = \cup_{n \geq 1} \mathcal{C}_n$. Give an algorithm for efficiently exactly learning $\mathcal{C}$ from membership and equivalence queries.

8.4. Consider modifying our algorithm for finite automata in the no-reset model so that the copy L_σ is halted only when its generalized classification tree T_σ has $2s$ leaves rather than just $s + 1$, where s is the number of states in the target automaton. Note that this increases the running time of the algorithm by only a constant. Show that this modification increases the probability that we improve our candidate homing sequence from $1/s^2$ to $1/s$.

8.6 Bibliographic Notes

The model of exact learning with membership and equivalence queries, and the algorithm given here for learning finite automata, is due to Angluin [5]. Her seminal paper inspired a tremendous amount of subsequent research in the model, and has yielded many positive results. These include efficient algorithms for learning the class of decision trees, due to Bshouty [25]; for learning conjunctions of Horn clauses, a restricted form of DNF formulae, due to Angluin, Frazier and Pitt [7]; for learning a subclass of context-free languages accepted by counter machines, due to Berman and Roos [15]; for learning read-once boolean formulae, due to Angluin, Hellerstein and Karpinski [8]; for learning sparse multivariate polynomials, due to Schapire and Sellie [83]; and for many other concept classes. The algorithm for learning monotone DNF that is the subject of Exercise 8.3 is due to Angluin [6]; this paper also provides many general resource bounds for query learning (also see the work of Kannan [54]). The monotone DNF algorithm was subsequently extended by Angluin and Slonim [11] to tolerate certain types of errors in the query responses.

However, there are still limitations: Angluin and Kharitonov [9] demonstrate that for the class of DNF formulae, membership queries provide no additional power to the learner over the PAC model for some input distributions (under certain cryptographic assumptions), and subsequently Kharitonov [62] greatly strengthened the hardness results we derived in Chapter 6 when he proved that boolean formulae cannot be efficiently learned from random examples and membership queries, even when the input distribution is uniform (again under cryptographic assumptions).

The extension of Angluin's algorithm to the problem of learning finite automata without a reset mechanism is due to Rivest and Schapire [80], who also study learning algorithms using an alternative representation for finite automata based on a quantity called the diversity [79]. A recent paper of Freund et al. [37] gives algorithms for learning finite automata on the basis of a single long walk in an average-case setting.

There is actually a huge literature on finite automata learning problems that predates the computational learning theory work. While there was less explicit emphasis in this previous work on efficiency considerations, there are still many efficient algorithms and other fundamental results in the older literature. It is far too large to survey here, but the book of Trakhtenbrot and Barzdin' [90] provides a thorough investigation.

9

Appendix: Some Tools for Probabilistic Analysis

In this brief appendix, we state some fundamental results from probability theory that we invoke repeatedly in our study.

9.1 The Union Bound

Perhaps the most basic fact we will need is what we shall call the **union bound**. It simply states that for any probability space and for any two events A and B over that space, $\mathbf{Pr}[A \cup B] \leq \mathbf{Pr}[A] + \mathbf{Pr}[B]$.

9.2 Markov's Inequality

Markov's inequality provides a coarse bound on the probability that a random variable deviates from it expected value:

Theorem 9.1 *(Markov's Inequality) Let χ be any nonnegative random variable with expected value μ. Then $\mathbf{Pr}[\chi \geq k\mu] \leq 1/k$.*

9.3   Chernoff Bounds

Let $X_1, \ldots, X_m$ denote the outcomes of m independent Bernoulli trials (coin flips), with $\mathbf{Pr}[X_i = 1] = p$ and $\mathbf{Pr}[X_i = 0] = 1 - p$. Let $S = X_1 + \cdots + X_m$ be the number of heads in the m coin flips. Then $E[S] = E[X_1] + \cdots + E[X_m] = pm$. The Chernoff bounds given below state that the probability that S deviates from its mean pm by an amount ℓ decreases exponentially in ℓ:

Theorem 9.2 *Let $X_1, \ldots, X_m$ be a sequence of m independent Bernoulli trials, each with probability of success $\mathbf{E}[X_i] = p$. Let $S = X_1 + \cdots + X_m$ be a random variable indicating the total number of successes, so $\mathbf{E}[S] = pm$. Then for $0 \leq \gamma \leq 1$, the following bounds hold:*

- *(Additive Form)*

$$\mathbf{Pr}[S > (p + \gamma)m] \leq e^{-2m\gamma^2}$$

  and

$$\mathbf{Pr}[S < (p - \gamma)m] \leq e^{-2m\gamma^2}.$$

- *(Multiplicative Form)*

$$\mathbf{Pr}[S > (1 + \gamma)pm] \leq e^{-mp\gamma^2/3}$$

  and

$$\mathbf{Pr}[S < (1 - \gamma)pm] \leq e^{-mp\gamma^2/2}.$$

The Additive Form of the bound is usually credited to Hoeffding and the Multiplicative Form to Chernoff; in the computer science literature, both forms àre often referred to by the name *Chernoff bounds*.

The multiplicative form of the Chernoff bound can be restated in terms of the standard deviation σ of the random variable S as follows: $\mathbf{Pr}[|S - E[S]| \geq k\sigma] \leq 2e^{k^2/6}$. To see this, first note that we have

$\sigma = \sqrt{mp(1-p)} \geq \sqrt{pm/2}$. Therefore $k\sigma \geq k\sqrt{pm/2} = k(\sqrt{2/pm})pm$. Substituting in the multiplicative form of the Chernoff bound with $\gamma = k\sqrt{2/pm}$ gives the above bound.

It is sometimes convenient to consider the observed success probability $\hat{p}$ rather than the actual number of successes S; $\hat{p}$ is simply S/m. In this light, Theorem 9.2 tells us how rapidly the estimate $\hat{p}$ converges to p as a function of m. For instance, in the additive form, simply divide each side of the inequality inside the $\mathbf{Pr}[\cdot]$ by m and we see that the probability that the estimate $\hat{p}$ exceeds p by more than γ is at most $e^{-2m\gamma^2}$.

Our most common application of the Chernoff bounds will be to provide an upper bound on the number of trials m required to ensure that the estimate $\hat{p}$ is "close" to the true value p with high confidence. Especially important is the case where p is small. In this case, by "close" we will mean that $\hat{p}$ be within a multiplicative factor of 2 of p, that is, $p/2 \leq \hat{p} \leq 2p$. Let $m(p, \delta)$ be the number of trials required to ensure that $\hat{p}$ is within a multiplicative factor of 2 of p with confidence at least $1 - \delta$. Setting $\gamma = 1$ in the first Multiplicative Form bound of Theorem 9.2, we obtain
$$\mathbf{Pr}[\hat{p} > 2p] \leq e^{-mp/3}.$$

Setting $\gamma = 1/2$ in the second Multiplicative Form bound of Theorem 9.2, we obtain
$$\mathbf{Pr}[\hat{p} < p/2] \leq e^{-mp/8}.$$

Thus we may write
$$\begin{aligned}
\mathbf{Pr}[(\hat{p} > 2p) \vee (\hat{p} < p/2)] &= \mathbf{Pr}[\hat{p} > 2p] + \mathbf{Pr}[\hat{p} < p/2] \\
&\leq e^{-mp/3} + e^{-mp/8} \\
&\leq 2e^{-mp/8}.
\end{aligned}$$

Solving $2e^{-mp/8} \leq \delta$ gives that $m(p, \delta) \geq (8/p)\ln(2/\delta)$ suffices. The most important aspect of this bound is that the dependence on p is $O(1/p)$.

We can also bound the number of trials m required to ensure that the estimate $\hat{p}$ is within an additive factor of ϵ of p (that is, $p - \epsilon \leq \hat{p} \leq p + \epsilon$)

with confidence at least $1 - \delta$. This bound is conveniently derived from the additive form of the Chernoff bound, which implies that

$$\mathbf{Pr}[|\hat{p} - p| \geq \epsilon] \leq 2e^{2m\epsilon^2}$$

The right hand side is less than δ for $m = \Omega((1/\epsilon^2) \ln(1/\delta))$. We will often apply Chernoff bounds in a rather informal manner to avoid tedious detail when it is clear that these details may be verified in a straightforward way.

Bibliography

[1] Y. S. Abu-Mostafa. The Vapnik-Chervonenkis dimension: Information versus complexity in learning. *Neural Computation*, 1(3):312–317, 1989.

[2] A. Aho, J. Hopcroft, and J. Ullman. *The Design and Analysis of Computer Algorithms*. Addison-Wesley, 1974.

[3] D. Aldous and U. Vazirani. A Markovian extension of Valiant's learning model. In *Proceedings of the 31st IEEE Symposium on the Foundations of Computer Science*, pages 392–396. IEEE Computer Society Press, Los Alamitos, CA, 1990.

[4] N. Alon, S. Ben-David, N. Cesa-Bianchi, and D. Haussler. Scale-sensitive dimensions, uniform convergence, and learnability. In *Proceedings of the 34th IEEE Symposium on the Foundations of Computer Science*, pages 292–301. IEEE Computer Society Press, Los Alamitos, CA, 1993.

[5] D. Angluin. Learning regular sets from queries and counterexamples. *Information and Computation*, 75(2):87–106, 1987.

[6] D. Angluin. Queries and concept learning. *Machine Learning*, 2(4):319–342, 1988.

[7] D. Angluin, M. Frazier, and L. Pitt. Learning conjunctions of Horn clauses. *Machine Learning*, 9:147–164, 1992.

[8] D. Angluin, L. Hellerstein, and M. Karpinski. Learning read-once formulas with queries. *Journal of the ACM*, 40:185–210, 1993.

[9] D. Angluin and M. Kharitonov. When won't membership queries help? In *Proceedings of the 23rd ACM Symposium on the Theory of Computing*, pages 444–454. ACM Press, New York, NY, 1991.

[10] D. Angluin and P. Laird. Learning from noisy examples. *Machine Learning*, 2(4):343–370, 1988.

[11] D. Angluin and D.K. Slonim. Randomly fallible teachers: learning monotone DNF with an incomplete membership oracle. *Machine Learning*, 14:7–26, 1994.

[12] J. A. Aslam and S. E. Decatur. General bounds on statistical query learning and PAC learning with noise via hypothesis boosting. In *Proceedings of the 35th IEEE Symposium on the Foundations of Computer Science*, pages 282–291. IEEE Computer Society Press, Los Alamitos, CA, 1993.

[13] E. Baum and D. Haussler. What size net gives valid generalization? *Neural Computation*, 1(1):151–160, 1989.

[14] P.W. Beame, S.A. Cook, and H.J. Hoover. Log-depth circuits for division and related problems. *SIAM Journal on Computing*, 15(4):994–1003, 1986.

[15] P. Berman and R. Roos. Learning one-counter languages in polynomial time. In *Proceedings of the 28th IEEE Symposium on the Foundations of Computer Science*, pages 61–67. IEEE Computer Society Press, Los Alamitos, CA, 1987.

[16] A. Blum. On the computational complexity of training simple neural networks. Master's thesis, MIT Department of Electrical Engineering and Computer Science, May 1989. Published as Laboratory for Computer Science Technical Report MIT/LCS/TR-445, May, 1989.

[17] A. Blum. Learning boolean functions in an infinite attribute space. *Machine Learning*, 9(4):373–386, 1992.

[18] A. Blum, M. Furst, J. Jackson, M. Kearns, Y. Mansour, and S. Rudich. Weakly learning DNF and characterizing statistical query learning using Fourier analysis. In *Proceedings of the 26th ACM Symposium on the Theory of Computing*. ACM Press, New York, NY, 1994.

[19] A. Blum, M. Furst, M. Kearns, and R. Lipton. Cryptographic primitives based on hard learning problems. In *Proceedings of CRYPTO*, 1993.

[20] A. Blum and R. L. Rivest. Training a 3-node neural net is NP-Complete. In David S. Touretzky, editor, *Advances in Neural Information Processing Systems I*, pages 494–501. Morgan Kaufmann, San Mateo, CA, 1989.

[21] A. Blumer, A. Ehrenfeucht, D. Haussler, and M. K. Warmuth. Occam's razor. *Information Processing Letters*, 24:377–380, 1987.

[22] A. Blumer, A. Ehrenfeucht, D. Haussler, and M. K. Warmuth. Learnability and the Vapnik-Chervonenkis dimension. *Journal of the ACM*, 36(4):929–965, 1989.

[23] R. Board and L. Pitt. On the necessity of Occam algorithms. *Theoretical Computer Science*, 100:157–184, 1992.

[24] D. Boneh and R. Lipton. Amplification of weak learning under the uniform distribution. In *Proceedings of the 6th Workshop on Computational Learning Theory*, pages 347–351. ACM Press, New York, NY, 1993.

[25] N. H. Bshouty. Exact learning via the monotone theory. In *Proceedings of the 34th IEEE Symposium on the Foundations of Computer Science*, pages 302–311. IEEE Computer Society Press, Los Alamitos, CA, 1993.

[26] V. Chvatal. A greedy heuristic for the set covering problem. *Mathematics of Operations Research*, 4(3):233–235, 1979.

[27] T. Cormen, C. Leiserson, and R. Rivest. *Introduction to Algorithms*. The MIT Press, Cambridge, Massachusetts, 1990.

[28] S. E. Decatur. Statistical queries and faulty PAC oracles. In *Proceedings of the 6th Workshop on Computational Learning Theory*, pages 262–268. ACM Press, New York, NY, 1993.

[29] A. DeSantis, G. Markowsky, and M. N. Wegman. Learning probabilistic prediction functions. In *Proceedings of the 29th IEEE Symposium on the Foundations of Computer Science*, pages 110–119. IEEE Computer Society Press, Los Alamitos, CA, 1988.

[30] H. Drucker, R. Schapire, and P. Simard. Improving performance in neural networks using a boosting algorithm. In S.J. Hanson, J.D. Cowan, and C.L. Giles, editors, *Advances in Neural Information Processing Systems*, pages 42–49. Morgan Kaufmann, San Mateo, CA, 1992.

[31] R.M. Dudley. A course on empirical processes. *Lecture Notes in Mathematics*, 1097:2–142, 1984.

[32] A. Ehrenfeucht and D. Haussler. Learning decision trees from random examples. In *Proceedings of the 1st Workshop on Computational Learning Theory*, pages 182–194. Morgan Kaufmann, San Mateo, CA, 1988.

[33] A. Ehrenfeucht, D. Haussler, M. Kearns, and L. Valiant. A general lower bound on the number of examples needed for learning. *Information and Computation*, 82(3):247–251, 1989.

[34] W. Evans, S. Rajagopalan, and U. Vazirani. Choosing a reliable hypothesis. In *Proceedings of the 6th Workshop on Computational Learning Theory*, pages 269–276. ACM Press, New York, NY, 1993.

[35] Y. Freund. Boosting a weak learning algorithm by majority. In *Proceedings of the 3rd Workshop on Computational Learning Theory*, pages 202–216. Morgan Kaufmann, San Mateo, CA, 1990.

[36] Y. Freund. An improved boosting algorithm and its implications on learning complexity. In *Proceedings of the 5th Workshop on Computational Learning Theory*, pages 391–398. ACM Press, New York, NY, 1992.

[37] Y. Freund, M. Kearns, D. Ron, R. Rubinfeld, R. Schapire, and L. Sellie. Efficient learning of typical finite automata from random walks. In *Proceedings of the 25th ACM Symposium on the Theory of Computing*, pages 315–324. ACM Press, New York, NY, 1993.

[38] M. Garey and D. Johnson. *Computers and Intractability: A Guide to the Theory of NP-Completeness*. Freeman, San Francisco, California, 1979.

[39] M. Gereb-Graus. Complexity of learning from one-sided examples. Unpublished manuscript, Harvard University, 1989.

[40] E. M. Gold. Complexity of automaton identification from given data. *Information and Control*, 37:302–320, 1978.

[41] S. Goldman and R. Sloan. The difficulty of random attribute noise. Technical Report WUCS-91-92, Washington University Department of Computer Science, 1991.

[42] S. A. Goldman, M. J. Kearns, and R. E. Schapire. On the sample complexity of weak learning. In *Proceedings of the 3rd Workshop on Computational Learning Theory*, pages 217–231. Morgan Kaufmann, San Mateo, CA, 1990.

[43] O. Goldreich, S. Goldwasser, and S. Micali. How to construct random functions. *Journal of the ACM*, 33(4):792–807, 1986.

[44] D. Haussler. Bias, version spaces, and Valiant's learning framework. In *Proceedings of the 4th International Workshop on Machine Learning*, pages 324–336. Morgan Kaufmann, San Mateo, CA, 1987.

[45] D. Haussler. Quantifying inductive bias: AI learning algorithms and Valiant's learning framework. *Artificial Intelligence*, 36:177–221, 1988.

[46] D. Haussler. Learning conjunctive concepts in structural domains. *Machine Learning*, 4(1):7–40, 1989.

[47] D. Haussler. Probably approximately correct learning. In *Proceedings of the 8th National Conference on Artificial Intelligence*, pages 1101–1108. Morgan Kaufmann, San Mateo, CA, 1990.

[48] D. Haussler. Decision-theoretic generalizations of the PAC model for neural net and other learning applications. *Information and Computation*, 100(1):78–150, 1992.

[49] D. Haussler, M. Kearns, N. Littlestone, and M. K. Warmuth. Equivalence of models for polynomial learnability. *Information and Computation*, 95(2):129–161, 1991.

[50] D. Haussler, M. Kearns, and R. E. Schapire. Bounds on the sample complexity of Bayesian learning using information theory and the VC dimension. *Machine Learning*, 14:83–113, 1994.

[51] D. Haussler, N. Littlestone, and M. K. Warmuth. Predicting $\{0,1\}$ functions on randomly drawn points. In *Proceedings of the 29th IEEE Symposium on the Foundations of Computer Science*, pages 100–109. IEEE Computer Society Press, Los Alamitos, CA, 1988.

[52] D. P. Helmbold and M. K. Warmuth. Some weak learning results. In *Proceedings of the 5th Workshop on Computational Learning Theory*, pages 399–412. ACM Press, New York, NY, 1992.

[53] S. Judd. *Neural Network Design and the Complexity of Learning*. MIT Press, 1990.

[54] S. Kannan. On the query complexity of learning. In *Proceedings of the Sixth Workshop on Computational Learning Theory*, pages 58–66. ACM Press, New York, NY, 1993.

[55] M. Kearns. *The Computational Complexity of Machine Learning.* MIT Press, Cambridge, MA, 1990.

[56] M. Kearns. Efficient noise-tolerant learning from statistical queries. In *Proceedings of the 25th ACM Symposium on the Theory of Computing*, pages 392–401. ACM Press, New York, NY, 1993.

[57] M. Kearns and M. Li. Learning in the presence of malicious errors. *SIAM Journal on Computing*, 22(4):807–837, 1993.

[58] M. Kearns, M. Li, L. Pitt, and L. Valiant. On the learnability of boolean formulae. In *Proceedings of the 19th ACM Symposium on the Theory of Computing*, pages 285–294. ACM Press, New York, NY, 1987.

[59] M. Kearns, M. Li, L. Pitt, and L. Valiant. Recent results on boolean concept learning. In Pat Langley, editor, *Proceedings of the Fourth International Workshop on Machine Learning*, pages 337–352. Morgan Kaufmann, San Mateo, CA, 1987.

[60] M. Kearns and L. G. Valiant. Cryptographic limitations on learning boolean formulae and finite automata. *Journal of the ACM*, 41(1):67–95, 1994.

[61] M. J. Kearns and R. E. Schapire. Efficient distribution-free learning of probabilistic concepts. In *Proceedings of the 31st IEEE Symposium on the Foundations of Computer Science*, pages 382–391. IEEE Computer Society Press, Los Alamitos, CA, 1990.

[62] M. Kharitonov. Cryptographic hardness of distribution-specific learning. In *Proceedings of the 25th ACM Symposium on the Theory of Computing*, pages 372–381. ACM Press, New York, NY, 1993.

[63] P. D. Laird. *Learning from Good and Bad Data.* Kluwer Academic Publishers, Boston, MA, 1988.

[64] N. Linial, Y. Mansour, and N. Nisan. Constant depth circuits, Fourier transform, and learnability. In *Proceedings of the 31st IEEE*

Symposium on the Foundations of Computer Science, pages 574–579. IEEE Computer Society Press, 1989.

[65] N. Littlestone. Learning when irrelevant attributes abound: A new linear-threshold algorithm. *Machine Learning*, 2:285–318, 1988.

[66] N. Littlestone. *Mistake Bounds and Logarithmic Linear-threshold Learning Algorithms*. PhD thesis, University of California Santa Cruz, 1989.

[67] N. Littlestone. Redundant noisy attributes, attribute errors, and linear threshold learning using Winnow. In *Proceedings of the 4th Workshop on Computational Learning Theory*, pages 147–156. Morgan Kaufmann, San Mateo, CA, 1991.

[68] P. M. Long and M. K. Warmuth. Composite geometric concepts and polynomial predictability. In *Proceedings of the 3rd Workshop on Computational Learning Theory*, pages 273–287. Morgan Kaufmann, 1990.

[69] W. Maass and G. Turán. On the complexity of learning from counterexamples. In *Proceedings of the 30th IEEE Symposium on the Foundations of Computer Science*, pages 262–267. IEEE Computer Society Press, Los Alamitos, CA, 1989.

[70] B. K. Natarajan. Occam's razor for functions. In *Proceedings of the 6th Workshop on Computational Learning Theory*, pages 370–376. ACM Press, New York, NY, 1993.

[71] L. Pitt and L. Valiant. Computational limitations on learning from examples. *Journal of the ACM*, 35:965–984, 1988.

[72] L. Pitt and M. Warmuth. The minimum consistent DFA problem cannot be approximated within any polynomial. *Journal of the ACM*, 40(1):95–142, 1993.

[73] L. Pitt and M. K. Warmuth. Prediction-preserving reducibility. *Journal of Computer and System Science*, 41(3):430–467, 1990.

[74] D. Pollard. *Convergence of Stochastic Processes.* Springer-Verlag, 1984.

[75] J. R. Quinlan and R. L. Rivest. Inferring decision trees using the minimum description length principle. *Information and Computation,* 80(3):227–248, 1989.

[76] J. Reif. On threshold circuits and polynomial computations. In *Proceedings of the 2nd Confernce on Structure in Complexity Theory,* pages 118–125, 1987.

[77] J. Rissanen. Modeling by shortest data description. *Automatica,* 14:465–471, 1978.

[78] R. L. Rivest. Learning decision lists. *Machine Learning,* 2(3):229–246, 1987.

[79] R. L. Rivest and R. E. Schapire. Diversity-based inference of finite automata. In *Proceedings of the 28th IEEE Symposium on the Foundations of Computer Science,* pages 78–87. IEEE Computer Society Press, Los Alamitos, CA, 1987.

[80] R. L. Rivest and R. E. Schapire. Inference of finite automata using homing sequences. *Information and Computation,* 103(2):299–347, 1993.

[81] R. L. Rivest, A. Shamir, and L. Adleman. A method for obtaining digital signatures and public key cryptosytems. *Communications of the ACM,* 21(2):120–126, 1978.

[82] Y. Sakakibara. *Algorithmic Learning of Formal Languages and Decision Trees.* PhD thesis, Tokyo Institute of Technology, 1991. International Institute for Advanced Study of Social Information Science, Fujitsu Laboratories Ltd, Research Report IIAS-RR-91-22E.

[83] R. Schapire and L. Sellie. Learning sparse multivariate polynomials over a field with queries and counterexamples. In *Proceedings of the 6th Workshop on Computational Learning Theory,* pages 17–26. ACM Press, New York, NY, 1993.

[84] R. E. Schapire. The strength of weak learnability. *Machine Learning*, 5(2):197–227, 1990.

[85] R. E. Schapire. *The Design and Analysis of Efficient Learning Algorithms*. MIT Press, Cambridge, MA, 1992.

[86] H. S. Seung, H. Sompolinsky, and N. Tishby. Statistical mechanics of learning from examples. *Physical Review*, A45:6056–6091, 1992.

[87] G. Shackelford and D. Volper. Learning k-DNF with noise in the attributes. In *Proceedings of the 1st Workshop on Computational Learning Theory*, pages 97–103. Morgan Kaufmann, San Mateo, CA, 1988.

[88] R. H. Sloan. *Computational Learning Theory: New Models and Algorithms*. PhD thesis, MIT, 1989. Issued as MIT/LCS/TR-448.

[89] G. Tesauro and D. Cohn. Can neural networks do better than the Vapnik-Chervonenkis bounds? In R. Lippmann, J. Moody, and D. Touretzky, editors, *Advances in Neural Information Processing, Vol. 3*, pages 911–917. Morgan Kaufmann, San Mateo, CA, 1991.

[90] B.A. Trakhtenbrot and Ya. M. Barzdin'. *Finite Automata: Behavior and Synthesis*. North-Holland, New York, 1973.

[91] L. Valiant. Deductive learning. *Philosophical Transactions of the Royal Society of London A*, 312:441–446, 1984.

[92] L. G. Valiant. A theory of the learnable. *Communications of the ACM*, 27(11):1134–1142, 1984.

[93] L. G. Valiant. Learning disjunctions of conjunctions. In *Proceedings of the 9th International Joint Conference on Artificial Intelligence*, pages 560–566. International Joint Committee for Artificial Intelligence, 1985.

[94] V. N. Vapnik. *Estimation of Dependences Based on Empirical Data*. Springer-Verlag, New York, 1982.

[95] V. N. Vapnik and A. Y. Chervonenkis. On the uniform convergence of relative frequencies of events to their probabilities. *Theory of Probability and its Applications*, 16(2):264–280, 1971.

Index

access strings 160
accuracy boosting 78
active learning 153
architecture
      of a neural network 67
axis-aligned
      rectangles 1,12,26,52,120

behaviors on a sample 51
boolean circuits 131
boolean formulae 134,149
boosting 76,78

cardinality of hypothesis class 32,35
Chernoff bounds 190
classification noise 103,105
classification tree 161
compositions of concepts,
      VC dimension 64
compression 34
concept 7
concept class 8
confidence parameter δ 10
confidence boosting 76
conjunctions of literals
      16,37,38,67,106,111,119
conjunctive normal form 22

consistent hypothesis 19
convex polygons 54,68
counterexample 158

decision lists 42,67,119
decision trees 44
dichotomy of a sample 51
dimensionality of
      instance space 12
discrete cube root assumption 127
discrete cube root problem 124
discrete square root problem 140
disjunctive normal
      form 18,22,27,144,153
distinguishing strings 160
distribution 9

efficient learning 10
epsilon-net 57
equivalence queries 158
error of a hypothesis 9
error parameter ϵ 10
error regions 57
exact learning 158
examples oracle 9
experimentation 153